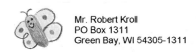

The Compendium of NCEA Notes
"Legal Issues"
Articles: 1990–2007

Mary Angela Shaughnessy
SCN, J.D., Ph.D.

National Catholic Educational Association

DEDICATION

This text is dedicated to the Sisters of Charity of Nazareth, my religious community, and in particular to those sisters who have served in leadership during the writing of the articles comprising this work. Their support of and challenge to me have made all the difference.

Most especially, I express my gratitude to
Emily Nabholz, SCN
Elizabeth Wendeln, SCN
Maria Vincent Brocato, SCN
Marilyn Spink, SCN +
Elizabeth Blandford, SCN
and Susan Gatz, SCN

Caritas urget nos.
The love of Christ urges us.

May it continue to be the force that gives urgency to
the mission of the Sisters of Charity of Nazareth.

Table of Contents

Violence, Abuse, and Harassment

Confidentiality, Privacy, and Defamation

Health Issues

ACKNOWLEDGMENTS

When the idea of compiling 17 years of legal issues columns first arose, I have to admit to thinking that the task would not be too time consuming. Many months later, I realized that compiling this book was just as time consuming, if not more, than any other. I have made very few changes to the actual text of the articles. I chose to add notes throughout the articles to reflect more recent legal thinking, new developments, and case law. I am most grateful to Sister Mary Frances Taymans, executive director of the National Catholic Educational Association's Department of Secondary Schools, and her assistants, Kenneth Lee and Chris Scalise, for their encouragement in the writing process.

I thank the many readers across the country who have encouraged and challenged me as they read these bimonthly articles for almost two decades. Their questions, comments, and critiques often prompted new ideas and new ways of thinking.

As always, I thank my family and my religious community, the Sisters of Charity of Nazareth, for their constant affection and support. I thank my two dear friends, Dr. Karen M. Juliano and Father Michael Huggins, for their support, friendship, and very real help. Karen, a Catholic school administrator for 29 years, is always ready to respond to my questions of "What would you do if this happened at your school?" Father Mike patiently answers my queries about church law and practice and parish administration while giving me insight into a priest's view of many thorny situations.

In many ways, rereading, editing, and commenting on these articles was a trip down memory lane. The history of Catholic education law is both changing and constant. As we live our holy vocation of educator, let us always be faithful to prayer and to faith; then, surely the One whose Gospel we follow will be with us every step of our journey.

Mary Angela Shaughnessy, SCN
February 2007

Constitutional

 and CONTRACT ISSUES

September 1990

The Catholic School and the Constitution: Is There a Fit?

Constitutional law is one of the major sources of civil law affecting education in the United States today and is the main source of the law for the public school. In the majority of public school student and teacher dismissal cases, plaintiffs allege deprivation of constitutional rights.

Educators are probably familiar with certain constitutional rights. The First Amendment guarantees freedom of speech, press, assembly, and religion; the Fourth Amendment protects against unlawful searches and seizures; the Fifth and 14th Amendments guarantee due process.

Public school teachers and students, of course, can claim constitutional rights because the public school is a government agency and those who administer public schools are government agents. The Constitution protects people from arbitrary governmental deprivation of their constitutional freedoms. People in Catholic schools, however, cannot claim such protections because Catholic schools are private institutions administered by private persons.

These restrictions may seem unfair, yet a similar price is paid by anyone who works in a private institution. If a person goes to work in a supermarket, the person will probably be required to wear a uniform. The employee will not be permitted to wear a button advertising a different supermarket chain.

The bottom line is that when one enters a private institution such as a Catholic school, one voluntarily surrenders the protections of the Constitution. A Catholic school teacher or student can always leave the Catholic school, but as long as the person remains in the institution, constitutional protections are not available. Thus, the Catholic school does not have to accept behaviors about which the public school has no choice and even is required to protect.

What cannot lawfully be done in a public school may be done in a Catholic school. For example, the First Amendment to the Constitution protects an individual's rights to free speech. Administrators in public schools, therefore, may not make rules prohibiting the expression of an unpopular viewpoint. Most educators have heard of the landmark Tinker case, which produced the now-famous line: "Students and teachers don't shed their constitutional rights at the schoolhouse gate" (Tinker v. Des Moines Independent School District, 393 U.S. 503 1969). Since no such constitutional protection exists in the Catholic school, administrators may restrict the speech of both students and teachers. Free speech issues in the Catholic school rarely reach courts; other constitutional issues often do.

Fairness and Due Process

The U.S. Supreme Court ruled in 1985 in *New Jersey v. T.L.O.*, 105 S.Ct 733, that public school officials may use a reasonableness, rather than a probable cause, standard in conducting student searches. Catholic schools are not bound by this case, but common sense and Gospel respect for students as people should govern searches in Catholic schools.

Public schools must be concerned about constitutional issues. Catholic schools, while not bound to grant constitutional freedoms per se, are bound to act in a manner characterized by fairness. Some legal experts talk about a "smell" test. If an action "smells" wrong when a person examines it, it may be suspect. In the end, the actions expected of Catholic schools may appear much like constitutional protections. In no area is this more evident than in due process considerations.

The Fifth Amendment to the Constitution guarantees that the federal government will not deprive someone of "life, liberty, or property without due process of law." The 14th Amendment made the Fifth Amendment and all other amendments in the Bill of Rights applicable to the states. Individuals entitled to constitutional due process have substantive due process rights, property interests (that which can be the subject of ownership, including jobs and education), and liberty interests (freedom, reputation). Substantive due process involves moral as well as legal ramifications: Is this action fair and reasonable? Substantive due process applies whenever property or liberty interests can be shown.

The Constitution also guarantees procedural due process, or how a deprivation occurs. In the public school, procedural due process includes *notice* (a presentation of the allegations against the accused), *hearing* (an opportunity to respond) *before an impartial tribunal,* opportunity to *confront* and *cross-examine* accusers, and the opportunity to call *witnesses on one's own behalf.* In serious disciplinary cases, a person in the public school has the right to have an attorney present.

Catholic schools, while not bound to provide the whole panoply of procedural due process protections that public schools must provide, are nonetheless expected to be fair. An Ohio court, ruling 12 years ago in a Catholic school discipline case, stated that courts could intervene in private school disciplinary cases if "the proceedings do not comport with fundamental fairness" (Geraci v. St. Xavier High School, 13 Ohio Op. 3d 146 Ohio, 1978). Fundamental fairness in a Catholic school is akin to, but not synonymous with, constitutional due process.

Federal and State Statutes

Federal and state statutes and regulations, many of which have constitutional bases, comprise a second source of the law affecting Catholic school personnel. If a statute requires that all who operate an educational institution in a given state follow a certain directive, both Catholic and public schools are bound. As long as what is required does not unfairly impinge on the rights of Catholic schools and can be shown to have some legitimate educational purposes, Catholic schools can be compelled to comply with state constitutional and legislative requirements.

The only situation in which a Catholic school can be required to grant federal constitutional protections is when state action can be found to be so pervasive in the school that the school can fairly be said to be acting as an agent of an individual state. The key factor in state action is the nexus or relationship between the state and the challenged activity. Although litigants have alleged state action in Catholic schools, no court of record has found state action present in private school teacher or student dismissal cases.

In a 1982 teacher dismissal case, *Rendell-Baker v. Kohn*, 102 S.Ct. 2764, the Supreme Court ruled such a dismissal in a private school that received 90 to 99% of its funding from the state did not constitute state action. *Rendell-Baker* seems to render the state action issue moot in cases alleging violation of constitutional due process protections. A different situation exists in cases alleging violations of federal antidiscrimination and civil rights legislation. In those cases, the presence of federal funding can result in an institution's being required to abide by the legislation.

Since Catholic schools are not bound to grant constitutional protections unless significant state action is found, litigants alleging a denial of constitutional due process will have to prove the existence of significant state action in the institution before the court will grant relief. It is very important for Catholic school administrators to keep these facts in mind.

It is not uncommon for parents, students, or teachers to claim that their constitutional rights have been violated in the Catholic school when, in fact, no constitutional rights ever existed in the first place. These realities need to be clarified very early in a relationship between a Catholic school system and its staff, students, and parents. One way to prevent possible misunderstandings is to develop and disseminate comprehensive handbooks that outline the rights and responsibilities of all individuals in the Catholic school.

Recent Developments: Negligence

The law governing negligence applies to both public and private schools. Two recent negligence cases are worthy of note.

In *Brown v. Tesack,* 556 So.2d 84 (La.App. 4 Cir. 1989), two students removed partially used cans of duplicating fluid from a dumpster, carried them to the apartment complex where they lived, played with them, and ultimately set them afire. A third child was severely injured when the fluid cans exploded. The injured child's mother alleged that the school district's disposal of the fluid containers was negligent and the school district should be liable for the injuries sustained by her son.

The court clarified the concept of causation: "[N]egligent conduct is a cause-in-fact of harm to another if it is a substantial factor in bringing about that harm." The court found that the school district had not breached its duty of care in disposing of the fluid; the actual cause-in-fact was the two boys' negligent misuse of the duplicating fluid. [Note: if this case were heard today, the result might be different. Regulations governing disposal of toxic waste have become much more demanding.]

In a New York case, *James v. Gloversville Enlarged School District,* 548 N.Y.S.2d 87 (A.D.3 Dept. 1989), a student was injured in a playground altercation and maintained that, before this incident, he had told his teacher the attacking student had tripped him. The plaintiff further alleged that the supervising aides were, in fact, talking with the each other with their backs to the students, in violation of written policy.

The school contended it had adequately fulfilled its duty of supervision by having four or five supervisors on the playground, the proximate cause of the injury was the action of the student who attacked the plaintiff, there was no issue of triable fact, and summary judgment should have been entered for the defendant school.

The court, finding that there were issues of fact for jury determination, denied the summary judgment motion. Both adequacy of supervision and foreseeability of harm to the student because of previous incidents are questions of fact that must be decided by a jury, not a judge. [Note: This case illustrates the mental aspect of supervision. Supervision is both a mental and a physical act. It is not enough to be physically present. One must know what is going on in the areas and with the people being supervised. Failure to exercise mental supervision is at least as grave as leaving students unattended for an insufficient reason.]

These two cases illustrate the dilemma facing many courts today. Courts must hold schools and school officials to the duties of providing supervision of children and protecting them from foreseeable harm. At the same time, schools cannot be held liable for every injury that occurs through a cause-in-fact other than the school. Both cases serve as reminders to administrators that the greatest of care must be taken in supervising students and their safety. Courts expect principals and other school officials to conduct ongoing examinations of buildings and grounds, eliminate hazards, and develop policies and procedures that protect the safety of all.

MAY 1996

SCHOOL INVOLVEMENT IN POLITICAL ACTION

Catholic educators and administrators may find the concept of political action a bit intimidating. Dire stories abound of the potential for losing tax-exempt status because of political activity. Principals, pastors, and other administrators worry: How far can the Catholic administrator go?

The administrator might consider the following five situations to determine whether the activity is permissible or impermissible:

1. A pulpit announcement urging parishioners to vote for candidate "x," who will support tuition vouchers

2. Distributing a pamphlet listing the pros and cons of tuition vouchers

3. Sending home to parents via children the campaign literature of a candidate who has indicated a pro-life position

4. Sending home a list of state or federal representatives with their addresses and phone numbers

5. Including a "legislative update" section containing information on tuition vouchers or charitable gaming laws in a school newsletter

Statements 1 and 3 are impermissible activities, while statements 2, 4, and 5 are permissible. The following discussion is offered as a basis for understanding the rationale behind permissible and impermissible activities.

Constitutional Issues

The U.S. Constitution does not address the issue of political activity by religious organizations. The First Amendment contains two important clauses, the establishment clause and the free exercise clause, in the first few words of the amendment: "Congress shall make no law respecting an establishment of religion nor prohibiting the free exercise thereof." These clauses mean that the government cannot promote one religion or even religion in general. At the same time, it cannot interfere with the practice of religion. Attempts to balance these two realities have occupied lawyers and government officials for years.

The balancing attempts have resulted in the concept of *accommodation of religion.* Government may, and perhaps should, accommodate religion. One type of accommodation, and perhaps the most well known, is that of tax-exempt status. Churches, institutions operated by religious organizations, and religious congregations of members with vows of poverty can be given tax-exempt status. The Internal Revenue Code, in Section 501 (c) (3), defines institutions that can be tax exempt.

Prohibition Against Political Activity

A prohibition is placed on tax-exempt institutions: a stricture against political activity, in particular lobbying. There are two kinds of lobbying, direct and grassroots. *Direct lobbying* is defined as "any attempt to influence legislation through communication with (a) [a]ny member or employee of a legislative body; or (b) [a]ny government official or employee . . . who may participate in the formulation of legislation" (IRC sec. 4911 (d)) (1), Regs. sec. 56.4911-2 (b) (1) (ii) (B)). *Grassroots lobbying* is defined as "any attempt to influence legislation through an attempt to affect the opinions of the general public" (IRC set. 4911 (d) (a) (A), Regs. Sec. 56.4911-2 (b) (1) (i)).

While the definitions may seem rather straightforward, the applications can be problematic. For example, the Catholic Church clearly does not sanction abortion. The Catholic Church and its members have the right to express their opinions on this moral topic. The tough part comes when a church member or official attempts to exercise freedom of religious expression while remaining within the strictures of IRS regulations that were clearly not part of the Founding Fathers' constitutional vision.

Endorsement of Candidates

One absolute prohibition for 501 (c) (3) organizations is the endorsement of political candidates. While many may remember the 1960 election of President Kennedy, which was urged by many teachers in Catholic classrooms and for which Catholic school children earnestly prayed, the 1960 election predated tax law reform. Today, such endorsements of candidates can result in a loss of tax-exempt status at worst. What is the Catholic educator to do when faced with students and parents asking questions about whether they are free to support a candidate with a pro-choice stance?

One of the best ways to deal with such situations is to reiterate clearly the church's teachings on abortion and to emphasize the individual's solemn duty to follow his or her conscience. Such an approach gives the information needed to make a reasonable decision, but does not indicate which candidate should be endorsed.

Tuition vouchers as a means of ensuring educational choice and aid for Catholic school parents are often supported by Catholic educators. The National Congress for Catholic Schools for the 21st Century (1991) adopted a goal of working toward full and fair parental choice in education. However, specific suggestions to endorse a candidate with pro-choice in education views must be avoided.

An approach that achieves much the same purpose but poses no legal threat to tax-exempt status is sending home information on parental choice and tuition vouchers along with the positions or voting records of all candidates or officials. Such a course of action is seen as educational rather than political, but the goal of educating parents and others on the importance of parental choice is met.

Tests for Political Action

Two types of tests for the presence of political action in nonprofit, 501 (c) (3) organizations are *substantial part* and *election*. The *substantial part* test demands that no substantial part of a charity's activity can consist of legislative or political activity. This test governs the activity of religious organizations. To date, no court has offered a clear definition of what constitutes substantial. Thus, it appears that courts are using a case-by-case basis of determination, deciding each case on its own merits rather than on black-letter law.

Some 501 (c) (3) organizations are permitted to use election, which allows them to stay within a predetermined percentage of political activity. However, the law specifically excludes churches and religious organizations from the election option. Thus, the Catholic administrator must keep in mind the prohibition against a substantial amount of political activity, although no one seems certain what constitutes a substantial amount.

Losing Tax-Exempt Status

To date, no Catholic entity has lost its tax-exempt status for political activity, but test cases have been filed and decided. Interested people might wish to consult *Abortion Rights Mobilization, Inc. v. Reagan*, 495 U.S. 918, 110 S. Ct. 1946 (1990), and *In re United States Catholic Conference*, 885 F.2d 1020 (2nd Cir. 1989), *Cert. den.*, 110 S.Ct. 1946 (1990).

Church-related institutions can lose tax-exempt status, as the case of *Bob Jones University v. United States*, 103 S.Ct. 2017 (1983), illustrates. The university, a religiously affiliated institution, had racially discriminatory admissions and discipline policies. The U.S. Supreme Court determined that racism is against public policy and permitted the IRS to revoke the school's tax-exempt status. Thus, there is a precedent for the revocation of a church-related institution's tax-exempt status.

Recommendations

The following recommendations are offered:

- Send information, not recommendations for action.
- Do not make statements favoring specific legislation of candidates to the media.
- Keep records of expenditures dealing with legislation.
- Avoid devoting a substantial part of the organization's activity to the dissemination of legislative or political information.
- Do not allow the school's name to be used in connection with any specific legislation of a political candidate.
- Consider forming a separate organization for lobbying purposes. Such an organization, which could be considered if an institution contemplates a great deal of political activity, can be tax exempt. However, it is not a 501 (c) (3) organization and donations to it cannot be taken as income tax deductions.

Recent Developments: Negligence and Teacher Unions

In the recent public school case Hernandez v. Renville Public School District, 542N.W. 2d 671 (Minn. App. 1996), "a parent brought a suit alleging negligence when her 4-year-old preschool child was injured falling from monkey bars." After examining all the facts, the court ruled that a school is not required to provide constant supervision of "all of the movement of all of the pupils all of the time." The incident could not have been prevented by any reasonable effort on the part of the teacher. Thus, the school was found not liable in this case.

Monkey bars and other playground equipment can pose dangers for children. The wise administrator carefully monitors the placement and maintenance of all playground equipment. Further, supervisory policies and procedures must be implemented. Nonetheless, this case indicates that at least one court recognizes that spontaneous accidents can occur in such instances, and neither the school nor the teacher should be held liable for injury.

The outcome of Association of *Catholic School Teachers Local 1776, Margaret J. Doyle, and Brian Fagari v. Pennsylvania Labor Relations Board and Norwood-Fontbonne Academy,* 671 A2d, 1207 (1996), demonstrates a judicial commitment to uphold the findings of National Labor Relations Board v. The Catholic Bishop of Chicago, 440 U.S. 490, 99 S.Ct. 1313, 59 L. Ed. 2d 533 (1979).

In the 1996 case, the academy appealed a lower court decision that determined that two of its employees were "public" and that the Pennsylvania Labor Relations Board had jurisdiction to consider a petition from the association requesting that it be certified as the representative of the lay teachers at the academy.

In 1979, the U.S. Supreme Court found that the NLRB does not have jurisdiction over the employees of a religiously affiliated educational institution. State labor relations boards do not have jurisdiction unless state law indicates specifically that employees of such institutions are covered.

Thus, employees of Catholic educational institutions cannot claim protection under state and federal laws as "public employees," nor can a Catholic educational institution be forced to recognize a union as the bargaining agent for its teachers.

While this case reaffirms the findings of the 1979 Supreme Court, it is important to remember that the Catholic Church does espouse the principles of justice and fair treatment of employees in *Rerum Novarum* and other documents. Catholic educational administrators should strive to treat people fairly and openly. The Catholic educational administrator who strives to be true to the message of the Gospel will seek to do the right thing for employees. Many Catholic schools cannot afford to meet the levels of compensation and benefits found in public schools, but they also cannot afford to be arbitrary or unjust in dealing with employees. 𝓝

May 2000

Free Speech and the Catholic Church

Recently, I was asked to participate in a public forum at Providence College in Rhode Island to address a situation involving three students who used an image of the Blessed Virgin and the statement "How's this for an immaculate concept: Keep abortion safe and legal" on a flyer. The president of Providence College disciplined the students by suspending them for the rest of the semester. In this issue of *NCEA Notes*, I would like to share some of the comments I made at the forum.

Oliver Wendell Holmes is reputed to have said: "I have a right to swing my arm, but my right to swing my arm ends where your nose begins." The question we must answer is "Who swung too close?" Sometimes people believe they have no rights in the Catholic Church. People do have rights but, as every reader should know, they do not come from the U.S. Constitution. They come from contract and statutory law. In a very real sense, one leaves the protections of the Constitution at the church or school door. One can always retrieve them, of course, but one has to leave the institution to do that.

While this reality may appear hard to swallow, it is not limited in applicability to religious institutions. Any private institution can enforce rules that may seem to deny the expression of constitutional rights. For example, if I work at McDonald's, do I have the right to express my opinion that Pizza Hut has the better buy? Most assuredly, I have that right. But I do not have any constitutional right to express that opinion in McDonald's. While working at McDonald's, I will not be permitted to tell people that Pizza Hut has a better deal.

The First Amendment states: "Congress shall make no law respecting an establishment of religion nor prohibiting the free exercise thereof." This clause is the basis for the separation of church and state doctrine. The state cannot intervene in matters of religion unless a compelling reason exists and there is no less-restrictive means to meet the demands of the compelling reason.

One of our founding fathers' most deeply held convictions was the necessity to keep church and state separate. The state cannot tell a church-related institution how to run its programs or develop its policies. As long as religion is not used as a smoke screen for some action, religious doctrine and practice can determine the permissibility of given actions. Next to Jesus Christ, the Virgin Mary is the most honored human person in the Catholic tradition. To use her image and part of her title, Immaculate Conception, in a pro-choice flyer is heresy to many.

Could the college have made a different decision? Legally, the college could have. Does the college have to do that? No. Just because a college can do something does not mean it should take that action. But Providence College and its administrators made the tough decision to express their disapproval of the three students' actions by separating them from the college community for a time, in an effort, no doubt, to underscore the importance of respecting, even if not accepting, the religious tenets of the institution and its sponsors.

Some believe that the punishment was too severe. But as long as the punishment does not "shock the conscience of the court," it can generally be upheld. Reasonable people can disagree on discipline. No one is necessarily wrong in personal beliefs. However, the college has a clear right to expect adherence to certain behaviors and to punish those who cross the line.

In this case, the students swung their collective arm too far. Just as Justice Black once observed, "You can't yell fire in a crowded theater. You can't enter a Jewish synagogue and utter anti-Semitic words," neither can one trivialize or mock the religious teachings of the church that sponsors a college, school, parish, or parish program without penalty. The students' arm made contact with the church's belief, and church officials are well within their rights to defend the institution and to discipline those who attacked or mocked a central religious figure.

Is this reality sometimes hard to live with? Of course. But remember that no one has to live with it. The door is always unlocked. One can leave the private institution and enter a public institution with different rules.

Further Comments

In the question-and-answer period, one student asked why the college did not provide forums on Catholic beliefs. The college's enrollment is over 80 percent Catholic and theology courses are required. If these college students perceive themselves as not knowing the tenets of the Catholic faith, all who work with children and teenagers must ask themselves, "How can I be sure that students know and understand the teachings of the Catholic Church?" ✒

January 2003

Search and Seizure:
If You Have to Do It, How Should You Do It?

∽𝕸𝕸∽

Many educators are reviewing the need for policies and procedures on student searches. Problems occur when a student alleges injury from a search of person or property. In 1985 the U.S. Supreme Court ruled in New Jersey v. T.L.O. that public school administrators did not need search warrants or probable cause to search students and their belongings. Probable cause is a stricter standard than reasonable cause and exists when a school official has reliable knowledge about the whereabouts of dangerous or potentially dangerous material on campus. Reasonable cause is a suspicion with some basis in fact. A phone call, a note, or a suspicious appearance can constitute reasonable cause.

The Catholic educator, obviously, is not bound to Fourth Amendment search-and-seizure requirements. However, parishes and schools could be subject to suits for damages if a young person alleges harm as a result of an unreasonable search. Teachers and administrators could be sued under tort law for assault and battery and invasion of privacy if appropriate search-and-seizure procedures are not followed. Commonsense precautions are in order. Teachers and other staff members should be given guidelines for any search of student belongings or students. Procedures for searching students should be more stringent than those for searching mere possessions. Strip searches should never be permitted.

School or parish property does not belong to the student. Schools and programs strengthen their legal positions by including a policy in the parent/student handbook stating "The school/parish is cotenant of lockers and desks and reserves the right to search them at any time without notice."

At the recent meeting of the Chief Administrators of Catholic Education, the author was asked to suggest some guidelines for search and seizure protocols. These follow.

General Considerations

1. Ask yourself if what you are looking for is worth the search. Looking for a lost dollar bill is generally not worth the effort beyond a general question, "Has anyone seen Tommy's dollar?"

2. Ask everyone to search around desks and lockers and in personal items. Approach is everything. A teacher might say, "Let's all look in our pockets and see if Mary's ring might have fallen in" (as the teacher looks in his or her pockets). In a secondary school setting, a teacher might say, "Mary has lost her ring. Does anyone have any idea where it might be?

Could you look in your belongings to see if it may have ended up with your things by mistake?" The teacher can then deal with the student who has the item, but the approach is not accusatory.

3. Have another staff member present in any searches of individual students or property.

Searching Lockers and Desks

1. Ask the student if there is anything he or she wishes to show you.

2. Ask the student to remove the items from the desk and open any you direct him or her to open.

3. Put any contraband in a separate container (if it will fit). Have the student sign a statement that the items were found in the locker or desk. Take the items to the office where the administrator can take over, talk with the student, and contact parents, if necessary.

4. If there is nothing "illegal" in the desk or locker, thank the student for his or her cooperation and state that you are glad that the matter has been resolved (in age-appropriate language, of course).

Searching Students and Purses, Coats or Book Bags (Considered Extensions of the Person)

1. Ask the student if you may search his or her pockets, coat, book bag, or purse.

2. If the answer is yes, ask the student to take everything out and show it to you.

3. If the answer is no, isolate the student and the purse or bag under someone's supervision.

4. Call the parent, explain the situation, tell the parent you would like to clear the student's name, and ask him or her to either tell the student to cooperate or to come to school and conduct the search himself or herself. If the parent refuses, tell the parent that the school/parental partnership is broken and ask the parent to consider where he or she will send the student to school.

If Police Ask to Search a Student

1. Ask for identification.

2. Ask if the officer has a warrant. If he or she has one, let the officer proceed. If there is no warrant, politely tell the officer that once one is obtained and presented, you will make the student available for a search. Exception: If a clear threat to health or safety is involved, use your best judgment and let the officer search the student on the school or church premises.

Administrators should not hesitate to consult with police officers and attorneys when needed.

When controversy arises, the best defense is having followed clear policies and procedures. ✒️

September 2004

Legal Victory for Catholic High School in Rhode Island: Implications for All Catholic Educators

A July 15, 2004, opinion for the Rhode Island Supreme Court, *Russell Gorman, Jr. et al. v. St. Raphael Academy,* No. 2003-371-Appeal (PC 01-4821), represents a victory for all Catholic schools. The decision clearly supports the right of Catholic schools and programs to establish reasonable rules and regulations. Courts have no right to interfere in private school disciplinary regulations unless they violate law or public policy.

The Facts

Russell Gorman, Jr., entered St. Raphael Academy in Pawtucket, RI, in fall 2001. Russell wears his hair six to eight inches below the shirt collar in the back. Shortly after the beginning of his freshman year, school officials instructed him to cut his hair or face expulsion. Russell, with his parents' support, refused. The parents sought and were granted a temporary restraining order keeping the school from expelling Russell for his hair length.

The principal revised the school handbook for the 2002–03 school year to include a new hair-length regulation stipulating that the hair of male students could be no longer than the bottom of the shirt collar. School officials testified that Russell's parents were notified of the impending rule change before the end of the school year. The parents claimed that they did not know of the change until the summer and were not given a new handbook until August of that year when they filed an amended complaint alleging breach of contract and seeking injunctive relief.

Legal Arguments and Decisions

The trial judge, relying on a public school case, held that the rule was arbitrary and capricious and that the school's rules had to be related to the mission of the school. In effect, the judge violated the principle of judicial restraint, which holds that courts do not generally substitute their opinions for those of the professionals. St. Raphael appealed the decision, which could have had the effect of making virtually every Catholic school rule subject to judicial scrutiny.

The Gormans alleged breach of contract; St. Raphael's argued that they did not identify the alleged contract, its terms, or breach. St. Raphael's further argued that the judge improperly placed the burden of proof on the school.

The state supreme court found that the trial judge applied equitable, rather than legal, contract principles to the claim. An equitable remedy is available only when there is no adequate remedy at law. The long-standing general principle has been that the remedy for breach of a contract for personal services (e.g., education) is damages, not reinstatement, because courts will not compel performance of such a contract if one of the parties does not wish to perform.

Additionally, the school argued that, since the parents did not sign the 2002–03 contract in the school handbook, no valid contract could exist.

The trial judge suggested that the Gormans had a four-year contract for Russell's education, a suggestion that the state supreme court rejected while it held that the contract was an annual one subject to renewal.

Question of First Impression

The state supreme court opinion held that this decision was one of first impression, the first time such a conflict had been litigated. Further, the justices observed that they could find no published case in any jurisdiction that dealt with hair-length rules in private educational institutions. Thus, this decision is groundbreaking.

Contract Law Rulings

The court stated, "Because contracts for private education have unique qualities, we must construe them in a manner that leaves the school administration broad discretion to meet its educational and doctrinal responsibilities." School handbooks can be considered contracts. Parents of St. Raphael's students are required to sign tuition contracts agreeing to the terms of the student handbook. Therefore, the court held that the relationship between students/parents and the school has to be a contractual one. The court held that, ". . . absent a violation of law or public policy, it is not within the province of the court to inject itself in the rule-making authority of a private school."

The court recognized that some public school litigants have alleged that the right to wear one's hair the way one wishes is a constitutional freedom guaranteed by the First Amendment, but, following earlier federal decisions, held that a private school would have to be a state agent before it would be required to recognize constitutional rights. Therefore, no constitutional protections exist.

Conclusion

Catholic schools and programs everywhere owe a debt of gratitude to St. Raphael's Academy. The willingness of the school and the diocese to fight for the right of Catholic schools to enact and enforce rules makes administration an easier task and underscores the reality that contract law, not constitutional law, governs the relationship of a Catholic school with its students.

November 2006

Freedom of Expression and Catholic Educators

⌘

"Why can't I express my personal opinion outside the school or parish? I understand that I don't have First Amendment freedom-of-speech rights while I am working, but I don't think that what I do outside the parish or school is the administrator's or pastor's business."

Administrators hear such statements more and more. However honest the complaint may be, it ignores a basic reality: Religious institutions have the legal right to set certain requirements for the conduct of personnel, especially when that conduct violates a religious belief.

Cases involving violation or public repudiation of the sponsoring religion's beliefs are definitely increasing. This is not only a Catholic issue, but also one that can affect virtually every religion. The reader is probably most familiar with Catholic disputes, which can include but are not limited to abortion, cohabitation, living with a partner in an openly gay lifestyle, divorce and remarriage without an annulment, pregnancy of an unmarried woman, artificial insemination, supporting birth control methods not approved by the church, euthanasia, and women's ordination. People are perhaps more aware of such issues and violations now than they would have been 30 years or a century ago. However, as the old adage instructs, there is "nothing new under the sun." Nothing that happens today was impossible a century ago—although bad behavior probably was not public knowledge and may have been hushed up. The author has had conversations with elderly members of her religious community and others who report similar situations occurring 50 to 60 years ago.

So the question still remains: "How Catholic do Catholic school teachers and parish volunteers have to be?" The answer is, on one level, quite simple. One must publicly support or, at least not repudiate, the teachings of the Catholic Church. If one does not support or if one repudiates church teachings, one's position may be terminated.

Three cases will illustrate. In 1980, plaintiff Ms. Dolter, an unmarried pregnant teacher in a Catholic high school, brought a sexual discrimination claim against the school when her contract was not renewed. The school claimed that freedom of religion protections shielded it from liability because sex outside marriage is against the religious beliefs of the Catholic Church. The plaintiff introduced evidence that unmarried male teachers who fathered children were treated differently than unmarried pregnant teachers, although both had engaged in premarital sex. Rejecting the school's claim, the court held that the case was not about freedom of religion or about violating religious beliefs; rather it was about the unequal application of those beliefs on the basis of sex. Had the school introduced clear evidence that males who fathered children out of wedlock were dismissed, its action may have been upheld. (See *Dolter v. Whalert High School,* 483 F.Supp. 266.)

In the 1991 case of *Little v. St. Mary Magdalene School,* 929 F.2d 944, a non-Catholic teacher was fired after she married a divorced Catholic whose first marriage had not been annulled. Such a marriage was perfectly acceptable in her religion. She had signed a contract containing a Cardinal's Clause, however, which required her to live a life consistent with the teachings of the Catholic Church. The court ruled in favor of the school.

In June 2006 the Third Circuit Court of Appeals rendered a precedent-setting decision in *Curay-Cramer v. Ursuline Academy of Wilmington,* No. 04-4628. The plaintiff had signed a pro-choice ad that was printed in the newspaper and the school terminated her employment. She filed suit, alleging violation of her rights under Title VII and the Pregnancy Discrimination Act. Upholding the lower court's ruling in favor of the school, District Judge Kent Jordan noted that Title VII has a specific provision exempting religious employers from the prohibition against religious discrimination. Further, her claims were without merit:

> *Short of a declaration that the Pope should pass draft encyclicals through the courts for approval, it is hard to conceive of a more obvious violation of the free exercise rights of the Catholic Church or a clearer case of inappropriate entanglement of church and state.*

The religious exemption allows religious institutions to make hiring and firing decisions on the basis of religion. In any other type of institution, such decisions cannot be made on the basis of religious principles. As long as the religious belief is sincerely held, courts will not judge the rightness or wrongness of the belief, since such judgment would violate the required separation of church and state.

Conclusion

When one works in a religious institution, freedom of speech as guaranteed by the First Amendment does not exist. An employee or volunteer must support the religious beliefs of the sponsor. There is no legal requirement that one agree with the beliefs, but courts will generally uphold employment decisions based on an employee's behavior that is inconsistent with the tenets of the sponsoring religion.

Ethics

September 1997

Law and Ethics

⌘

"The last temptation is the greatest treason; to do the right deed for the wrong reason."

These lines by T.S. Eliot from *Murder in the Cathedral* offer fruitful meditation for administrators who face complex situations calling for the wisdom of Solomon, the tact of a public relations firm, and the faith to move mountains. Many crises do not lend themselves to textbook solutions. Sometimes civil law may dictate or allow one course of action, but conscience may require another. Why not simply decline to renew a troublesome teacher's contract and avoid another year of trying to work with the individual? The decision is certainly legal, the apparent right thing to do. When and how such decisions are made are ethical issues. Or consider the parent who has complained bitterly about the school and its staff, and who perhaps has also attempted to organize other parents to express discontent. It is tempting to refuse registration forms and fees for the parent's children for the following school year.

In both of these scenarios, the law is on the side of the administrator. Since contract law governs private education, administrators of Catholic programs do not have to be concerned about constitutional rights of parents, students, and teachers because such rights do not exist in a Catholic school. It can be truthfully said that one leaves one's constitutional rights at the door when entering a Catholic school or program. Hence, administrators may believe that they are a law unto themselves and can take actions that might appear arbitrary to others. Because the remedy for breach of contract is damages, a Catholic institution will never have to take back an unwanted individual.

Requirements of the Law

Civil law requires that parties to contracts act in good faith and treat each other fairly. Individuals are assumed to know what they are agreeing to do when they enter into the agreement. Courts will generally not intervene in matters that may touch on religion because of the separation of church and state required by the First Amendment to the U.S. Constitution. Yet a wise observer might comment, "You say that you are Christian. Would Jesus hold people to standards they did not know existed? Would Jesus change the rules or add new ones?"

In 1988, the noted columnist Delores Curran observed, "Our church can be a lousy employer." What is a 55-year-old single woman who has taught at a school for 30 years going to do if her contract is not renewed? The answer to that question is not the legal responsibility of the administrator who made the nonrenewal decision. But is it the moral responsibility?

These questions are not meant to suggest that every teacher or employee should be rehired even if incompetent. Rather, these questions suggest that just policies should be in place and people should be given ample time and help to improve before their employment is ended.

Student Behavior

Student behavior poses dilemmas as well. For example, it is not just for an administrator to dismiss a student for an offense while looking the other way when another student does the same thing. Just policies can allow for flexibility in extenuating circumstances without destroying credibility. All policy action should reflect a reasoned, prayerful approach to decision-making.

Conclusion

It is fairly easy to identify legal principles and decide what one can and can't do. It is not so easy to decide what one should do. The question should not be "Is this what we can do?" but rather "Is this what Jesus would do?" It is tempting to identify the legal issues and forget the rest. One should remember Jesus' words: "You hypocrites. You see the mote in your brother's eye and ignore the plank in your own."

Those of us with responsibility for the lives of others should always ask, "Is this the right thing to do? How will I feel about this decision in a year? 10 years? Is this what I would want done if I were in this situation? Is this what would Jesus would do?"

In the final analysis, Jesus' opinion, not an earthly court's ruling, is what matters.

The Overturning of Aguilar

On June 23, 1997, the U.S. Supreme Court reversed its 1985 decision in Aguilar v. Felton, which in effect outlawed the provision of Title I services in educational institutions with religious ties. In Agostini v. Felton, 117 S.Ct. 1997, 138 L.Ed.2d 391, the court ruled that such services could lawfully be provided.

September 1997

Legal and Ethical Issue of september 11, 2001

ᏯᎢᎻᎢᏋ

What Do We Say to Our Young People?

I write this column a few days after the world as we knew it changed forever. The words of Psalm 30 echo in my mind: "In my security, I thought I could never be disturbed." My 4-year-old nephew greeted me that fateful evening with an account of the day's events. He and his classmates watched the tragedy on television in his preschool classroom. His 8-year-old brother, disturbed by the accounts of planes crashing into buildings and people being killed, did not want to go to school the next day.

Families all over America met similar situations and those in school and parish leadership positions now deal with this situation and all the accompanying fallout. By the time this column appears, months will have passed and hopefully some of the terror will have subsided. But the real, legal, ethical, and human questions will remain. How do we keep our young people safe? How do we prepare them for the reality that we are all vulnerable?

Most administrators develop crisis plans and practice what to do when the unthinkable happens, but few were prepared for the tragedies of New York, Washington, D.C., and Pennsylvania. What do we do in times of tragedy? This column will attempt to address some of the questions that rose from the wreckage of September 11, 2001.

A Crisis Plan in Time of National Tragedy

Crisis plans are written to help both students and staff deal with horrible situations. Although most crisis plan writers envision individual crises in single institutions, the same principles of action should apply in national, large-scale emergencies. Administrators may decide to gather the entire community together for prayer and conversation. Leaders should rely on their own knowledge and experience; if something does not feel right, it probably is not right.

Should We Cancel School or Religious Education?

Resist the temptation to send everyone home to be with parents and family. Administrators have the same legal supervisory responsibilities in times of crisis as in times of normalcy. Children cannot just be sent home. Most schools in the United States kept young people in class on September 11, 2001, following as normal a schedule as possible. Psychologists report that routine is important in times of shock and grief.

Should We Let Young People Watch Television?

One can advance an argument that it is better for young people to discuss tragedy in a structured environment than to leave students to their own unguided thoughts. Given the human fascination with tragedy, educators need to provide a steadying, calm, and reasoned response to tragedy, as well as an atmosphere of respectful questioning and reflection. The age of the child must also be a consideration. Adults should be careful that their desire to stay informed does not overshadow meeting the needs of students.

What if a Parent Wants to Take a Child Out of School?

As always, parents have the absolute legal right to take their children out of school. This right remains whether the absence is for a good reason or no reason at all. If a parent insists on a doctor's appointment during the school day, the school cannot refuse to release the child. The school must return the child to his or her parents (subject, of course, to any legal custodial arrangements). Some principals commented that concerned parents called schools on September 11, but were willing to allow the children to stay in school when officials explained that students were safe and that the school was taking all reasonable precautions.

How Can We Reassure Students?

As one high school principal put it, "In times like these, our faith sustains us." We cannot guarantee students that they will always be safe and that nothing bad will ever happen to them. We can assure them that a loving God and a loving religious community will stand with them to face whatever happens.

What Does this Column Have to Do With the Law?

Actually, this author believes the answer to this question is "everything." We cannot educate students unless we meet our legal responsibilities to keep them physically and emotionally as safe as possible. All of us who work with young people need to reflect on our legal responsibilities, first and foremost, to provide a Catholic education rooted in the faith of the Gospel.

Students

and FAMILIES

January 1991

Student Rights and School Responsibilities

∽⁓

All school administrators face the challenge of respecting student rights while upholding discipline and order. Common law and common sense indicate that people and institutions responsible for the education of youth are expected to hold students to standards of behavior. The main source of law governing Catholic school and student conflicts is contract law.

Nonetheless, the Catholic school administrator needs to understand the constitutional protections available in the public sector. Recent decisions have indicated that courts, using contractual doctrines of fair play and arm's-length dealing, can require Catholic schools to provide protections very similar to those required in the public school.

Due Process and Fairness

The Fifth Amendment to the Constitution requires that no person shall "be deprived of life, liberty, or property" without due process of law. There are two types of due process: substantive and procedural.

Substantive due process can be defined as fundamental fairness involving moral as well as legal ramifications: Is this action fair and reasonable? Substantive due process applies when property (a right of ownership) or liberty (right to freedom or reputation) interests can be demonstrated.

Although not protected by the Constitution, Catholic students and parents have property rights in the contract between the parent and the school. Courts can consider parent and student handbooks or similar documents as conferring property rights. Failure to protect the reputation of students can result in defamation liability in the Catholic school in the same way such a failure can result in constitutional violation of liberty interests in the public school.

Catholic school officials should naturally be concerned about protecting the good name of all entrusted to their care. Disciplinary procedures, records, etc., may have an impact on a student's reputation. Care must be taken to guard against unnecessary harm.

Procedural due process has been defined as a question: What process is due? In the public sector, several elements are present. In meeting the requirements of fairness, Catholic school administrators should ask themselves these questions:

- What are our disciplinary procedures?
- Are they reasonable?

- Are all students treated fairly and, as far as reasonably possible, in the same way?
- Is there a clear procedure that students and parents can expect will be followed?

Privacy and Access

Student privacy must be protected. Disciplinary and other nonacademic records should be stored in files separate from permanent records. When a student transfers or graduates, only the permanent records should be sent to the new school. Parents have a right to inspect any and all records. All other persons should be denied access without written parental permission or a court order.

Historical Perspective

Before the 1960s, judgments were rarely made in favor of students. Courts instead invoked the doctrine of in loco parentis, which holds that schools act in the place of parents, even if the school makes decisions that parents would not reasonably make. The right of both public and private schools to discipline was seen as absolute.

This doctrine was largely abandoned in a series of cases beginning with *Tinker v. Des Moines Ind. School District,* 393 U.S. 503 (1969), in which the Supreme Court held that students in public elementary and secondary schools had First Amendment rights. Although *Tinker* has no direct bearing on Catholic school administration, it does reflect the willingness of the court to uphold student rights.

In a 1974 landmark case, *Goss v. Lopez,* 19 U.S. 565, the Supreme Court held that a student facing suspension should, at the very least, be given notice and some kind of hearing. The court's comments provide fruitful reflection for educators in both the public and private sector: "[I]t would be a strange disciplinary system in an educational institution if no communication was sought by the disciplinarian in an effort to . . . inform him [the student] of his dereliction and to let him tell his side of the story in order to make sure that injustice is not done" (p. 580).

One of the most significant Catholic school cases is *Geraci v. St. Xavier High School,* 13 Ohio Opinions 3d 146 (Ohio 1978), in which the state supreme court indicated that courts would intervene in private school disciplinary cases if procedures were not fair.

Most school officials and attorneys would agree that the best school law is, like medicine, preventive. The best defense is having tried to follow the right course in the first place. School administrators must realize that, despite their best efforts in any and all areas of school life, they may face lawsuits.

Courts look for evidence of good faith: Did the institution have a rule promulgated? Did the student know of the rule? The court does not concern itself with the wisdom of the rule—or even with the rightness or wrongness of the professional opinion of educators.

The court is concerned only with the existence of a properly promulgated rule and with the institution's acting in good faith according to stated procedures. Courts look for basic fairness in the execution of the contract existing between the student/parent and the school when the student alleges that a school acted improperly.

Principals must understand that it is impossible to identify everything a student might do that could result in suspension or expulsion. Therefore, it is advisable to have some kind of catchall clause, such as "other inappropriate conduct" or "conduct, whether inside or outside the school, that is detrimental to the reputation of the school." No court will expect a school to have listed all possible offenses, but courts will expect that something is written and that students and parents have a reasonable idea of the school's expectations.

Guidelines

The beginning point for rules development should be the school's philosophy. All students, even first graders, can be brought to some understanding of philosophy: "At our school we try to treat each other the way we want to be treated." The life of the school should be seen as flowing from the philosophy.

Rules should be clear and understandable. The test that might be applied by the court is "Would two persons of average intelligence reading this rule have the same understanding of it?"

A rule stating "Students arriving at class after the bell will be marked tardy" is clear, while a rule such as "Late students will be marked tardy" is open to such questions as "How late is late? After the bell? After the teacher begins class?"

Whenever possible, rules should be written. It is easier to refer to the written rule when emotions run high than to insist, "This rule was announced at the beginning of the school year."

Every school should have a written handbook. Parents should be required to sign a form stating that they have read the rules and agree to be governed by them.

When considering the development of student guidelines, educators should be aware that a time investment is involved. If a teacher allows a student to tell his or her story instead of summarily imposing punishment ("All students whose names are on the board will remain after school"), the teacher makes a commitment to spending time with a student who faces discipline.

The principal or disciplinarian makes a commitment to listening to the student's side of the story as well as to the teacher's, but the benefit should be obvious: Students will perceive teachers and administrators as trying to be fair and, hopefully, will internalize the values modeled.

Somewhat more extensive procedures should be developed if the penalty is suspension. One-day suspensions, at minimum, require that the principal or vice-principal be involved and that the parents be notified. Longer suspensions should involve a written notice of the charges and a hearing.

Cases involving the possibility of expulsion require both formal notification and a hearing at which the student normally should be able to confront accusers. Careful documentation must be kept in all major disciplinary proceedings. There is no requirement, however, that a student be allowed to have legal counsel present at any stage of the school's disciplinary proceedings.

The guiding principle in any consideration of student rights and discipline should be the desire to act in a Christian manner characterized by fairness and compassion.

Recent Developments: Corporal Punishment Revisited

One of the more emotional topics in education is corporal punishment. Since the 1977 case of *Ingraham v. Wright,* 430 U.S. 65, in which the Supreme Court ruled that public school students do not have Eighth Amendment protections against cruel and unusual punishment, states have been embroiled in controversies. The majority of states still permit corporal punishment. Only a handful of states outlaw it in both public and private sectors. [In 2007 the vast majority of states outlaw corporal punishment, many taking such actions as a result of *Ingraham.*]

Two recent cases indicate that the controversy continues. In the Texas case, *Fee v. Herndon,* 900 F.2d 804 (5th Cir. 1990), the court ruled that reasonable corporal punishment does not conflict with the due process clause. Echoing Ingraham, the court referred the student to other remedies, civil and criminal, for excessive corporal punishment and refused to support a constitutional claim for due process relief under the Fifth and 14th Amendments. The court did note that excessive corporal punishment could be deemed child abuse.

In a Wisconsin case, *Thrasher v. General Casualty Co. of Wisconsin,* 732 F.Supp. 966 (W.D. Wisc. 1990), the court sought to determine whether throwing or pushing a student into a blackboard exceeded acceptable limits of corporal punishment. The court declined to find Eighth Amendment protections and rejected a claim that the teacher's action constituted an unreasonable seizure under the Fourth Amendment.

The court, however, refused to grant summary judgment for the teacher. Citing the 1980 case of *Hall v. Tawney,* 621 D. 2d 607, which held that substantive due process violations could result from excessive corporal punishment, the court remanded the case to the lower court for a determination of whether the student's substantive due process right to be free from unnecessary bodily harm had been violated.

Thrasher illustrates the notion that corporal punishment can be defined as any punitive touching. Although constitutional issues are not present in corporal punishment cases in the private sector, Catholic school principals would be well advised to prohibit corporal punishment. The risks of a student's sustaining psychological or physical harm and of the school's incurring legal liability are too great. [Note: The majority of states now outlaw corporal punishment in schools. Sixteen years after the publication of this article, the author can only reiterate the importance of avoiding corporal punishment and punitive touching. Courts are increasingly unwilling to uphold corporal punishment as a legitimate means of discipline. From a legal standpoint, educators should make it a practice to always employ an alternative means of discipline and correction.] 🖉

March 1994

Students With Special Needs in Catholic Schools

⁶〰〰〰⁹

Today's Catholic school principals face many challenges. Litigation against Catholic schools and their administrators is on the rise. Students with special needs present special concerns. Section 504 of the Rehabilitation Act of 1973 and the 1992 Americans with Disabilities Act (ADA) can seem legal quagmires for the educator. Myths and half-truths abound. Some consultants and lawyers have advised principals that schools must be made totally accessible. Many administrators fear that the cost of accommodations will be so high as to force schools out of existence. Other administrators question accepting students with special needs. Can the average Catholic school provide the proper program adjustments these students need? Catholic school personnel need a clear understanding of legal requirements.

Discrimination Law

Federal law prohibits discrimination on the basis of race, sex, disability, age, and national origin. Although discrimination on the basis of religion or creed is also prohibited, the right of religious institutions to give preference to their own members is upheld. Practically, this means that Catholic schools may give preference to Catholic students and may give hiring preference to Catholic teachers and other employees.

Public Law 94-142

Catholic school administrators must understand the law governing students with special needs. Public Law 94-142, the Education of All Handicapped Children Act, ensures a "free and appropriate education" for all children. It does not require Catholic schools to provide the "free and appropriate education." However, in situations in which the only school for the handicapped or disabled is one operated by the Catholic Church or some other private organization, the state may place a child in a private school if that placement seems to provide the most appropriate education. In such a case, the state would be responsible for the tuition.

Catholic schools are not required to meet every need of every child. Most private schools are not equipped to offer educational services to everyone. The fact that a school does not have to offer services does not mean that a student attending that school has no right to such services. Public Law 94-142 gives students rights. A private school student has a right to request and receive an evaluation and, if necessary, an Individualized Education Program (IEP). The public school must make every reasonable effort to provide the student with services needed even if the student remains in the private school.

If it is not practical to offer such services to a private school student, public school officials can draw up an IEP that calls for public school education. A parent is always free to accept or reject such an IEP. If a parent elects to keep a child in a private school over the objections of the professional educators working with that child, the public school cannot be held responsible for the child's progress nor can the public school be required to pay private school tuition.

It is important to note that the private school student and the public school student have the same federal protections. The private school student is entitled to the same services a public school student is entitled to receive. However, the private school student may not be able to insist that the services be provided within a private school as part of an IEP.

Standards of Supervision

Principals, many of whom are familiar with the adage "the younger the child chronologically or mentally, the greater the standard of care," may ask: "If we accept students with special needs, are we committing ourselves to higher levels of supervision?"

Teachers can be held to different standards. For example, a teacher supervising a senior honors class will probably be held to a lower standard than an individual teaching kindergarten children. Courts assume that older children can take some responsibility for themselves.

Chronological age is concerned with the effect that a disability may have on a child. If a Catholic school accepts a student with a mental disability, teachers must accommodate the disability. If a child performs well below grade level and exhibits immature behavior, a teacher may be expected to provide more stringent supervision than that given to other students.

Some disabilities are not mental, of course. If a child is an amputee, the child will need more supervision and help in physical activities than others may need.

Discipline

All students need to be accountable to people in authority. Special needs children are no exception. Schools have the right to require that all students abide by a code of conduct. Every student in a Catholic school should be expected to obey the rules.

Exceptions are in order only when the infraction is the result of the disability. If students who use walkers or crutches could not get to class on time because they simply could not move fast enough, it would be unfair to penalize them for being late. Another example is presented by a student with Tourette Syndrome, which is often characterized by bizarre behavior such as swearing. If a student suffering from Tourette Syndrome were to use profanity, it might be unfair to discipline the student if the behavior is beyond the student's control.

ADA Requirements

The Americans with Disabilities Act, like Section 504 of the Rehabilitation Act of 1973, requires that disabled persons be offered reasonable accommodation, those that an institution could be expected to fund. It would not be reasonable to suppose that a Catholic school should institute a special program with special teachers for a blind student or a profoundly mentally handicapped student.

Neither Section 504 of the Rehabilitation Act nor the ADA requires that institutions create programs to meet the needs of the disabled. These laws do require that institutions not discriminate against people who seek admission to their programs.

If a disabled person can participate in the program with a reasonable amount of accommodation, the institution must provide the accommodation. If providing that support system would create a significant hardship, the institution does not have to provide it. For example, if a blind student were to seek admission, and acceptance of that student would require that a special teacher be employed for the student and that all teachers learn Braille, the school would probably not be expected to incur those expenses.

Frankly, however, simply because one is not legally required to do something, it does not follow that one should not do it if it is the right thing to do. If a school has significant assets and could afford a sign language interpreter for a deaf student or instructions in signing for the faculty and staff, the administrator may have a moral and ethical duty to provide for the student even though the law does not require such provision. Indeed, the *Pastoral Statement of U.S. Catholic Bishops on Handicapped People* (1978) seems to demand such action: "If handicapped people are to become equal partners in the Christian community, injustices must be eliminated." Certainly, Catholic schools should be leaders in fighting injustice wherever it is found, especially as it affects people whose disabilities place them among those for whom Christ manifested special concern.

Students' Rights

"All students have the right to a free and appropriate education," according to Public Law 94-142, the Education of All Handicapped Children Act. Students must be evaluated for special services at parental request, but the law does not entitle students to a special needs program. Catholic school students have the same rights to evaluation as public school students. However, the program recommended as a result of the evaluation may not be available in the Catholic school, which is only required to make reasonable accommodations.

Public Law 94-142 requires that students receive a "free and appropriate" education, but it does not require that the education be the best available. To require the best education would mean that school systems would constantly be meeting parental demands for instructional services that could "better" student performance.

Much apprehension could be alleviated if administrators clearly understood what the law does and does not require. In the final analysis, though, the question is not "Did you do what you had to do?" but "Did you do what you could?" [Note: PL 94-142 has been succeeded by the No Child Left Behind Act and other laws.]

Recent Developments

In a recent case under the Individuals with Disabilities Education Act, the U.S. District Court for the Southern District of Texas held that the parents of a hearing-impaired student were not entitled to reimbursement from the public school district for their unilateral change of their child to a private program. The parents disagreed with the particular program the Individualized Education Program (IEP) offered the student.

They argued that since they did not believe the public school program offered their child the best possible education, they should be allowed to enroll their child in the school they believed provided the best program. Further, the parents claimed that the public school district was legally bound to reimburse them for the cost of private school tuition.

The student, however, was making progress in an appropriate manner in the public school program in which she had been enrolled. Thus, the court found that no reimbursement was in order. (*Bonnie Ann F. by John R. v. Calallen Independent School Dist. (S.D. Tex.)*, Civ. No. C-91-259, Sept. 9, 1993.)

In a similar case, *Doe By and Through Doe v. Board of Education Tullahoma City Schools* (C.A. Tenn.), No. 92-5996, Nov. 5, 1993, a federal appeals court held that a student's IEP met the standards of the Individuals with Disabilities Education Act. The student suffered from a neurological impairment, which hindered his ability to process auditory information and use normal language and thinking skills.

The IEP offered mainstreaming, with a provision for oral rather than written examinations and tutorial assistance. Although the parents contested the IEP, the court found that an appropriate education was being provided. Thus, the court declined to require the school board to reimburse parents for private tuition when they removed the student to a private program.

Both cases indicate that courts are reluctant to require reimbursement for private school tuition if the program developed for a special needs student appears to provide an appropriate education. Catholic school administrators should be wary of any parent of a special needs student who claims that tuition will be paid by a public school district.

May 1994

Parents and Catholic Education:
Rights and Responsibilities

⌇⌇⌇

When a parent enrolls a child in a Catholic school or other educational program, that parent has expectations of the school, parish, and administrators. Some parents, like some employees, really do not understand the law as it affects private education. They do not realize that public education and private education are governed by different rules. This difference, if not understood, can seriously affect the parent's relationship with the school.

Constitutional Law

Parents and students generally expect that they have the same rights as their public school counterparts. A parent may quickly come to a student's defense if the student faces discipline for wearing nonuniform clothing or for being groomed in a manner deemed unacceptable by the school.

However, a Catholic school may restrict the wearing of articles such as long chains, gaudy jewelry, sneakers, and sweatshirts containing slogans considered inappropriate for a Catholic school, and school officials may prohibit extreme hairstyles. A parent may assert that the student's actions are protected by the First Amendment when, in fact, there is no such protection.

Constitutional protections are guaranteed by the government, which pledges to respect certain rights outlined in the U.S. Constitution. Since a public school is a government agency, it is held to the same constitutional requirements that bind any government agency.

The Catholic school or other educational program is a private agency administered by private agents, and such agents do not have to enforce constitutional protections. Thus, one can legislate in a Catholic school what cannot lawfully be mandated in a public school. In effect, a parent enrolling a child in a Catholic school surrenders constitutional protections because the Catholic school is not a government entity. When one enters a private organization such as a Catholic school, one leaves constitutional rights at the door. Those rights can always be reclaimed when one leaves the private sector. While one is in the private institution, sources other than the Constitution must provide protection.

It is not unusual for parents to claim that their constitutional rights have been violated in the Catholic school when, in fact, no constitutional rights existed in the first place. These realities need to be clarified very early in the relationship between a Catholic school system and parents. One way to prevent possible misunderstandings is to develop and disseminate comprehensive handbooks that outline the rights and responsibilities of all people in the school.

Contract Law

Although not protected by the Constitution, Catholic school students and parents have rights conferred by the contract, oral or written, existing between the parents and the school. Oral contracts can be upheld. For example, a court can decide that, in enrolling a child in a Catholic school, a parent agrees to follow the rules of that school. When the Catholic school administrator accepts the parent's payment of tuition or other consideration, the Catholic school has entered into a contract to educate the student. While oral contracts may be recognized, it is a far better practice to commit the contract to a signed writing between the two parties. Having such a written document enables everyone to determine exactly what was agreed on by the parties.

Breach of Contract

When parents object to the treatment of their children or themselves, they may threaten or even initiate lawsuits. Unless the lawsuit alleges negligence (such as a child's injury resulting from the presence of some safety hazard in the school), a court will generally have to determine whether a breach of contract has occurred. Courts look for evidence of good faith: Did the school have a rule promulgated? Did the parents and students know of the rule?

The court does not concern itself with the wisdom of the rule—or even with the rightness or wrongness of the professional opinion of those who wrote the rule. The court is concerned only with the existence of a properly promulgated rule and with the institution's acting in good faith according to stated procedures. Courts look for basic fairness in the execution of the contract between the parent and the school when the parent alleges that school officials acted improperly.

Administrators must understand that it is impossible to identify every possible situation in a handbook. Therefore, it is advisable to have some kind of catchall clauses. In student discipline matters, a handbook might include statements such as "other inappropriate conduct" or "conduct, whether inside or outside the school, that is detrimental to the reputation of the school." No court will expect an administrator to have listed all possible offenses, but courts will expect that something is written and that students and parents have a reasonable idea of the expectations of the school.

Whenever possible, rules should be written. It is easier to refer to the written rule when emotions run high than to insist, "Before Christmas, you were told about this rule." Every school should have some kind of written handbook, even if it is only a few pages long. Parents should be required to sign a form stating that they have read the handbook and agree to be governed by it. The signatures serve as evidence that the parent entered into the contract and that the parent understood the provisions of the contract.

Rights of Parents

It is not uncommon to hear Catholic school parents declare that they have no rights in the Catholic school. Such a statement is simply untrue. Parental rights do exist and are grounded in contract law, as discussed above. Parents also have rights under statutory law and commonly accepted standards of fair play, known as common law.

For example, federal and state statutes against racial discrimination protect Catholic school parents. State statutes can also provide additional protection, if they apply to both public and private schools. For example, it is generally considered acceptable to withhold student records for nonpayment of tuition. However, a few states, such as Massachusetts, have statutes mandating the release of student records within a certain number of days, regardless of unpaid tuition or other debts.

Parents may ask, "What rights do we have in a Catholic school?" A complete listing and thorough discussion of all rights is beyond the scope of this brief essay. However, one would be well advised to consider some sort of parental bill of rights or school commitment to parents that could be included in a handbook. At the very least, parents have the following legal rights:

- To have children receive an academically sound education in a Catholic environment
- To talk with school personnel and to have requests for meetings answered in a timely manner
- To receive fair hearings of concerns and grievances
- To have students supervised in a safe and appropriate manner
- To review records and respond
- To participate in the life of the school

Pertinent NCEA Publications

Readers may find the following NCEA publications by this author helpful in studying legal issues concerning parents and in constructing legally sound policies, procedures, and handbooks: *A Primer on School Law, School Handbooks, Catholic Preschools, Extended Care Programs in Catholic Schools, Catholic Schools and the Law: Approaching the New Millennium, Ethics and the Law, Volunteers in Catholic Schools,* and *A Primer on Law for DREs and Youth Ministers.* (A small pamphlet on parent rights and responsibilities, suitable for distribution to parents, is in progress.) [Note: The pamphlet, *Your Rights and Responsibilities in a Catholic School,* is now in its second edition.]

March 1998

Conflicts with Parents

Almost every administrator and teacher has experienced the dilemmas posed by parents who cannot or will not support school policies, procedures, rules, or personnel. Reasonable people do differ in interpretations of situations and most people can work through their differences to a solution that everyone can accept, even if the solution is not an individual's personal preference. Problems result when parents refuse to accept reasonable actions by school officials.

Don't Take It Personally

The educator should avoid regarding disagreements as personal. Words said in anger in the heat of an argument can come back to haunt the speaker. All educators must guard against saying harsh words or making accusations that could be repeated in a manner detrimental to the speaker, both for commonsense and legal reasons. Depending on the nature of what is actually said, angry statements could be used as evidence of defamation of character or to prove points in a lawsuit.

What Rights Does a Parent Have?

When parents enroll their children in Catholic schools or programs, they should have certain expectations: The children will be provided with an excellent Catholic education, they will pay tuition or support the school or programs in other ways, their children's safety will be paramount, they will have reasonable access to instructors and administrators, they can present concerns and receive fair hearings, and they will accept the rules and regulations of the school or program.

The U.S. Constitution does not govern private institutions. Many parents do not know this fact, and will argue that constitutional rights have been violated when no such rights ever existed. Administrators should be aware, however, that statutory law enacted by legislatures can apply to private institutions. Contract law governs private institutions. All parents and guardians enrolling students should sign an enrollment agreement, which should include a provision agreeing to be governed by the parent/student handbook.

Who Broke the Contract?

In any parent/school disputes on discipline or other policies and procedures that result in lawsuits, courts will have to determine if a contract has been broken and, if so, whether the parent and student or the school broke it. Courts look for evidence of good faith: Did the school have a rule promulgated? Did the parents and students know about the rules?

Courts generally are not concerned about the wisdom or advisability of policies and procedures, as long as they do not "shock the conscience of the court." The court is concerned only with the existence of a properly promulgated rule and with the institution's acting in good faith according to stated procedures.

Courts look for basic fairness in the implementation of contracts when a parent alleges that officials have acted improperly. Because situations can arise that were not foreseen when the handbook was written, administrators are well advised to include a catchall clause such as "other inappropriate conduct" to allow for action on unforeseen, yet unacceptable, conduct.

What's the Bottom Line?

The bottom line is to be fair. Act the way Jesus would and you will not have to worry about whether you did the right thing, even if you are sued. You will also be able to present evidence that you acted in good faith.

Hear concerns calmly. Be sure to have a grievance procedure and adhere to it. Point out the appropriate rule or regulation. Answer any questions the parent has. Consider reasonable requests. Remind the parent that he or she has signed an agreement to be governed by the handbook and/or rules and regulations of the school. Offer to assist the parent in finding another school if a serious impasse exists.

What if all efforts fail? The administrator should consider asking the parent to transfer his or her child at the end of the semester or year if no solution can be reached. The student's interests are most important and cannot be served if parents and education officials cannot work together. Some handbooks contain statements such as "The school reserves the right to require the parent to withdraw from a working partnership." Every administrator should hope that such extreme actions would be rare.

Supervisors, pastors, and diocesan officials, of course, should be kept informed. Not every school or program is right for every child or parent, and appropriate action must be taken when mutual cooperation cannot be sustained.

November 2000

Special Education:
What Can We Do? What Should We Do?

⟨≈⟩

Every Catholic educator has encountered at least one student with special needs. The topic of special education both challenges and frightens. As Sister Antoinette Dudek writes in her excellent book about special education in Catholic schools, *Is There Room for Me?*, the issues confronting the Catholic educator working with special needs students are complex. It can be time consuming to offer oral tests or inconvenient to allow taping of classes, but these accommodations are not unrealistic. There are often reasonable accommodations that can be made, but far too often are not.

Surely Catholic educators have a serious duty to consider carefully all requests related to children with special needs. It may be easier to say "We do not have a special needs program at this school" than it is to say "We do not discriminate against students with special needs, if with reasonable accommodations, the student can meet the bona fide educational requirements of this school." Surely Jesus, who said, "Suffer the little children to come unto me," expects Catholic educators to make every possible effort to help challenged students in our schools.

Section 504 of the Rehabilitation Act of 1973 (amended 1974) and the 1992 Americans with Disabilities Act can seem ponderous and sometimes practically incomprehensible. Myths and half-truths abound. Catholic board members and educators fear that the cost of accommodations will be so high as to force schools and parish programs out of existence. Some lawyers advise church officials that they must do everything necessary to accommodate a student with special needs, but such is not the case. If, for example, a student needs an elevator to get to important areas such as labs on a second or third floor, most Catholic schools and parishes could not reasonably be expected to finance its installation. All disability law recognizes the concept of financial exigency. An institution is not required to make accommodations that would bankrupt or financially cripple the institution because such accommodations would not be reasonable ones regulated by law.

Education Access Laws

Public Law 94-142, the Education of All Handicapped Children Act, and its successor law, the Individuals with Disabilities Education Act, ensure a free and appropriate education for all children. There is no requirement that Catholic schools provide the free and appropriate education. Catholic schools and programs are not required to meet every need of every child. Most private schools are not equipped to offer all educational services to everyone. The fact that a school or program does not have to offer services does not mean that a student attending the school has no right to such services.

Both laws cited above give students rights, and a private school student has a right to request and receive an evaluation and, if necessary, an Individualized Education Program (IEP). The public school must make every reasonable effort to provide the student with needed services, even if the student remains in the private school. If it is not practical to offer such services to a private school student, the public school officials can devise an IEP that calls for public school education. A parent is always free to accept or reject an IEP. If a parent elects to keep a child in a private school over the objections of the professional educators working with that child, the public school cannot be held responsible for the child's progress, nor can the public school be required to pay private school tuition.

Neither of the cited laws requires that institutions create programs to meet the needs of the disabled. What these laws require is that institutions not discriminate against otherwise qualified individuals who seek admission to their programs. If a disabled person can participate in the program with a reasonable amount of accommodation, then the institution must provide the accommodation. If the accommodation would unreasonably burden the institution, it does not have to be made.

Simply because one is not legally required to do something, it does not follow that one should not do that thing if it is the right thing to do. If a school or parish has assets that could fund a sign language interpreter for a deaf student or instructions in signing for faculty and staff, the administrator may have a moral and ethical duty to provide for the student, even though the law may not require such provision. "Welcome and Justice for Persons with Disabilities," the U.S. Catholic bishops' 1978 pastoral, seems to demand such action. If handicapped people are to become equal partners in the Christian community, injustices must be eliminated. Certainly, Catholic parishes and schools should be leaders in fighting injustice wherever it is found, especially as it affects those whose disabilities place them among people for whom Christ manifested special concern.

March 2001

The Nontraditional Family:
Emerging Legal Issues

A high school principal commented recently, "I've just gone over our school directory and discovered that 61% of our students are from nontraditional families. Of course, there are a whole group of students whose status I'm not exactly sure of, so the percentage is probably larger." As a grade school student in the mid 1950s, the author remembers that only one girl in the whole 1,200- student enrollment had divorced parents and she was considered a minor celebrity. Today's divorce and family statistics reveal that what was once the nontraditional family is quickly becoming the norm. Old ways of conducting business must adapt to the challenges presented by new demographics. This article will deal with some of the major legal issues involving the nontraditional family.

Establishing Who Has Custody

The first task an administrator must undertake is establishing who has custody. Parents do not always volunteer this information and registration forms are often incomplete. A form on which the space for the father's name is left blank does not automatically mean the father is dead, missing, or unknown. Registration forms and handbooks should contain a policy statement such as

"Divorced or separated parents must file a court-certified copy of the custody section of the divorce or separation decree with the principal's office. The school will not be held responsible for failing to honor arrangements that have not been made known."

Unfortunately, receipt of a form is not the end of the administrator's responsibility. A responsible official must carefully read the forms and note in a readily accessible place what the requirements are. If one parent has sole custody, there is very little problem with access to the child. The person with sole custody makes the educational decisions and is considered the primary caregiver.

Today, sole custody is rarely the rule. Parents may have shared custody, but one has physical custody. In that situation, visiting rights must be noted. If the noncustodial parent has the child every other weekend, he or she may pick the child up at school and school officials have to know whether to let the child go. Further, the custodial decree may allow the noncustodial parent some say in educational decision-making. More difficult problems ensue when there is joint custody, in which one parent may have physical custody but both parents have the right to be involved in decision-making.

What happens when the two parties cannot agree? In such an instance, the administrator should contact the judge who signed the order and follow his or her directions.

Another situation is posed by joint custody in which physical custody is shared. Dad may have the child Monday through Thursday and Mom Thursday through Sunday. Or there may be the situation in which the child stays three days with Dad one week and four days with Mom, followed by a week of four days with Dad and three days with Mom. Still another situation is presented by the arrangement in which Dad has the child for one week and Mom has the next week.

People Who Are Not Parents

Grandparents, aunts, uncles, and older siblings can function as the primary parent with or without formal custody or guardianship. People living in homosexual relationships may wish partners to be considered parents. Parents may wish stepparents or live-in girlfriends or boyfriends to assume parental obligations and, in fact, most regulations recognize a person who provides primary care as a parent.

One can easily see how confusing these arrangements can be. One practical way of dealing with these situations is to have a Rolodex or file card box containing each child's name and specific custody arrangements. For schools and programs with the appropriate technology, computers can access such information, but administrators must be careful to ensure privacy and accessibility.

Recommendations for Dealing With Custody Issues

1. Make collecting and updating custody information a priority.

2. Have a readily accessible system of recording and monitoring custody arrangements.

3. Know that a parent does not stop being a parent when custody is lost. The Buckley Amendment requires that noncustodial parents be given information about the student's progress in school as well as unofficial copies of report cards unless there is a court order to the contrary.

4. Be calm when a parent demands that you do what he or she wants. Consult the documents on file and call the appropriate judge if necessary.

5. If a parent presents a new custody order, call the judge and ask for directions.

6. When in doubt, do not release children into an individual's custody until you have reached someone in authority who can give you clear directives.

7. Tell staff members to refer any doubtful situation to you.

8. Show compassion to all involved, even if you can't meet their requests. 𝕵𝕽

January 2004

Custody Issues:
What's an Educator To Do?

⟨✦⟩

The days are long past when the vast majority of students lived with both biological parents in the family unit. Today the traditional family is the exception, and educators are being asked to figure out custody arrangements and negotiate conflicts between parents. This article attempts to demystify some of the legal realities surrounding custody issues.

Which Parent Does the Law Favor?

While mothers do tend to retain custody more often than fathers, the law requires the judge to do what is in the best interests of the child. It must be noted, however, that two reasonable, intelligent justices can come to different conclusions about what a child's best interests are. Therefore, no one can predict the outcome of a custody battle.

Judges require that social workers and other advocates conduct detailed, painstaking studies of the environments available to the child and offer recommendations to the court. Educators and child service providers can find themselves caught on the horns of a dilemma when separation occurs or divorce proceedings begin: Which parent has the greater right? Further questions arise when other relatives—aunts, uncles, and grandparents—become involved and ask the school to intervene or take a particular action.

Educators must remember that, unless altered by the court, both parents have rights. One cannot simply defer to the wishes of the parent one knows best or the parent one considers more responsible. When a separation agreement is in place, a director or principal can simply call the judge and ask for help. Parents can be required to furnish the school or parish with a court-certified copy of the custody section of the separation agreement or divorce decree. In the absence of any of the above, administrators must assume that both parents have custodial rights.

What Does the Law Say About Parents Who Are Separated, but Not Divorced?

The law requires that each parent's rights be recognized. So if a mother comes to the minister and states that she plans to leave her husband and she wants him to have no contact with the children, the minister or administrator must insist that a court-certified document be given to the parish or school that clearly states that the father is to be given no access to and information about his children before the mother's wishes can be honored. While the rule of law is often clear, its application may be problematic. If a mother comes to the parish administrator and states that she is terrified for her and her children's safety, the administrator must use common sense. No administrator who believes a mother's fear of abuse will release a child into the custody of the father without proper legal authorization. As demonstrated by the Elian Gonzales case, involving a father in Cuba fighting for and ultimately winning custody of a son who had been living with relatives in the United States, allegations of abuse can be made on both sides. In such situations, the administrator or pastor should contact local police and the diocesan or parish attorney. Child protective services may also be contacted. Once a separation or divorce decree is given, officials should comply with its directives.

What Are a Noncustodial Parent's Rights to Information About the Child?

In the school setting, the Buckley Amendment of 1975 provides clear guidelines governing access to academic progress information. By extension and through local laws and regulations, administrators should follow the guidelines of the Buckley Amendment in dealing with nonschool cases. The amendment clearly gives noncustodial parents rights in regard to the academic performance of their children. Unless a court has ruled otherwise, noncustodial parents have the right to copies of their children's academic records, although address and other identifying information can be excluded.

The noncustodial parent also has a right to discuss his or child's progress with school or program personnel. While a parish or school official may be required to provide access to each parent, it may not be necessary to hold duplicate conferences. The administrator may decide to require a joint conference. Caution is in order in such situations. If one parent has a restraining order against the other, a joint conference cannot be held. Although it may be inconvenient to provide duplicate services, the educator or minister must keep in mind that the primary responsibility ethically, even if not absolutely legally required, is to protect the child and his or her interests. If a child's interests appear to be best served by separate conferences, the administrator should provide them.

How Can I Construct a Policy to Govern Custody Situations?

School officials, relying on the Buckley Amendment, can place a statement such as this in its parent/student handbook: "The school abides by the provisions of the Buckley Amendment. Thus, noncustodial parents will be given access to the academic records and to information on the academic progress of their children unless there is a court order specifically stating that the noncustodial parent is denied access to such information."

Another approach is to require that all separated and divorced parents provide the school with a court-certified copy of the custody section of the appropriate decree. If the parent is to be denied access to the child's academic records, that denial should be noted in this section. The custody section should also provide information about the noncustodial parent's right of access to the child: May the parent call for the child at school or at a parish program on the Friday before weekend visitation?

Nonschool program administrators can adapt the suggestions offered above to their specific needs. In any case, all programs would be well advised to gather as much data as possible about separated and divorced parents and their custodial rights and privileges so that all will act in the best interests of the child and in a manner recognized by civil law. Jesus Himself has admonished us, "Woe to you who leads one of these little ones astray. Better for that you that you should have a millstone placed around your neck and be drowned in the sea." The days of millstones may be over, but the need to care for the little children of whom the Bible speaks continues. Finally, administrators, ministers, educators, and other supervising personnel should ask themselves that oft-quoted question, "What would Jesus do?" and act accordingly. Surely, the One who has called us to our respective ministries will give us the grace to both obey the law and protect the child.. 🕮

Teachers,

STAFF, and VOLUNTEERS

November 1990

Teacher Contracts and the Law: Who is Protected?

⟨⟨⟨⟩⟩⟩

The prevailing law in Catholic schools is contract law. A contract is an agreement between two parties who both incur detriments and derive benefits from the contract.

A teacher agrees to teach (a detriment in that one is unable to perform other employment during that time) and receives a benefit (salary, etc.). The school incurs a detriment (payment of salary) and a benefit (the students are being taught).

Breach of Contract

Breach of contract occurs when one party fails to perform. When a Catholic school is involved in litigation with personnel, the court will examine the provisions of the contract. *Weithoff v. St. Veronica School*, 210 N.W.2d 108 (Mich. 1973), an early but significant case, illustrates. The school terminated Ms. Weithoff's contract after her marriage to a priest who had not been laicized. She had signed a contract of employment that bound her to observe the "promulgated" policies of the sponsoring school. A policy requiring teachers to be practicing Catholics had been adopted by the governing body, but the policy was filed and never published to teachers. Therefore, Ms. Weithoff alleged that the school's dismissal of her was breach of contract. The court agreed and ordered the school to pay damages, since the remedy for breach of contract in the private sector is damages, not reinstatement.

Weithoff illustrates the importance of contract language. Had there been no clause requiring "promulgation," there is a strong possibility that the school would have won this case. The court might well have maintained that a person who teaches in a Catholic school should expect to be held to the requirements of church law.

Either party to the contract, the school or the teacher, can commit breach of contract. It is generally conceded, however, that it is futile for a Catholic school to bring breach of contract charges against a teacher who wants to terminate a contract because to compel a person to teach would be tantamount to involuntary servitude. Courts have stated that since replacements are readily available, a school sustains no injury. Without injury, there can be no lawsuit. As frustrating as this reality can be for principals (especially when a teacher phones over Labor Day weekend to inform the principal that the public school has offered a job and the teacher must report on Tuesday), it is simply a fact of life.

Some people suggest including liquidated damages clauses in contracts requiring a teacher who breaches a contract to pay a fee toward the cost of finding a replacement. The labor laws of most states do not permit withholding monies from salaries, so a school could be forced to pursue a small claims action, which might result in a teacher's paying an amount as low as $1 a week. Thus, a school might be advised to forego the liquidated damages scenario.

Personnel Policies

Schools are responsible for developing policies that protect the contractual rights of personnel. A court can consider the faculty handbook as part of the contract. Contracts place certain obligations on the employer. It is important that the school's policies be in line with those of the diocese, especially in view of the fact that most teacher contracts bind the teacher to observe the policies and regulations of the diocese or other sponsoring organization.

Nonrenewal of Contract and Dismissal

Policies governing nonrenewal of contract and dismissal from employment should be in place in all schools. Nonrenewal of contract and dismissal from employment are not synonymous terms. Nonrenewal of contract does not carry the same connotations and stigma that dismissal from employment, or being fired, does.

Sometimes, the terms are used synonymously. Indeed, according to the way many contracts are written throughout the country, teachers in Catholic schools may face nonrenewal of contract every year because the contract contains a clause such as "This contract expires June 30 unless definitely renewed." In many of these situations, there is little real difference between nonrenewal of contract and dismissal. If a principal wants to dismiss a teacher, he or she simply does not renew the teacher's contract for the next year.

The situation is different if a school has a policy whereby a teacher can expect continuing employment after a given number of years. Even if no policy exists, de facto tenure (discussed later in this article) could be held to exist if an expectation of continuing employment is created.

Documentation: Creating a Paper Trail

The faculty handbook and/or the employment contract should state, at least in general terms, the reasons for which a teacher may be terminated. The most important factor to keep in mind in any termination or nonrenewal situation is documentation. The best protection against a lawsuit is a written record of the reasons and events leading to termination.

The principal should document all events that illustrate what makes an employee ineffective or undesirable. Administrators should keep in mind that teachers and other professional employees may do an adequate job in the classroom, but may behave outside the classroom in ways that are unacceptable. Examples are excessive absenteeism, tardiness, lack of cooperation, etc. Documentation should describe behaviors and avoid judgments. It would be better to record "Ms. Smith sent 20 students to the office for misconduct in a three-day period" than to state "Ms. Jones is having difficulty keeping order."

It is crucial that a principal have a paper trail indicating that the teacher was told of problems and given an opportunity to improve. One way to ensure appropriate communication and documentation is to follow a seven-point checklist when conferencing with problem teachers:

1. Enumerate precisely what is wrong and needs improvement.

2. State that the school wants the teacher to improve.

3. State what the school will do to help the teacher.

4. Set a deadline when all parties will sit down and review improvement or lack thereof.

5. Tell the employee that if there is no improvement within the time frame stated, disciplinary action will result.

6. Give the teacher a copy of the conference documentation stating the first five points and ask the teacher to comment on the document to ensure understanding.

7. Have the teacher sign the document and add any comments he or she wishes to include. If the teacher refuses to sign, have another person witness that fact.

Due Process: Fairness Considerations

In the public sector, due process demands that an accused person be given notice and a hearing before an impartial tribunal. Further, the accused has the right to question accusers, provide witnesses, have an attorney present, and appeal the decision. Recently many courts have required at least the first three elements (notice and a hearing before an impartial tribunal) as essential components of basic fairness in the nonpublic school. At a minimum, schools should develop policies requiring that a teacher facing suspension or dismissal be told of the charges and be given an opportunity to refute them. Some process for appeal should be in place. In most dioceses, the bishop is the "last court of appeal."

The concept of de facto tenure (in fact, there is an expectation of continuing employment) merits mention here. If a Catholic school terminated a teacher who had worked in that school for 10 years, a court would look at the policies, procedures, and past practices of the school or diocese. If teachers are routinely retained after a certain number of years and rarely, if ever, face nonrenewal of contract, it is possible that de facto tenure exists. [Note: The concept of de facto tenure appears to be on again/off again in popularity. While no Catholic school to this author's knowledge has ever had to reinstate a dismissed teacher or one whose contract has not been renewed, damages can be awarded, particularly if the judge accepts the de facto tenure argument. It is simply impossible to predict accurately the outcome of every hearing or trial or the basis for a particular judge's decision.]

While Catholic schools are not bound by constitutional due process, they are bound by common law considerations of fundamental fairness. Further, the Gospel demands that those in authority treat others as Jesus would. Thus, some job protection should be available in Catholic schools. A teacher facing termination, for example, should be given a hearing if the teacher requests one.

Local school boards and dioceses should carefully develop and review policies on teacher discipline and dismissal. Reasons for dismissal should be listed. Generally, the following are recognized as legitimate grounds for dismissal: incompetence, insubordination, immorality, neglect of duty, incapacity, and unprofessional conduct.

Some argue that a teacher facing disciplinary measures should be allowed to have an attorney present at every stage of the process. There is no civil law requirement that this be done and, indeed, the presence of attorneys can often create an adversarial atmosphere; such a presence can lessen the possibility of attaining Christian reconciliation. Policy-makers may wish to allow a person facing dismissal or nonrenewal of contract the opportunity to bring a witness who is not allowed to speak.

Catholic school leaders must understand that the law is a parameter in which they must operate. It is appropriate to be concerned about the legal considerations affecting personnel issues in Catholic schools. Sometimes it is difficult to balance legal and Gospel considerations when developing and implementing personnel policies, but such is the challenge Catholic schools face.

New Development: Administrator Job Protection (or Lack Thereof)

A California appellate court in *Tollefson v. Roman Catholic Bishop of San Diego,* 268 Cal.Rptr. 550 (Cal.App.4 Dist. 1990), ruled that no cause of action existed in the case of a Catholic high school assistant principal whose administrative contract was not renewed, but who was offered a teaching contract in the school.

Ms. Tollefson had been employed at Marian High School as assistant principal for seven years. Separate one-year contracts ensured each year's employment. The contract specifically stated that there was no obligation to renew and that the administrator could be transferred to other positions at the school upon expiration of the contract.

Five years after Ms. Tollefson's initial appointment as assistant principal, a new principal was appointed. Two years later he informed Ms. Tollefson that he had decided on an administrative reorganization plan that would not include her. He expressed hope that she would remain on the staff as a teacher.

Ms. Tollefson alleged wrongful termination. The trial court granted summary judgment for the school. Ms. Tollefson appealed. The appellate court held that the express language of the contract limiting its duration to one year made any expectation of employment in that position beyond that time span impossible. The court held further that nothing in the record indicated that an agreement to continue to employ Ms. Tollefson as an administrator "absent good cause" existed.

The *Tollefson* case suggests that an employee whose administrative contract is not renewed will have no legal recourse if a nonadministrative position is offered. Demotion is not grounds for legal action.

[Note: Demotion remains a particularly sore topic in Catholic education. A new principal suddenly tells the assistant principal who has held the position for 15 years that he or she will have to return to teaching; the demoted individual believes the action is unfair and believes that there must be some recourse. But there is none. Demotion is not actionable; the only exception would be if the decision were made on discriminatory grounds, such as race, sex, etc. It is simply a fact of life that the chief administrator has the legal right to choose his or her own administrative team, regardless of whose feelings are hurt in the process or whose status or salary is affected by the decision.]

MAY 1992

THE CATHOLIC CHURCH AND TERMINATION OF EMPLOYMENT

The Catholic Church has long been an advocate of worker's rights. The encyclical Rerum Novarum stated unequivocally that employers must guard the human rights of their employees. Like any other employer, however, the Catholic Church has found itself the defendant in lawsuits brought by employees. Catholic school educators may find a discussion of some pertinent cases and points of law helpful.

Catholic school employees do not enjoy constitutional rights, but they do have rights. Administrators must honor the provisions of the contract with the teacher or be able to give a legitimate reason for breaking the contract. Courts will scrutinize the contract to ensure that its provisions have been followed.

Tenure Questions

In most dioceses, tenure does not appear to exist. One exception would be dioceses with unions. A 1979 Supreme Court decision, *NLRB v. the Catholic Bishop of Chicago*, held that Catholic schools did not have to allow union representation. Unions that were in place in Catholic schools before this ruling were not affected by it.

Historically, private sector employment was said to be at will and private sector employers generally may hire and fire whom they please. Recent case law in private industry suggests that courts may be moving away from absolute at-will employment. One can usually dismiss employees for no reason or for a good reason, but not for a bad reason (e.g., discrimination).

Dismissal at will may not be an option if a school has a policy whereby a teacher can expect continuing employment after a given number of years. Even if no policy exists, de facto tenure could be held to exist if an expectation of continuing employment is documented (e.g., teachers in a Catholic institution are routinely offered contracts after a given number of years of employment). Although no court has yet held that Catholic schools can be compelled to reinstate wrongfully terminated teachers, courts have ordered Catholic schools to pay damages to teachers whose contracts were breached. (See *Dolter v. Wahlert,* 483 F.Supp. 266, N.D. Iowa 1980).

Breach of Contract

One example of an allegation of breach of contract is presented by the 1973 case of *Weithoff v. St. Veronica School,* 210 N.W. 2d 108 (Michigan). A teacher was terminated after her marriage to a priest who had not been dispensed from his vow of celibacy in the church. The plaintiff had signed a contract of employment that bound her to observe the "promulgated" policies of the sponsoring school. A policy requiring teachers to be practicing Catholics had been adopted by the governing body, but the policy was filed and never published to teachers. The court held that the teacher could not be held responsible for meeting the demands of the unpromulgated policy.

In *Bischoff v. Brothers of the Sacred Heart,* 416 So.2d 348 (1982), a newly hired teacher, whose contract was canceled when the principal discovered that the plaintiff had divorced and remarried without obtaining an annulment of the first marriage, brought suit. The court ruled in favor of the school; the contract contained no loopholes.

Unemployment Case

Cases in which dismissed Catholic school employees allege they were unfairly denied unemployment benefits are on the rise. In *Holy Name School v. Retlick,* 109 Wis.2d 381, a Catholic school appealed a circuit court order that directed that a teacher whose employment contract was not renewed because she married a divorced man who had not obtained an annulment was entitled to unemployment benefits. The school allowed the teacher to finish the year after contracting the marriage and the principal even suggested to the teacher that she live with the man rather than contract an illicit marriage. The court recognized the right of the school to hold teachers to a moral code, but found that school officials had not been reasonable in their conduct.

In the 1989 case, *Bishop Carroll High School v. Commonwealth of Pennsylvania,* 557 A.2d 1141, a high school teacher informed his principal that he was cohabiting with a divorced woman whose previous marriage had not been annulled. After being discharged, the teacher filed for unemployment and the school contested. The court ruled that the teacher effectively waived any constitutional or statutory requirements when he signed the employment contract.

Thus, the Catholic Church, like any religious organization, can determine the discipline it requires of both its members and employees. People who do not wish to live in accordance with church teachings are not compelled to act against their desires. They simply cannot act as they wish and continue as church employees.

In a 1989 Rhode Island case, *St. Pius X Parish Corp. v. Murray,* 557 A.2d 1214, resembling the *Retlick* case, a different decision was reached. The teacher had informed school officials in April that she intended to contract a marriage outside the church. School officials allowed her to finish teaching for the remainder of the academic year, but did not offer her a contract for the next year.

The court ruled that the school's action in permitting her to finish the school year prohibited officials from calling the nonrenewal of her contract a "discharge." In still another unemployment compensation case, *Bishop Leonard Regional Catholic School v. Unemployment Compensation,* 593 A.2d 28, a 1991 Pennsylvania court heard the arguments of a Catholic grade school that a teacher's actions in marrying a divorced man was disqualifying willful misconduct because it was in violation of a school policy that forbade teachers to publicly reject official teaching, doctrines, or laws of the Catholic Church. [Note: In the past 15 years, courts have shown an increasing willingness to allow Catholic institutions to hold employees to the rules of the Catholic Church governing behavior, as long as the expectation and requirement of following those rules is made clear in a written contract or policy statement.]

The above cases involving Catholic institutions illustrate that administrators cannot hide behind the First Amendment's separation of church and state guarantee as a cover for any actions they wish to take. The courts have made it clear that they do have jurisdiction over the elements of a contract made with a religious entity, particularly on nondoctrinal issues.

(Readers desiring discussion of documentation and reporting issues in employment termination should consult the author's column in the November 1990 issue of *NCEA Notes.*)

Although the Catholic Church is not bound by all the employment constraints that oblige the public sector, officials are expected to be fair in the development of employment policies. The church's own teachings and documents demand just treatment of all employees.

Recent Developments

A Florida public high school and its officials were found liable in the wrongful death of a student who fell through a skylight on the school roof while posing with other students for a yearbook photograph. Evidence indicated that a single teacher was responsible for the supervision of 30 students on the roof and that the teacher herself was posing for the photograph.

The court concluded that the conduct of school officials was negligent and the proximate cause of the student's death. The reasonable person standard required extraordinary care in the supervision of students on a roof. Further, the court held that severe injury, including death, was foreseeable in the situation. The court ruled that the potential danger warranted, at minimum, (a) instructions to students about the layout of the roof, (b) clear warnings about the danger of being on a roof, and (d) instructions to students on the exact procedures to follow. Absent these three factors, the court ruled that the school was liable for the fatal injury sustained by the student. (See *Dade County School Board v. Gutierrez*, 592 So.2d 25, 1991.)

This case illustrates the very real dangers present in school activities. Administrators should ensure that no student activity is undertaken unless dangers have been assessed, foreseeable injuries discussed, and appropriate instructions given. Parental permission should be sought for out-of-the-ordinary situations such as the one in this case. Finally, administrators should weigh carefully the benefits and risks of an activity before permitting it.

November 1992

Staff and Student Relationships in Catholic Schools

Teachers and other staff members care about students. That care extends to all areas of student life. Educators often find themselves counseling students in personal matters, and it is not unusual for a teacher to find himself or herself in the position of surrogate parent. Students often entrust teachers with confidential information. Teachers, many with little training in professional counseling, often question what is appropriate in interacting with students outside the classroom setting.

Few guidelines are available. Teachers and other personnel may deal with situations that pose personal and legal risks for the adults as well as the students. The author is familiar with several situations in which parents threatened or pursued legal action against a teacher whose actions they viewed as unwise, inappropriate, sexually motivated, or interfering with the parent/child relationship. Thus, all adults working in the educational ministry of the church should be aware of the legal ramifications involved in student/staff relationships.

Confidentiality

Most educators rightfully consider student confidences sacred. If a student confides in a teacher, the student should be able to presume that the confidential information normally will not be shared with anyone. Educators may believe that some type of immunity protects them from legal liability if they refuse to share student information given in confidence.

However, the facts indicate that very few states provide any sort of immunity or privilege for teachers who receive confidential information from students. If a teacher were subpoenaed, placed on the stand, and asked for confidential information, most judges would require the teacher to answer. The teacher does not enjoy the type of privilege that doctor and patient, lawyer and client, priest and penitent, or husband and wife enjoy.

Another fairly common situation involves the student who tells a teacher that suicide or other violent action is being considered. Such information must be shared with appropriate people or the educator risks being found liable for negligence if injury occurs.

To avoid misunderstanding, teachers should establish ground rules for confidences early in the relationship. Teachers who require journal writing or other exercises that may involve sharing personal feelings should inform the entire class of the rules. Basically, teachers should honor the confidences of students unless health or safety is involved. In such an instance, the student should know that the greater good requires that the information be revealed.

Sexual Misconduct

One end of the student/staff relationship spectrum is represented by sexual misconduct. Sexual misconduct can be alleged in apparently innocent situations. Students can misinterpret touching, and a teacher could find himself or herself facing child abuse charges. Extreme caution is in order whenever a teacher touches a student.

The situation in which a student believes that a teacher has not responded to efforts to achieve a closer relationship can pose a problem. Such a student may accuse a teacher of inappropriate conduct as a retaliatory measure. Educators must be aware that serious consequences can result from an allegation of child abuse, even if that allegation is eventually proven false.

At the very least, such a false allegation can be extremely embarrassing for the teacher. If a child abuse report is made, the teacher will be questioned by authorities and the investigation will be recorded. In some states, lists of suspected child abusers are kept.

Thus, it is imperative that educators protect themselves and the students they teach by practicing appropriate behavior with students. To avoid even the slightest hint of impropriety, a teacher should avoid being alone with a single student behind closed doors unless a window or other opening permits outsiders to see into the area. A good question to ask might be "If this were my child, would I have any objection to a teacher relating with him or her in this manner?"

Fear of teachers facing child abuse allegations has caused some public school districts in this country to adopt school rules that prohibit any faculty touching of students. Such rules preclude putting one's arm around students, patting a student on the back, or giving a student a hug. No Catholic school administrators would want to take such a position, but commonsense precautions must be taken for the protection of all.

Other Physical Contact

Educators can also be charged with child abuse that is not sexual. Corporal punishment, prohibited by regulation in most Catholic schools, can set the stage for allegations of physical abuse. Corporal punishment can be defined as "any touching that can be construed as punitive." The author is aware of a case in which a teacher tapped a child on the shoulder with a folder while reprimanding the child for not having his homework done. The child's mother filed a child abuse report against the teacher and threatened to file charges of assault and battery. Although this case is outrageous, it does indicate the dangers that can exist. Thus, educators are well advised to adopt an operating rule: Never touch a child in a way that can be construed as punitive.

Other Behaviors

Teachers and other staff members must bear in mind that they are professionals rendering a service. Just as a counselor or psychiatrist is professionally bound to avoid emotional involvement with a client, a teacher should strive to avoid becoming so emotionally involved with a student that objectivity and fairness are compromised. Teachers must remember that they have many students for whom they are responsible and who need and may desire the teacher's attention. If a relationship with a student keeps a teacher from responding to other student needs on a regular basis, the teacher should seriously examine the appropriateness of the relationship.

In seeking to assess the appropriateness of a teacher/student relationship, some mental health professionals recommend asking questions such as these: "Whose needs are being met? Is there a boundary? Where is it?"

The following adult behavior could be considered inappropriate, depending on the totality of the circumstances: dropping by a student's home, particularly if no parent is present; telephoning a student frequently; taking social trips with a student; or sharing the teacher's personal problems with a student.

Serving as a Catholic educator in these times is a privilege and a gift. It is indeed sad when an educator is forced to relinquish that gift because of inappropriate choices. Thoughtful reflection and prudent behavior will keep educators both legally protected and professionally fulfilled.

Recent Developments: Negligence Litigation

Three recent negligence cases will be of interest to school administrators. The first, *Espinosa v. Fresno Unified School District,* a 1992 California case, involved a 7-year-old student who was burned when he spilled hot food on himself in the school cafeteria. In denying the school district's motion for a directed verdict, the court ruled that a jury could determine that (a) the school was negligent in serving food hot enough to burn a person, and (b) the school should have foreseen student conduct that could result in spilled food and student injury.

In the second case, *Peck v. Siau,* a 1992 Washington case, the state appellate court declined to find a school district negligent in its hiring or supervision of a librarian who had sexual contact with a high school student. The court ruled that there was no evidence that the school district knew or should have known of the librarian's potential misconduct.

In a third case in Ohio, *Caston et al. v. Buckeye Union Insurance Co.*, 456 N.E.2d 1970 (1982), a student was injured while on an overnight trip. The priest in charge of the trip had asked that students use their family cars to transport other students to the site. After arriving, one student asked if he could go get a hamburger. The priest gave permission and another student accompanied the driver. The car was involved in an accident and the passenger was injured.

The school's insurance policy covered "hired automobiles," and the court ruled that the student car involved in the accident was "loaned" to the school and was within the definition of "hired" automobile. This case illustrates both the liability to which schools can be exposed if volunteer drivers are involved in accidents and the extreme importance of carefully monitoring the use of nonschool vehicles while on school trips.

January 1993

Volunteers in Catholic Schools: An Analysis of Legal Concerns

∽𝕴𝕴𝕴𝕴𝕴✑

Volunteers have served a valuable function in schools for many years. Most Catholic educators will recall lunchroom and library mothers as part of their own school experiences. Today, the use of volunteers is growing in schools, and Catholic schools are no exception.

Administrators are rightly concerned about using volunteer service effectively while ensuring that legal considerations have been adequately addressed. The principal should seek to ensure that only competent individuals are accepted as volunteers and that those accepted are given the help necessary to perform their tasks in a satisfactory manner. This column will address some of the major concerns in selecting and training volunteers.

Negligence: A Lawsuit Waiting to Happen

Every person reading this column has probably heard at least one story of a volunteer whose action or inaction caused or exacerbated a student injury. Students can certainly be injured in settings in which no negligence occurred. However, negligence is the allegation most likely to be raised if a student is injured while under the supervision of a volunteer.

If a volunteer is sued for negligence, the odds are fairly high that the supervisor will be sued for negligence as well under the doctrine of *respondeat superior,* let the superior answer. It is extremely important, therefore, that principals develop policies and procedures for volunteers that ensure that every volunteer knows what is expected of him or her.

A second type of negligence case can be brought against school administrators. This type of case arises most often in situations alleging sexual abuse. The volunteer is not charged with negligence, but with some intentional tort such as sexual assault or rape. The volunteer's supervisor can be charged with negligence for failing to properly investigate the volunteer's background before accepting the volunteer's presence in the school setting. Thus, background screening of volunteers in imperative.

Background Screening

Two main types of background screening procedures exist. The first is a fingerprint check. Several states now have laws that require anyone who works with young people to be fingerprinted. The fingerprints are sent to a state agency that checks them to determine if the person has a criminal record.

The mere existence of a criminal record does not automatically make an individual unsuitable as a volunteer. The nature of the offense and the time elapsed since the offense should be considered.

For example, a person with a record of sexual offense should never be allowed to work with young people. However, a person who has a 20-year-old conviction for larceny but has a clean record since then might be accepted.

The second type of background search involves checking references. Volunteers should be asked to complete an application and to give the names of references. The administrator should ensure that the references are checked.

Neither fingerprinting nor background checking is foolproof. However, each provides excellent data for use in assessing whether a person should be entrusted with young people. When a student injury occurs, the principal and the institution will be in a much sounder legal position if background searches have been made on people who volunteer on a regular basis.

Should an injury occur and a lawsuit be filed, courts will consider the foreseeability of that injury. No one is expected to foresee everything that could possibly happen, but one is expected to foresee reasonable happenings and to take appropriate precautions.

In the case of *Poelker v. Macon Community School District*, 212 Ill.App.3d 312, 571 N.E.2d 479 (1990), a student was hit by a discus thrown by another student during a warm-up session supervised by a volunteer. The court, declining to find the volunteer liable for the injury, ruled that "School district owed duty to participant to provide supervision during warm-ups." The supervision provided must be competent. If an adult volunteer is not familiar with an activity assigned for supervision, some instruction must be given [to the volunteer and his or her competency assessed before supervision of the activity commences] so that foreseeable injuries can be avoided.

Not every injury is foreseeable. In *Bender v. First Church of the Nazarene,* 59 Ohio App.3d 69, 571 (1989), a 14-year-old volunteer raped a 4-year-old. The court, finding that the event was not reasonably foreseeable, declined to find the church responsible.

The principal or other administrator will immediately ask: "How practical is such information? Surely, we are not expected to run a background check on every parent who volunteers to go on a field trip."

The likelihood that a court would require background checks on every parent who volunteers on an occasional basis is probably slim. In light of the exploding litigation in our society, however, the day of requiring background checks on any individual who intends to volunteer any service requiring supervision of students may not be too far in the future.

[Note: That future is here. Administrators must run background/criminal checks on all parents and other adults involved in supervising children. The old standard of running checks on only those who "would have ongoing or regular duties involving supervision of students" is gone and has been replaced by the more restrictive standard expressed in the previous sentence. The writer believes that schools will soon run checks on all parents and guardians before their children attend. While such a policy may be extreme, it provides the best protection for all children and adolescents. Indeed, were the writer to return to being a principal, that is the procedure she would implement. The following two paragraphs are the text as written in 1993; they should be read in light of this note.]

For the present, it seems that background checks should be done on all parents who will volunteer on a regular basis in situations in which young people are present. Such situations might include cafeteria, playground, and classroom supervision; lunchroom monitoring; and working alone with individual children or small groups of students.

Some educators may be concerned that parents will resent being subject to background searches. The principal who explains that this is a standard procedure undertaken to protect all children should find the majority of parents understanding and cooperative. Parents who do not wish to follow the procedure simply will not participate as volunteers.

Training Volunteers

The best way to avoid student injury and subsequent litigation is to provide every volunteer with some in-service training. Such training need not be lengthy. Topics might include the following:

- School philosophy and goals
- Importance of volunteers in the school
- Duties of the volunteer
- Student discipline procedures, with a clear indication of when offending students should be referred to a staff member
- Health and safety measures
- Duties specific to given activities, such as field trips
- An explanation of supervision as both a mental and physical activity.

For the last item, it is not sufficient to be only physically present with students; one must be mentally present as well. This means that a volunteer cannot be engaged in doing something other than supervision. For example, volunteers should not be reading the newspaper while supervising students in the library, nor should a volunteer, while supervising the playground or lunchroom, be engaged in conversation with another volunteer or teacher if such conversation distracts the teacher from giving students necessary attention. Such activities, unrelated to the supervisory function, could be problematic if a student is injured and can demonstrate that the supervising volunteer's attention was not on the students.

Finally, a principal might consider developing a volunteer handbook that includes the items listed above and any other items the principal considers important.

Conclusion

Protecting students and avoiding litigation are certainly goals of any Catholic educator. As in many other areas of professional concern, common sense is a good guide in selecting and training volunteers. Asking how one would wish the volunteers in his or her child's school to be selected and trained is a means of ensuring sound policies.

Recent Developments

In the 1992 case *Woodall v. Marion School District,* 414 S.E.2d 794 (S.C.App.), the guardian of a student, injured when another student assaulted her at school, brought suit against the school district for negligence. The complaint alleged that the school was grossly negligent in its supervision of both victim and assailant. The trial court granted the school's motion to dismiss the case, but the appellate court reversed the trial court's decision and remanded the case for trial.

Referring to South Carolina law, the court stated, "A governmental entity may be liable to a student for loss when the entity's responsibility to supervise, protect, or control a student is exercised in a grossly negligent manner." If a governmental entity can be held liable for gross negligence, a Catholic school, which is a private entity, can certainly be held liable for gross negligence as well. Thus, all educators must strive to provide adequate supervision for all students, and administrators must adequately supervise all professional staff and volunteers who supervise students.

January 1995

Documentation of Employee Behaviors: What and How Should You Document?

⚜

Educational administrators often ask questions about written documentation of faculty and student behavior. Twenty years ago it was rare to find much written documentation about either faculty or student discipline cases. Administrators often expressed a belief that little or no documentation was good, since it gave a person a second chance. Today, increasing litigation against administrators demonstrates that such a belief is not good operational theory. On the contrary, documentation is an absolute necessity to protect both institutions and administrators. Good documentation also ensures that employee rights are protected. This article will address the main issues in documentation and offer a model for good record keeping.

[Note: Between 1995 and 2007, the author has served as consultant and expert witness in cases alleging that a school's failure to keep adequate written documentation has resulted in injury to the plaintiff. For example, if a plaintiff alleges that a teacher sexually abused him 20 years ago, his attorney will seek copies of the teacher's permanent record or file. Unfortunately, it is not unusual for a school to have no records on former employees or to have seriously deficient records. In a few cases, the only document found in a former teacher's file was the employment application. Everything else, including supervisory records, certification, and transcripts had either never been filed or had been removed. It is only reasonable in such cases for the plaintiff's attorney to characterize the school and its administrators as negligent in record keeping.]

Contracts and Related Documents

The faculty handbook and/or employment contract should state, at least in general terms, the expectations for teacher and staff behavior. It is unfair to tell a teacher or staff member after the fact that certain behavior is unacceptable if no standards exist or if standards are vague. Obviously, there are some behaviors that everyone ought to know are unacceptable, such as theft and other dishonesty.

The faculty handbook and/or contract should also indicate what behaviors could result in termination of employment or in nonrenewal of contract. The important factor to keep mind in any such situation is documentation. The best protection against a successful lawsuit is a written record of the reasons and events leading to termination.

Some behaviors fall into gray areas. For example: What is inappropriate behavior with students? What is sexual harassment? Is it sexual harassment if the person is joking? (See the November 1994 *NCEA Notes* for a discussion of sexual harassment.)

When an administrator believes that an employee has done something unacceptable, the administrator should ask whether the school's documents make it clear that such behavior is inappropriate. If there is any possibility that a reasonable person might not have known that such an action was prohibited, the administrator should give the employee the benefit of the doubt, advise the employee that such behavior is not acceptable and that any such subsequent behavior will be documented, and immediately take steps to ensure that all employees are made aware of the school's expectations.

The principal or other administrator should document all events that illustrate what makes an employee ineffective or undesirable. Administrators should keep in mind that professional employees may perform adequately in the classroom, but may still behave in unacceptable ways outside the classroom.

Examples are lack of cooperation or criticizing school, parish, or church officials to students. All documentation should describe the inappropriate behavior in language that is specific and verifiable. It would be better to write "Mr. Thompson sent 20 students to the disciplinarian's office in a three-day period" than to record "Mr. Thompson is having difficulty keeping order."

In cases in which employee behavior does not meet administrative expectations, the principal or other supervisor should leave a paper trail indicating that the employee was told of problems and given an opportunity to improve. One way to ensure appropriate communication and documentation is to follow a seven-point checklist when conferring with teachers who present problems.

Checklist for Conferencing with Employees

The following checklist can be used in drafting a document that is presented to the employee and used to conduct the actual conference.

1. Enumerate precisely what is wrong and needs improvement. (Because it is difficult to correct other adults, administrators may fall into the trap of speaking too generally. The employee may not know exactly what he or she did that was not acceptable and may not understand what new behaviors are expected.)

2. State that the school wants the employee to improve. (Such a statement indicates good faith on the part of the administrator and can be important in subsequent litigation.)

3. State what the school will do to help the teacher. (A beginning teacher could be assigned a more experienced teacher as a mentor in matters of instruction and classroom management. A teacher could also be sent to another school to observe teachers with proven records of good teaching and discipline.)

4. Give a deadline for all parties to review improvement or lack thereof. (If no deadline is given and maintained, an employee could later claim, "I never heard back from you so I assumed everything was all right." Thus, it is absolutely imperative that the administrator give time parameters, such as two weeks, a month, or two months. A date and time for a follow-up meeting should be established before the end of the conference.)

5. Tell the employee that if there is no improvement within the time frame stated, disciplinary action will be taken. (Administrators may ask, "What sort of disciplinary action can I take?" An employee can be placed on probation, given notice of nonrenewal, or suspended for a specified time period.)

6. Give the teacher a copy of the conference document stating the first five points and ask the teacher to comment on the document to ensure understanding. (This procedure allows the employee the opportunity to ask for, and be given, clarification of any points.)

7. Have the employee sign the document and add any comments he or she wishes to include. If the employee refuses to sign, have another person witness the refusal. (This other person should be another administrator or the pastor. If neither is available, a secretary could serve as a witness. Asking a peer of the employee, such as a fellow teacher, should be avoided.)

Avoiding Problems

Although there is no foolproof formula for avoiding documentation problems, careful, objective recording of facts provides the best possible protection. Objective documentation lessens the possibility of misinterpretation or multiple interpretations. Specific documentation enables the administrator to work with the teacher to identify strategies to improve behavior.

Careful, accurate record keeping also protects an administrator against defamation allegations, should the records ever be shared with a third party. It is hard to deny that one said playground rules are stupid if there were witnesses to that fact; it is easy to deny that one has an "attitude problem" or a "problem with authority."

Practical Considerations

Some administrators ask if every problematic employee behavior should be formally documented in an employee's personnel file. The answer is "not necessarily." For example, if an administrator notices that a teacher is five minutes late for class one morning, but has never before been late, the administrator may decide not to confront the teacher. However, an administrator might note the tardiness in his or her calendar or log book. Whether the information would become part of a written personnel report would depend on whether subsequent problems occurred.

Problems and resentment can often be avoided if administrators ask themselves: "Is this the fair thing to do? Is it moral? Is this the action I would want or expect someone to take if I were in the employee's position? Is it the position Jesus would take?" Sometimes it is difficult to balance legal and Gospel issues, but such is the challenge facing Catholic educational administrators. 𝄞

March 1995

Supervision, Evaluation and Contract Renewal

Several recent research studies on the importance of and time allotted to certain administrative tasks indicate that principals consider staff supervision a primary responsibility. However, many administrators readily admit that supervision ranks low in terms of the amount of time they spend. More immediate and seemingly more pressing concerns clamor for administrative attention. But the supervision of teachers has to be one of a principal's most important legal and ethical responsibilities.

The administrator is responsible for ensuring that qualified personnel are employed. Principals must make decisions about teacher performance. Teachers who do not leave voluntarily when found professionally deficient should not have their contracts renewed if remedies for improvement have been exhausted. Conversely, competent teachers should find supervision and emulation procedures a protection for them.

Often administrators find themselves struggling with the ethical as well as legal dimensions of situations. No one wants to end the employment of a teacher whose family livelihood depends on his or her income, but justice demands that students be provided with competent teachers.

Not Synonymous Terms

Supervision and evaluation of teachers are not synonymous terms. As most principals learned in administrative preparation classes, supervision is a formative experience and evaluation is a summative one. Practically speaking, supervision is the observation of teachers in classrooms or other instructional situations. Principals should make regular visits to teachers' classrooms.

Supervision can be problematic for both the principal and the teacher. A principal who never taught any grade lower than the sixth may feel inadequate in a fifth-grade teacher's classroom. A high school principal who taught English may feel less than competent in a physics classroom. Nonetheless, administrators should be able to recognize good teaching within five to 10 minutes of entering a classroom. If supervision is an ongoing process, both principal and teacher can grow together and help each other improve the learning environment of the school.

If supervision is seen as punitive, something that is done only if the principal is "out to get the teacher," it will not be successful.

Evaluation is summative: An administrator sums up all the available data and makes a decision on contract renewal. Evaluation of teaching performance should be based on more than supervisory data. The principal will seek to answer such questions as "Does this person support the rules of the school? Does he or she look after the safety of the students?" as well as "Is he or she a good subject matter teacher?"

Evaluation, then, is a more encompassing concept than supervision, but both should be present in an effective school.

Teachers are in schools for the students. The students are not there for the teachers' employment. There is no more serious legal responsibility than ensuring that students are being taught by a capable, competent, caring professional and that all teachers are encouraged and given the means to become the best professionals they can be.

The importance of teachers knowing what is expected of them cannot be underestimated. The faculty handbook should contain a statement of the supervision and evaluation a teacher will experience. For example: Who will supervise? How often? What besides classroom observations will form the basis for evaluation?

Supervision enables a principal to make legally sound decisions about contract renewal. Declining to renew a contract seems unethical if the principal has never observed the teacher on the job. Yet people have lost teaching positions because they "couldn't keep order" or were judged "incompetent," even though no formal supervision had occurred. Consistent, careful supervision ensures that people are treated in appropriate legal and ethical ways.

A Teacher's Protection

Supervision is also the teacher's best defense against unjust termination. Should anyone allege that a teacher is not doing an adequate job, the supervisor's observations can protect the teacher. If a parent were to claim that a student now in the third grade could not read and the first- or second-grade teacher is to blame, it would be hard to prove the claim false if no professional had ever supervised the teachers. If, however, a supervisor could say, "I visited Mrs. Smith's class four times last year and students were being taught reading concepts, they were reading, and Mrs. Smith's lesson plans contained adequate time for the teaching of reading," it would be much harder, if not impossible, for an accusation to be supported.

Nonrenewal Decisions

If a decision is made not to renew a teacher's contract, administrators need to be clear about the teacher's employment status. Public school teachers may have tenure, an expectation of continuing employment, while Catholic school teachers, unless protected by a union contract, generally do not. Catholic schoolteachers are usually employed under one-year contracts.

Nonrenewal of contract and dismissal from employment are not synonymous terms. Nontenured teachers do not have the same rights as tenured teachers at the end of a given contract year. A nontenured teacher has no guarantee of continued employment.

Of course, one should not decide lightly against renewing the contract of a teacher who has been in a school for a substantial number of years. A nonrenewal decision in such a case has ethical as well as legal ramifications. Nonetheless, a person who has a year-to-year contract should not be seen as having a legal expectation of continued employment unless that person can give credible evidence supporting such an expectation.

It is good policy to state in the faculty handbook or contract the reasons and procedures for termination and nonrenewal of contract. Written procedures can make everyone's positions clearer and can give all parties guidance in working through termination.

Unless a faculty handbook or contract states otherwise, a nontenured teacher does not have to be given the reasons for nonrenewal of contract. It might seem that the ethical action would be to give the person the reasons so that self-improvement might be sought. Problems can result, however, when a teacher attempts to prove in court that the reasons are not true or sufficient. Such a situation is one example of an ethical and legal dilemma in which administrators can find themselves.

In a way, administrators are involved in a kind of juggling act—attempting to juggle the legal dimensions of one's position with the ethical ones. If, however, the principal has supervised properly and kept appropriate documentation, the decision of nonrenewal should not be a surprise.

Administrators might find the following suggestions helpful:

- Develop a planned, orderly procedure for supervising teachers.
- Publish and give the procedure to teachers.
- Treat all teachers consistently.
- Keep written records of observations and evaluations, being careful to do the following:
    - Stay with the facts.
    - Avoid speculation on motive or attitude.
    - Say nothing that doesn't have to be said.
    - Write with the certainty that others will read what is written.

Finally, one might consider these oft-quoted lines from Shakespeare's Hamlet: "This above all: to thine own self be true, / And it must follow, as the night the day, / Thou canst not then be false to any man" (I. iii, 75). If administrators strive to be true to their own best selves, they should be successful in both the ethical and legal responsibilities of supervision and evaluation.

Recent Developments

Continuing with the twin themes of law and ethics, a recent case from the U.S. District Court in Colorado illustrates the dilemma courts face today as they seek to balance First Amendment separation of church and state issues with the mandates of antidiscrimination legislation.

In *Powell v. Stafford,* 859 F. Supp. 1343, a religion teacher in a Denver Catholic high school brought an action under the Age Discrimination in Employment Act (ADEA) when his contract was not renewed. He had taught in the high school for 13 years under a series of one-year contracts. The ADEA makes it illegal for an employer to "fail or refuse to hire or to discharge any individual or otherwise discriminate against any individual with respect to his compensation, terms, conditions, or privileges of employment, because of such individual's age" (29 U.S.C. s 623 (a)). The Archdiocese of

Denver answered Mr. Powell's complaint by stating that it was not subject to the ADEA and if it were subject to the law, it could not be applied in this case because it violated the Free Exercise and Establishment clauses of the First Amendment.

Antidiscrimination legislation will be upheld if the state has a compelling interest in it and there is no less burdensome way to achieve that interest. However, age discrimination does not trigger the same compelling interest issues that racial discrimination does. As long as there is some rational basis for age classification, the classification will probably be upheld. For example, the right of commercial airlines to require pilots to retire at age 60 has been upheld.

Mr. Powell is a laicized Catholic priest whose responsibilities included only those of a religion teacher. He alleged that the nonrenewal of his contract after 13 years was because of his age. The archdiocese maintained that Mr. Powell's nonrenewal was based on a need for fewer teachers and an administrative decision that he was less qualified than other faculty members.

Applying the three prongs of the famous *Lemon* test, the court held that (a) antidiscrimination legislation has a secular purpose, (b) it neither advances nor inhibits religion, but (c) policing age discrimination issues in the decision to not renew the contract of a religion teacher in a Catholic school would impermissibly entangle the state in the affairs of a religious institution. The *Powell* case cites the landmark *NLRB v. the Catholic Bishop of Chicago* case, 440 US. 490 (1979), in which the U.S. Supreme Court ruled that Catholic schools were not bound by the provisions of the National Labor Relations Act because of the potential for entanglement.

The Powell decision indicates that religious institutions have broad discretion in dealing with employees whose duties are clearly religious in nature. Although the issue is not raised in this case, one cannot but wonder what the court's holding would have been if the plaintiff had been a geometry or physics teacher.

January 1997

Personal Conduct of Professional Staff

❧

At some time or other, Catholic educational administrators confront the issues of actual or perceived inappropriate staff conduct. They may wonder what legal rights they have to demand certain standards of behavior from staff members, particularly during off-campus times.

What a staff member does, both in and outside the educational setting, has an impact on the quality and integrity of ministry within the setting. The doctrine of separation of church and state allows administrators of religious institutions to set standards of personal behavior not permitted in the public sector.

Behavioral Expectations

Catholic educational administrators should ensure that documents governing employment state that staff members are expected to support the teachings of the Catholic Church through their behavior. Obviously, many programs have non-Catholic staff members, and one would not expect such individuals to attend Mass on a regular basis or to be participating members of a parish.

But non-Catholics who seek to acquire or retain positions in Catholic settings should expect that standards of behavior will be in force. For example, if the fact that an individual has an abortion becomes known and is a source of scandal, the administrator has every right to terminate that individual's employment or volunteer status. To do otherwise may send a confusing message to parents, students, and the larger community.

Issues of sexual preference pose special problems. While no one should condemn a homosexual orientation, a Catholic educational administrator, as an agent of the church, cannot ignore manifestations of a gay lifestyle that pose scandal. Equally difficult decisions must be made in situations involving divorced teachers who remarry without an annulment, if the fact becomes known. There is no easy solution, but the administrator has an obligation to see that the teachings of the Catholic Church are respected and not compromised in the witness given by staff members.

In summary, once an individual performs an act that is inconsistent with a teaching position in church ministry, that person may no longer be qualified as a minister in a given situation at a certain time. While such a reality may seem obvious, it is a good idea to have documents that state the requirement of supporting the teachings of the church.

Mary Angela Shaughnessy, SCN, J.D., Ph.D.

Illegal Activity

A person who has committed an illegal act may certainly have his or her employment terminated. One who is convicted of or who admits confession of a crime should be removed from professional or volunteer status. The harder question arises when a person is simply accused of or arrested on suspicion of a crime. Administrators may be sharply divided on the proper response to such a situation.

The United States has long operated under the principle of "innocent until proven guilty." It may appear that, until guilt is established, the fair approach would be to let the person continue in ministry, but the reality is often that effectiveness in such situations is severely compromised.

How, then, should one deal with an arrest of or serious accusation about a staff member? Every educational entity should have a policy in place that allows the administrator to place the accused individual on a leave of absence pending the outcome of an investigation or an adjudication of guilt. The time to enact a policy is not when it is needed. The prudent administrator and educational board will have a policy in place that anticipates such situations. It will be much easier to deal with an established policy and procedure when one is needed than to try to fashion a policy after the fact.

Relationships With Students

Past columns have offered discussion of the legal risks posed by student/staff relationships. Obviously, adult teachers and ministers want to demonstrate a personal interest in their students. It is a sad reality, however, that administrators must be vigilant in monitoring staff behavior to avoid even the appearance of impropriety.

Administrators should be especially concerned and seek to intervene in the following situations:

- A staff member appears to spend an inordinate amount of time with one student to the exclusion of others.

- A staff member makes frequent visits to a student's home for no discernable professional reason.

- A staff member takes social trips with one student.

- A staff member is present when students are engaged in drinking or taking recreational drugs and takes no action.

- A staff member shares intimate details of his or her life with students.

While realizing the complexity inherent in many of the situations discussed above, the Catholic educational administrator must ensure that both fidelity to the church and compliance with law characterize policies and procedures.

MARCH 1999

ADULT CHAPERONES:
WHAT THE ADMINISTRATOR NEEDS TO KNOW

Few educational administrators could imagine offering varied on- and off-site experiences without the services of adult volunteers. Field trips, dances, skating parties, etc., would be severely affected if only certified staff members were permitted to serve as chaperones. Increasing litigation demands that chaperones be screened, trained, and supervised for the protection of all. This article will address some of the more common administrative questions.

How Can You Identify Good Volunteer Chaperones?

No foolproof approach to selecting chaperones exists. Administrators must understand a basic fact: Everyone who volunteers to chaperone does not have to be accepted for the task. Some people do not possess the physical or mental competence or the maturity for the job. Others may see chaperoning as a popularity contest and take actions that are not appropriate. Still others may insist on bringing younger children on the trip or may focus exclusively on their own children.

Administrators must be willing to say to a volunteer, "I appreciate your interest, but at this time we cannot use your services." It is not necessary to enter into a prolonged debate about reasons. Simply declining to accept the person as a volunteer is enough.

Readers may say, "I understand that I do not have to continue with volunteers once I know they lack necessary skills. But how can I determine that they do not possess the necessary skills before I entrust them with other people's children?" The same methods used to screen other adult volunteers should be employed for chaperones. At the very least, prospective chaperones should have to submit a signed form indicating that they have not been convicted of a crime. In some situations, however, a decades-old conviction for a nonviolent crime should not be a barrier to volunteering. Some schools now require that all people who volunteer to work with students be fingerprinted. In the sad event that a chaperone's action or inaction injures a student, a school with a clear screening procedure will be in a much better position than a school without one.

Can Adult Volunteers Chaperone Students Without a Staff Member Present?

If volunteers have passed criminal background checks, the answer to this question is a resounding "yes." A few states require certified personnel to supervise playgrounds, but it is commonly accepted that a teacher cannot be everywhere, pay attention to everything, and supervise students and chaperones at all times. Courts expect that adult chaperones are reasonably prudent people who have been trained in the duties of their position and who can be expected to perform those duties.

What Kind of Training Should Chaperones Receive?

All volunteers should receive orientation, even if that orientation takes place 15 minutes before a field trip departure. Each volunteer should be given a written description of chaperoning duties, school rules, and consequences for breaking those rules. Chaperones must agree to enforce the rules. If for some reason a person ignores the rules, that person should not be allowed to chaperone again.

What Kinds of Problems are Common With Adult Chaperones?

One of the most common problems is administrative failure to orient or explain what is expected of the chaperone. When this author became a high school principal and attended the first school dance, she was amazed to find all the adult chaperones sitting in the faculty room drinking coffee while two teachers were frantically trying to keep order in a noisy gymnasium. When the principal asked the adults why they were not on the dance floor, she was told that no one had told them to do anything. Such an occurrence is more common than might be thought. Educators cannot afford to assume that chaperones know what to do.

A second problem arises frequently on grade school field trips. A parent chaperone appears with two younger children and announces that they are coming because he or she cannot leave them home alone. In such instances, administrators should thank the parents for their interest but explain that they will be unable to serve as chaperones because their attention will necessarily be on their own children, not on the ones they are assigned to supervise.

The parent who drives to a field trip and makes unauthorized stops such as at a fast food restaurant or ice cream shop to treat students presents a third problem. Should accidents or injuries occur, it would be difficult to avoid liability if the situation could have been avoided by following the rules in the first place.

Summary

Chaperones are an important part of the total educational experience. Administrators must be sure that (a) volunteers are properly screened, (b) volunteers receive some sort of orientation and written instructions, and (c) people who are unable or unwilling to follow school rules and procedures are not allowed to volunteer.

September 1999

Legal Issues:
Behavior and Lifestyles

Certain legal issues can dominate discussion in various professions. Such is the case with Catholic education. While traveling the country on the lecture circuit for several months, I have witnessed a marked increase in the number of inquiries on administrators', teachers', and other staff members' behavior and lifestyle.

The following is one question that has been put to the writer: "Should I be suspicious because two men [or women] are sharing a house or an apartment? You can never be too careful these days." While administrators must be vigilant, suspicions based on the fact that two people of the same sex live together are generally without merit. Much more definitive evidence is needed before any investigation or action should be taken. When should such a living situation be viewed as problematic? Only when the employee admits to an improper relationship that is going to come out or when the employee gives some sort of public witness to the status of the relationship. Behaviors such as wearing matching wedding bands, frequenting gay bars, and referring to the other as "my spouse" or "significant other" are problematic. Even in such a circumstance, the administrator is well advised to proceed slowly and cautiously.

Administrators can make statements in nonthreatening ways: "A few of the parents mentioned that they saw you and your housemate holding hands in the park. I thought you might want to know." Such a communication signals that the administrator is aware and watching. The staff member is, in effect, put on notice, and it is up to him or her to determine whether to deny the allegation, end the relationship, be more discreet, or leave the church employment situation.

Some prominent commentators have suggested that students are better served when teachers whose lifestyles are questioned are removed from the school or program. While no good Catholic administrator would wish to send a message that it is all right for teachers to do something that children are being taught not to do, there are clear imperatives in the Gospel: "Judge not, that ye be not judged. For the measure you measure with, will be measured back to you." Compassion, as well as justice, should always be an important concern. However, rumors are not facts, and all must guard against accepting them as such. Anyone who has ever played the game "Gossip" knows what happens when information is passed among several individuals; the result may be far different than the truth.

I have also been asked this question: "What should I do if I know that one of my teachers is living with her or his boyfriend or girlfriend? Can I just assume that they are in an immoral relationship?" One of the cardinal rules of administration is to "assume nothing." Rather than judge a relationship, the administrator could ask the individual to put his or her relationship in the context of propriety. All who hold positions of authority, as well as all Catholics, should avoid even the appearance of impropriety.

Once impropriety is surmised, other conclusions can be reached and the individual may be judged without any opportunity to be heard.

What's the bottom line for the administrator? The administrator must keep responsibility for the ministry of education and those who serve in it clearly in mind. The school or other entity exists for the young people, not for adult employment. Decisions must be made with the good of the students uppermost.

Can people who teach in Catholic education be required to adhere to a higher standard than those in public institutions? The answer is a definitive "yes." Catholic educators are supposed to be role models for the young people they serve. Several court decisions indicate that even non-Catholic teachers can be dismissed for conduct not acceptable to the Catholic Church, even if the conduct would be permitted in the teacher's own church.

The types of behaviors that can be problematic are numerous. One common question is what to do when an unmarried teacher becomes pregnant with no plans to marry. This is no easy question. One can certainly argue that the woman has failed as a role model, while others can argue that she will be a good example to her students of what not to do and of the importance of accepting responsibility for one's actions. This type of situation poses an ethical dilemma. Two reasonable persons can reach opposite conclusions. Sometimes the answer to "What does the law permit me to do?" is different than the answer to "What should I do?"

As disciples of Jesus Christ, all people with administrative responsibilities should ask, "What would Jesus do?" The answer to this question should aid administrators in making appropriate personnel decisions on individual lifestyles. ✣

November 2002

Supervising and Evaluating Teachers

The school head is legally responsible for both instructional quality and student well-being. Accomplishing these duties requires being present in the classroom. People, problems, and situations facing administrators on a daily basis claim time and attention. Many threats of lawsuits could be avoided if school heads and other administrators simply followed existing policy. An administrator's responsibilities include supervising and evaluating teachers. However, these tasks can be problematic for both the principal and the teacher.

Frequency and Format

A school head who has never taught any grade below sixth, for example, may feel inadequate in a primary teacher's classroom. A high school principal who taught English may feel less than competent in a physics classroom. Regardless, all effective educators will recognize good teaching. If a principal feels unqualified in a certain content area, someone with competence should assist the principal.

Supervision should not be viewed as a punitive activity. Such a view will weaken the relationship between the principal and teacher and the process will not succeed. Supervision as a continual, formative process allows both principal and teacher to grow. Together, they will improve the learning environment of the school by acknowledging strengths and identifying areas for progress.

Evaluation is a summative process. Written observations shared with teachers provide some of the best data for making employment decisions. A principal can use this data to plan and set goals with teachers. Evaluation of teaching performance, then, should be based on more than supervisory data. A principal should seek answers to such questions as "Does this teacher support school policy? Does he or she look after the safety of the children?" These factors should be considered in addition to a teacher's subject matter competence.

All school heads must understand that teachers and administrators work for the students; the students do not attend school to provide these adults with employment. Surely, there is no more sacred responsibility than ensuring that the capable, competent, caring professionals who teach students are given the opportunity for professional development and that all teachers are encouraged and given the means to become the best professionals they can be.

The handbook should clearly state the school policy on supervision and should identify who is responsible for supervising teachers: the principal, assistant principals, department heads, or others. How often teachers will be supervised and the format for supervision should be clearly defined.

Scheduled Versus Unscheduled Visits

Teachers have a right to know how supervision will be conducted. Supervision and evaluation of teachers are matters of personnel policy. The faculty handbook should clearly delineate policies and procedures so that every teacher knows what to expect. School heads should consider whether the supervisor's visits are scheduled or unscheduled. If the visits are normally scheduled for twice a year, the principal may choose to reserve the right to observe classes at unscheduled times. However, the teacher has a right to know when and how visits will occur. Missing scheduled supervisory visits unnerves teachers. Everyone understands that emergencies happen, but once normalcy returns, administrators should return to their regular supervisory and evaluative cycle.

School heads should determine how the supervisory visit data will be incorporated into an end-of-the-year evaluation and who will have access to this information. Questions to be considered include "Will the evaluation become part of the teacher's permanent file? Does the teacher have an opportunity to respond in writing to the evaluation? Will the teacher's response become part of the evaluation record?" Answers to these questions will lead to a fully developed policy on supervision and evaluation and administrators will be on firm legal ground.

Although most educators would agree that supervision is a formative experience and evaluation is a *summative* one, the distinction becomes blurred in many Catholic schools where one administrator serves as both supervisor and evaluator. Teachers may be reluctant to discuss problems with principals if they suspect that the information could be included later in evaluations. Administrators who wear both hats must be especially sensitive to allow for open dialogue with teachers.

Good practice and civil law demand that administrators supervise and evaluate teachers. Teachers should welcome these opportunities as a means for professional development and legal protection against accusations about their teaching competency. Justice is not served if the principal fails to supervise and evaluate teachers as part of an accurate assessment of their performance. 𝒯𝒥

March 2004

How Catholic Do We Have to Be?

❦

Today's Catholic educators talk a great deal about Catholic identity. What makes a school Catholic? How do a school and its staff claim Catholic heritage? What do we have to do to be Catholic? Do we have to agree with everything the church says? What should I say if a student asks me what I think and I don't agree with the church's position? Isn't it dishonest to support a position you think is wrong? These are all questions that most readers will have heard. The writer hears them on a weekly, sometimes daily basis. This article will attempt to offer some answers from a legal perspective.

What Makes a School Catholic?

Simply calling an institution Catholic does not make it so. Being Catholic requires a commitment to the Gospel, the teachings of Jesus Christ, and the teachings of the Roman Catholic Church, both when it is convenient to be committed and when it is not so convenient. If any of the above are compromised, the school is eroding its Catholicity, but one can legitimately argue that being Catholic is an either/or proposition: Either the school is Catholic or it isn't.

Cafeteria Approaches to Catholicism Not Permitted

In the 1970s, many in the church talked about a cafeteria approach to Catholicism: "I like the church's teachings on social justice, so I'll support them. I think the church is wrong about birth control, so I'll follow my conscience—after all, doesn't the church teach that conscience is primary?" These statements are probably familiar to many readers.

However, there is one basic bottom line. A Catholic educator's first legal duty is to be true to the teachings of the Catholic Church. A Catholic educator is an agent of the Catholic Church and has to hold the "company line," as this author often states. The situation is similar to that of any person who works for any organization. If I work for a company that makes umbrellas, I have to uphold the company's products. I probably won't be employed very long if I encourage people to buy plastic rain hoods as an alternative to umbrellas. Perhaps the analogy is a bit simplistic, but the underlying premise is not: If one cannot support the company that one works for and the products the company produces, the honest course of action is to find another job.

The product we sell is Catholic education. Parents send their children to Catholic schools and religious education programs for Catholic education, not for the private opinions of teachers and catechists, and they have a legal right to expect fidelity to church teaching.

Isn't Conscience Primary?

The Catholic Church does teach that one's conscience, properly formed, is primary. But the question of agency is still the sticking point. If I teach in a Catholic school and am asked my opinion about a matter on which I have a different personal position than the one the church takes, I am not at liberty to just share that opinion with the students in my classes because I am an agent of the church, the same way a bishop or the pope is an agent.

Sometimes, this reality is painful. The church does not claim to be perfect, but people responsible for the Catholic education of young people must teach them the precepts of the Catholic Church as the church has taught them, not as individual teachers might like them to be. To do less is to fail in one's primary legal obligation.

So What's an Educator to Do?

The Catholic educator must present the teachings of the Catholic Church. It is certainly permissible to say that some people do not agree with whatever the teaching is, but one must be clear about what the church's position is. The educator is not free to say, for example, "I think the church is wrong about birth control. Responsible people use artificial contraception" or "Women should be ordained. The pope is wrong." If pressed for one's personal opinion, one can say, "My personal opinion is not what we are discussing. The church teaches . . ."

Lifestyle Issues

There are certainly Catholic educators living with others in sexual relationships without benefit of clergy. At the very least, if an individual's lifestyle becomes a matter of scandal, the administrator must address it. Teaching in a Catholic institution is not the same as having a job in industry. What the Catholic educator does both inside and outside the institution matters because one has chosen to be a role model for young people. The Catholic Church, its parishes, and programs have the legal right to demand that its educators live lives and speak words consistent with the church's teachings. 𝓙𝓡

January 2005

Avoiding the Appearance of Impropriety: Recommendations for Keeping Boundaries

Today everyone seems to be talking about boundaries and the avoidance of litigation prompted by the appearance of impropriety. In response to many requests to develop a "don'ts" list for educators, the writer has prepared the following:

1. Do not stay alone in a room with a student unless there is a window permitting others to view the interior of the room or the door is open.

   Think before you act. Ask yourself how someone else might perceive what you are doing. If a student were to leave your classroom or other area and claim abuse, a closed area with no visual access would leave little room for a defense.

2. Do not allow students to become overly friendly or familiar with you. Students should never call teachers by their first names or nicknames.

   There is a difference between being "friendly" and being "friends" with students. Boundaries between adults and young people must be enforced.

   Insisting on proper titles is one way to keep boundaries.

3. Do not engage in private correspondence with students. If you receive personal communication from a student and the communication is not appropriate, keep a copy of the communication and do not respond unless you have received permission from a supervisor.

   It is not uncommon for students to develop crushes on teachers, fantasize about them, or try to communicate on a peer level. If one receives student letters, etc., that are romantic, sexual, or otherwise inappropriate, it is best not to respond and to report the occurrence to one's supervisor for everyone's protection.

4. Do not visit students in their homes unless their parents are present.

   Being alone with young people can give an appearance of impropriety. Many instances of sexual abuse are alleged to have occurred when adults were present in students' homes when the parents were absent. In particular, if there is no one home but the student, the situation can quickly become one of your word against the student's.

5. Do not invite students to your home.

The comments in #4 also apply here.

6. Do not transport students in your vehicle without the written permission of their parents and the consent of your supervisor.

   Obviously, the same problematic situation exists of an adult being alone with a student or students. Additionally, the adult may assume personal liability for any accident or injury. It can be tempting to give a student a needed ride home, but a better approach would be to wait in an open area with the student until transportation arrives or to direct the student to an administrator.

7. Do not take the role of surrogate parent with a student.

   Educators are not parents and do not have the responsibilities or privileges of parents. While being supportive and helpful, educators must respect the rights of parents. Some parents, feeling displaced in their children's affections by teachers, seek restraining orders against the educators.

8. Do not criticize a student's parents to the student.

   No matter how poorly parents parent, they are most likely the only parents their children will have. If you believe a child is abused or neglected, contact the appropriate authorities.

9. Do not give students your home phone number without the permission and knowledge of your supervisor.

   Communicating with students via telephone on a regular basis or encouraging students to call a teacher at home can give an appearance, even if not the reality, of impropriety. It is best to call students from school or parish phones if possible.

10. Do not communicate with students from your home e-mail address.

    E-mail was the topic of the November 2003 NCEA Notes article by this author and readers may want to refer to it. In brief, communicating with students from home e-mail addresses can give an appearance of secrecy. Educators should always use their school or parish e-mail accounts.

11. Do not hire students to work in your home without the express knowledge and consent of your supervisor.

    Mixing roles is not a good idea. Acting as both employer and teacher can muddy the waters where boundaries are concerned. For example, a male teacher taking a babysitter home at midnight is placing himself in a particularly vulnerable position should the student claim inappropriate conduct. Additionally, teachers can incur liability for injuries students sustain while in their employ.

Ask yourself: "How would I feel if what I am doing were to appear on the front page of the paper tomorrow?"

Many problems could be avoided if adults would routinely ask themselves this question in potentially problematic situations. An even better question might be "Would Jesus do this?" Fidelity to prayer and the exercise of common sense can help educators avoid boundary pitfalls and can protect everyone. 🕮

Extracurricular and
OFF-SITE ACTIVITIES

November 1991

Athletics: Some Legal Concerns

Athletics pose some of the greatest legal concerns to school administrators, and those in Catholic school are no exception. Principals and athletic directors constantly ask themselves how they can best protect student-athletes from injury and their schools from liability. This column will focus primarily on negligence issues arising from school athletics.

Avoiding Negligence

Most lawsuits alleging negligence begin in the classroom, since that is where students spend most of their time. Other areas, however, are potentially more dangerous than the classroom, so a greater standard of care is expected from staff and administrators. School athletic programs are clearly activities that are more dangerous than normal classroom activities.

Negligence is an unintentional act or omission that results in injury. People who bring successful negligence suits are usually awarded financial damages in an amount calculated to compensate for the actual injury suffered. It is possible, though rare, for a court to award punitive or exemplary damages if the court is shocked by the negligent behavior. In assessing whether a person's behavior is negligent, a court will use the "reasonable person" test: Would a reasonable person in the defendant's situation have acted in this manner? "Reasonable" is whatever the jury or other fact finder decides it is.

Before a court will find a defendant legally negligent, four elements must be present: duty, violation of duty, proximate cause, and injury. An examination of these four elements should prove helpful to people supervising athletic programs.

The Duty to Supervise

The individual charged with negligence must have a duty in the situation. Student athletes have a right to safety, and coaches and other officials have a responsibility to protect the well-being of all those entrusted to their care. Coaches are assumed to have a duty to provide reasonable supervision of their players. It is expected that principals and athletic directors will have developed and promulgated rules and regulations to guide coaches in providing for student safety. Coaches should develop and implement team practices consistent with safety and in harmony with administrative practices.

Violation of Duty

Negligence cannot exist if the second element, *violation of duty,* is not present. Courts understand that accidents and spontaneous actions can occur. The 1989 New York case *Benitez v. NYC Board of Education,* 543 N.Y.S. 2d 29, 541 N.E. 29, involved a high school football player who was injured during play. The player alleged negligence by the coach and principal for allowing him to play in a fatigued condition.

A lower court awarded the student damages, but the appellate court ruled that school officials had to provide only reasonable, not extraordinary, care and reversed the decision. Further, the court invoked the *assumption of the risk* doctrine. Students are under no compulsion to play sports; if they choose to participate, they voluntarily assume the risks of some injuries. Assumption of the risk is a defense against an allegation of negligence. [More recent judicial decisions have also relied on assumption of the risk as an affirmative defense to a charge of negligence.]

At first glance, it may appear that athletic directors and coaches would be the school officials found liable for violation of duty in the case of student injury. Under the doctrine of respondeat superior, let the superior answer, principals and other administrators can be found liable for the acts of subordinates.

For example, if a principal paid little or no attention to the administration of the athletic program, provided no supervision, or offered no guidance, he or she might well be found guilty of negligence if a student were injured while a dangerous practice or policy was in place.

Unfortunately, many administrators believe themselves woefully ignorant of the principles of athletics and are too often content to let coaches and athletic directors run the whole sports program. These same administrators would be shocked if someone were to suggest that the fifth-grade reading teacher is an expert, needs no supervision, and should be given carte blanche in directing the reading program.

Principals have an obligation to oversee athletics. While no one expects a principal to be an athletic expert, the principal should be sure that only qualified individuals are hired as coaches and athletic directors. The principal should insist that the athletic director and/or coaches keep the administrator informed about the operation of the program.

Every principal should seriously consider having an athletic handbook outlining the policies and procedures for each sport. [Note: Today schools must have athletic handbooks if they wish to be in the best possible legal position if charged with negligence in administering their athletic programs.] Parents and students should sign a statement agreeing to be governed by the provisions of the handbook.

Principals will not be held responsible for every employee mistake, but only for those that a reasonable person could have foreseen. In the 1979 Virginia case *Short v. Griffits,* 255 W.E. 2d 479, an athletic director was held liable for injuries sustained by a student who fell on broken glass while running laps. The school and the school board were exonerated. It was the athletic director's responsibility to ensure that the playing areas and equipment were in order. Unless the principal had some reason to believe that the employee was careless in his supervision, the principal would not be expected to check the area for hazards.

Proximate Cause

The third requirement for legal negligence is *proximate cause*. The violation of duty must be the proximate cause of the injury. Proximate cause is sometimes defined as a contributing factor. If a coach were to order a 250-pound student to wrestle a 125-pound student and the lighter-weight student were injured in the match, the coach is the proximate cause of the injury even though the physical actions of the heavier student would constitute the direct cause of the injury.

The court must decide whether proper performance of duty could have prevented the injury and, in so doing, the court has to look at the facts of each individual case. In an old but still applicable case, *Stehn v. MacFadden Foundations,* 434 F. 2d 811 (USCA 6th Cir., 1970), a private school and its officials were held liable for damages sustained by a student who suffered a severe spinal cord injury in a wrestling match. The court found that the maneuver that resulted in the injury was not listed in any reputable book on the subject of teaching wrestling, and the defense could produce no evidence that the maneuver was legitimate. The coach had very limited previous experience and was coaching without any supervision.

The court ruled that the school's violation of duty, its failure to ensure that the coach was qualified and experienced, was the proximate cause of the student's injury. Proximate cause is a complex doctrine. It is difficult to predict what a court will determine to be the proximate cause in any particular allegation of negligence.

Injury

The fourth element necessary for a finding of negligence is *injury*. To prevail in a lawsuit, a student must have sustained an injury for which the court can award a remedy. No matter how unreasonable the behavior of a coach, there is no legal negligence if there is no injury. Everyone must understand, however, that physical harm is not the only type of injury. Emotional or psychological harm can also constitute injury.

Two legal scholars, Clear and Bagley, have observed the following:
It is sufficient to state the coaches owe athletes a standard of care that includes the following: (1) proper precautions to prevent injuries from occurring in the first place and (2) treatment of injuries that normally occur in a manner that does not exacerbate the damage that has already been done. This standard, additionally, is based on what the coach *should have known* regarding the sport and/or injury, as well as what was actually known. (*NOLPE School Law Journal,* 1982, p. 185)

Conclusion

Even if every possible precaution were taken, the possibility for student injury is high. Administrators have very real duties to ensure that only competent personnel—trained in coaching techniques, theory of the sport, and first aid and safety procedures—are employed. Further, administrators are responsible for establishing policies that provide the following:

- Clear procedures to be followed when accidents occur
- Minimal delay in seeking medical attention when needed
- Hazard-free equipment and playing areas

There is no absolute protection against lawsuits, particularly in athletics. Nonetheless, a thorough handbook, as indicated above, can provide the best possible protection and can serve as evidence that both parents and students understand the risks involved in sports and the requirements of participation in the school athletic program.

Recent Developments

The 1991 New Jersey case of *The Princeton Montessori Society, Inc. v. Leff*, 591 A.2d 685, involved a lawsuit brought by a private school against the parent of a former student. The school sought to recover the balance of payments due pursuant to a tuition contract. A clause in the contract stated: "The Parent understands that the obligation to pay the fees for the full year is unconditional and that no portion of such fees paid or outstanding will be refunded or canceled in the event of absence, withdrawal or dismissal from the School of the above Student" (p. 686).

The school offered parents a tuition refund plan in which insurance could be bought for 2.2% of the annual tuition. This plan provided payment of tuition in the case of withdrawal. The parent in this case declined to participate in the plan.

About a month after the beginning of school, the parent withdrew her child from the school. The parent had paid $5,000 tuition, and a balance of $2,400 remained on the contract. The trial court ruled in favor of the parent, but the appellate court reversed that decision and held that the parent had no right to a refund and that the school had a right to collect the balance.

This case indicated that contracts between Catholic schools and parents might well be upheld. In these days of increasing financial pressures, Catholic schools might want to consider implementing a tuition contract that requires parents to pay tuition even if the child leaves the school. If mitigating circumstances are present, school officials can always make an exception to the payment requirement.

A tuition insurance option allows parents protection against unforeseen developments. Adopting a policy such as the plaintiff in this case offers the school a degree of financial security. As always, competent legal counsel should be retained for the construction of the tuition contract.

September 1992

Field Trips:
Balancing the Risk and Benefits

Field trips have long been part of the educational experience. Teachers and principals want students to see that learning is not confined to the school building. Field trips give students those opportunities and allow them to apply knowledge learned in the classroom to real-life situations. At the same time, educators are aware that field trips pose special legal considerations.

Most accidents occur in classrooms because that is where students spend most of their time. However, off-campus activities are more dangerous than classroom activities simply because of their nature and the hazards involved in transportation. Some attorneys adopt a "no field trips" position on the theory that if students aren't taken off campus, they can't get hurt off campus. Most educators, however, view field trips as an important part of a student's education. The challenge is to effectively balance the risks and the benefits.

Educational Purpose

Most attorneys and judges would agree that a field trip should have an educational purpose. If an accident were to occur, a school could much more easily justify an educational trip than one that is purely recreational.

The 1984 Michigan case *David v. Homestead Farms, et al.,* 359 N.W.2d 1, illustrates. A kindergarten student was bitten by a horse while she was on a field trip to a farm. The court found that the trip to the farm constituted a curricular activity. In the absence of any evidence indicating that the school failed to provide adequate supervision, the school was held blameless.

Educational purposes should be readily apparent. Eighth-grade rites of passage-type trips to amusement parks generally do not fall into the category of educational trips. In an effort to attract such trips, many amusement parks now distribute information suggesting that such trips can be educational.

Lesson plans, such as "Teaching Physics from the Ferris Wheel," may be offered. An argument can certainly be made that a trip to an amusement park can be educational. However, the administrator must ensure that educational preparation for the academic aspect of the trip is adequate and that the teacher does indeed use the experience as a basis for classroom teaching.

A cover letter stating the educational purpose of the trip should accompany each permission slip. In the unfortunate case in which a student is injured, a school will be in a much better legal position if the educational value of the trip is clearly evident. The school may find it difficult to justify a trip that was taken purely for pleasure.

Liability for Injury

Parents cannot sign away their children's rights to safety. Schools and their employees are required to protect the safety of children entrusted to their care. If a child is injured while participating in a field trip and evidence indicates that the supervising adults failed in their duty to supervise adequately, and if that failure was a significant factor in the student's sustaining an injury, the school and its employees can be held liable for the injury. In a 1989 Missouri case, *Walker v. St. Louis Board of Education,* 776 S.W.2d 474, teachers were held liable in the death of a sixth-grade student who drowned on a field trip.

Some people ask, "Why have a permission form if you can be held liable anyway?" While the permission form does not provide protection from absolute liability for injury, it does provide the best protection available. If an unforeseeable event occurs (a child is hit by a drunk driver or injured when a tool falls from a scaffold), there is a strong possibility that the school and its employees will be exonerated of any blame.

That mythical creative "the reasonable person" is the standard courts use when considering teacher liability. A court will ask, "Did the teacher supervise the student in a manner that a reasonable person in the same situation would have used? Had the parent signed a permission form? If so, what did the form say?" The answers to these questions will determine the nature and degree of liability. The wording of the permission form, then, is important.

Permission Forms

Whenever students are taken off campus, a permission form should be used. The following permission form is suggested:

I/we, the parent(s)/guardian(s) of _____ request that the school allow my/our son/daughter to participate in (insert activity/trip). In consideration for the making of the arrangements for this trip, we hereby release and save harmless the school and all its employees from any and all liability arising to my/our son/daughter as a result.

Both parents should sign the form when possible, and special conditions should be noted. If a trip poses particular risks, such as being near a body of water or walking in an area that poses industrial hazards, these should be noted.

Submitted permission slips should be checked for forgery. The teacher responsible for the field trip could be required to check signatures with those on file on a signature card. Perhaps the school secretary could be given the task of checking all field trip forms. When one person consistently checks all forms, the likelihood of finding forgeries increases.

A student who does not have a signed permission slip should not be allowed to go on the trip. Parent phone calls should not be accepted in place of a signed form. A nonstandard form, such as a note saying "Bobby can go with you today" should not be accepted, as a parent could always maintain that he or she was not aware of the real destination. Administrators should consider placing a sample slip in the handbook that parents could copy when necessary.

Transportation

The means of transportation should be clearly noted in the cover letter of the permission slip. As far as possible, buses should be used for field trips. If parent drivers are used, the permission slip should contain a clause in which the parent agrees to this mode of transportation. If the school does not provide insurance, parent drivers should be notified of that fact, should be required to place a copy of proof of insurance on file, and should be told that they can be held liable in the event of accident or injury. The same cautions apply when teachers use their own cars. Thus, the use of teacher cars should be discouraged. Administrators should consult their insurance agents in this matter; some policies cover volunteer and/or employee drivers.

Overnight Trips

Both elementary and high school students may participate in overnight trips, such as retreats or field trips to places of historical or educational significance such as Washington, D;C. Regular permission slips should be used. Chaperons should have notarized, medical releases for students, which allow them to seek medical attention for injured or ill students.

The permission slip should clearly state the penalties to be imposed if students break rules. For example, violations of civil law and use of alcohol or drugs will probably result in students being sent home. The permission slip should include a statement such as "We/I agree that it is our responsibility to arrange for our son/daughter to be transported home at our expense in the event of such an infraction."

Trips to foreign countries are also a concern, particularly for the secondary administrator. Principals should ensure that only reputable tour companies are involved and should require proof of insurance. A principal must understand that if the school advertises the trip and supplies the teachers who chaperone the trip, the school cannot evade its responsibility for the trip. In effect, this is a school trip.

Principals frequently ask about the possibility of parents being entirely responsible for trips and the school claiming no responsibility. If the administrator allows fund-raising, dissemination of materials, etc., in school, a court could well construe the trip as a school trip.

Thus, the decision to take a field trip is one that cannot be made lightly. The wise administrator weighs the risks and benefits posed by the trip in making a final determination. 𝓙𝓡

September 1993

Extracurricular Activities: What Educators Should Know About the Law

❧〰〰❧

Catholic schoolteachers, like teachers everywhere, understand that multiple duties accompany their chosen profession. While teachers may not like some of the requirements, they generally accept and perform their various responsibilities. Certain aspects of nonteaching duties may, however, prove less acceptable than others to the teacher. Nowhere is this more evident than in extracurricular activities.

Extracurricular events used to be the almost exclusive domain of the high school. Today elementary schools may have as many extracurricular programs as secondary schools. Athletics, yearbooks, and drama and music productions are all finding homes in elementary schools.

Almost every full-time teacher at the secondary level and many at the elementary level are expected to sponsor some sort of extracurricular activity. These activities can range from conducting candy drives and directing Christmas plays to coaching sports. Obviously, the supervision needed to oversee a candy drive is quite different from that required to coach an athletic event.

Teachers have a right to know what their extracurricular activities will be before they sign contracts and to be given as much direction in moderating these activities as necessary and possible. Principals must ensure that teachers understand their responsibilities as moderators. Simply being present during the club meeting or other activity is not sufficient supervision.

The faculty handbook should state the school's expectations for teacher sponsorship of extracurricular activities. Can each teacher be required to moderate one or more activities? Will more time-consuming activities carry compensation and, if so, what is the compensation scale?

The responsibilities of extracurricular moderators should be presented, perhaps in outline form. Activities such as dances or roller-skating parties might benefit from a checklist-type of approach so that teachers can easily see if they have met their responsibilities.

Negligence: The Reasonable Person Standard

The potential for student injury is always present in any school setting, but extracurricular activities are more problematic. While it is true that most accidents occur in classrooms because that is where students spend most of their time, it is also true that many extracurricular activities are inherently more dangerous than others. Student injury during an extracurricular activity may well result in the sponsoring teacher, principal, and school being sued for negligence.

Negligence is the cause of frequently litigated cases arising from school events. Negligence is the absence of the care that a reasonable person would exercise. In the case of a teacher, the question is "What would a reasonable teacher have done in this situation?"

The court must determine what the reasonable teacher would have done. In jury trials, the jury makes the determination; in nonjury trials, the judge functions as fact finder and decides the issue.

What Is Negligence?

While many writers define negligence as an absence of care, courts must determine whether legal negligence has occurred. It is possible for an action to be professionally negligent, but not legally negligent, if one of the elements of legal negligence is missing. Four elements constitute legal negligence. All four are necessary or the court must decline to find that negligence occurred.

The first element is *duty*. The individual accused of negligence must have had a duty in a given situation. If there is no duty, there is no negligence. For example, if the drama coach is attending a play at a local theater and one of the students is also present and engages in dangerous behavior, the drama coach has no legal duty to intervene, since the teacher/coach is not required to supervise a public theater. One could argue that, even if there is no legal duty, there is an ethical or moral duty to intervene. Such an ethical or moral duty cannot, however, be considered by a court in the circumstances described above.

If a duty is found to exist, the second element, *violation of duty* must be established. If the teacher/coach brought a group of students to the play as a drama club, the teacher does have a legal duty to supervise the students in the theater. If a student were to decide to jump from the balcony to the first floor and the teacher, knowing that the student was threatening to jump, failed to intervene, the teacher would have violated a legal duty. If the teacher had taken all reasonable precautions, did not know the student intended to jump, and tried to render all reasonable assistance after the occurrence, the teacher would probably not have violated a legal duty unless some other factors could demonstrate that he or she should have known that this particular student might do something of this nature.

The third element is *causation*. There are two types of causation: direct and proximate. Before an action can be considered legal negligence, that action must have been the proximate cause of the injury. It is possible to be the direct cause of an injury, but not be the proximate cause. If a sponsor were to tell a student to go to the store and the student was hit by a car, the person driving the car may well be the direct cause. A court might determine, however, that the injury occurred because the teacher sent the student, without proper parental permission, on a nonessential errand. Thus, the teacher's violation of duty is the proximate cause of the student's injury. Proximate cause means contributing factor. Thus, if the teacher had not done what should have been done or had done what he or she should not have done, proximate cause may be found.

The fourth element, *injury*, is perhaps the easiest to understand. An injury does not have to be physical; it can be psychological, emotional, or mental. Some courts have even recognized the possibility of spiritual injury. For negligence to be found, there must be an injury. If there is no injury, there is no negligence. If the drama coach directs a student to jump from a high balcony and the student is not injured, there can be no finding of legal negligence. Obviously, there is professional negligence. Since an element of legal negligence is missing, however, there can be no remedy.

Of course, no one would suggest that it is acceptable to be professionally negligent as long as one is not legally negligent. An educator's ethical responsibilities should always be a factor in decision-making.

Supervision of Students

One problematic area is supervision of students before, during, and after an extracurricular activity. All moderators must understand that they are responsible for supervising students. If a coach calls a practice for a Saturday or a yearbook moderator has the staff come to school on a vacation day, the staff member is responsible for the welfare of the young people. A moderator cannot arrive exactly on time or some minutes late, since students who arrive earlier will be left unsupervised. Thus, the sponsor must plan to arrive at a reasonable time before the activity begins. Students should clearly understand what the acceptable arrival time is, and students who arrive before that time can be warned and ultimately dismissed from the program if they do not obey the rules. Students' presence in school before or after activities offers an alarming and abundant potential for lawsuits.

Some moderators believe that they can depart as soon as an activity is concluded. Students whose rides haven't arrived might be told to wait outside or to remain in the building, with the teachers making sure the door is closed when they leave. If a student was injured while remaining after an activity and no supervision was present, the teacher and the school could be held responsible. Judges have indicated that they believe reasonable people should expect students to arrive early and stay late. Long-suffering moderators may wish to try a contract approach.

For the student to participate, his or her parents as well as the student must sign an activity contract that clearly states what will happen if students arrive before or stay after the appointed time. A moderator or principal contemplating such an approach must be prepared to implement the policy, even if the student who is dismissed or suspended from an activity is an integral part of the activity.

In no situation is it acceptable to have students unsupervised in an otherwise empty building, nor is it acceptable to tell young people to leave the property so the moderator can lock the facility. Reasonable people serving as extracurricular moderators do not leave students unsupervised. Getting teachers to understand the seriousness of supervision may be difficult, but it is essential for the well-being of students and for the legal protection of the school and its employees.

A Concluding Thought

Extracurricular activities are important components of any school program. People moderating such activities should be competent. It is the principal's responsibility to ensure that moderators are capable and responsible. The principal must supervise teachers in their extracurricular activities, as well as in their classroom experiences. Responsible supervision fosters an atmosphere of cooperation and accountability in which the welfare of students is constantly kept in mind.

Mary Angela Shaughnessy, SCN, J.D., Ph.D.

Recent Developments

In the case of *Osborne v. Olean Board of Education,* 586 N.Y.S. 2d 489 (A.D. 4 Dept. 1992), the parents of an 11-year-old boy who was injured when struck by a baseball on the school grounds sued the school district for negligence. The trial court denied the school district's motion for summary judgment and held that there were facts in question that a jury needed to decide. On appeal, the New York Supreme Court, Appellate Division, Fourth Department, reversed the trial court's decision, granted summary judgment, and dismissed the complaint against the school district. The appellate court held that the student assumed the risk of being struck by a baseball when he walked in front of or between two students who were playing catch. Thus, the child placed himself in danger and the school district could not be found negligent on the facts as presented.

While the school was exonerated in the above case, it is apparent that injured students and their parents may seek legal recourse and damage payments. Principals must ensure that proper safety procedures are in place. When such procedures are in place and are being implemented, a school may well escape liability in lawsuit if it can be demonstrated that the student's own conduct was a significant factor. In other words, if the student had not behaved inappropriately, the injury could have been avoided. *JP*

November 1995

Extracurricular and Curricular Activities

Autumn traditionally ushers in a season of extensive extracurricular and cocurricular activities. Both elementary and high schools host performances of drama, speech, and debate clubs; football and basketball games and intramurals; and choir recitals. With these and similar activities come an increased concern for legal issues.

Busy administrators may notice some problems with an activity and promise themselves that next year will be different. They will ensure that teachers who sponsor extracurricular activities understand and conscientiously perform their duties. Academic and behavioral requirements for extracurricular participation will be published to all affected and will be enforced. Some plan will be in place for dealing with students who are dropped off well before an adult supervisor is present or are still on campus long after activities are over. However, as any seasoned administrator knows, next year comes all too soon.

Extracurricular and cocurricular activities are, by their very nature, more dangerous than ordinary classroom activities. Participants and their parents can appear to care far more passionately about these programs than about academic offerings. An angry student or parent can threaten a lawsuit. The reasonable school administrator will not be unduly alarmed when threats are made if policies and procedures are properly developed and implemented.

This article will address three areas of legal concerns in extracurricular activities: assignment and training of moderators, student selection and standards for participation, and administrative monitoring.

Assignment of Moderators

Finding moderators at the beginning of the year or when vacancies occur can present near-crisis situations for the administrator. The temptation is great to make anyone who expresses interest in the activity the moderator. Such a procedure is particularly dangerous in athletics. While a person does not have to be an expert wrestler to coach wrestling or an outstanding actor to direct a play, the individual should be willing to study the requirements for coaching a team or directing a play. At the same time, people who played a sport or acted in a play may believe that they can direct the activity when, in fact, participation does not ensure the ability to teach another the skill.

Administrators must ensure that people who moderate activities possess at least minimum understanding of them. For example, administrators can provide released time or other incentives to allow a neophyte moderator to visit a more experienced one or to choose a mentor at another school. Such actions may be time consuming, but they provide the best protection for the safety of the students and the best defense against liability in the case of injury.

The administrator should verify the applicant's experience and qualifications to serve as a moderator. If one has no actual experience in the activity, one should be able to indicate how the necessary knowledge and skills will be acquired. The truly inexperienced moderator should not be assigned complete responsibility for the students participating in the activity, but could be assigned as an assistant to a more experienced faculty member.

Some administrators ask whether using a volunteer as a moderator is ever advisable. At certain times and on certain occasions such an action is possible. A student's mother with extensive experience in college musicals may be able to direct the school play and may be more qualified to do so than anyone on the faculty. A student's father who was a football captain may be able to serve as coach. While the use of volunteers is certainly legally acceptable, the administrator must ensure that the individual is a person of integrity and trustworthiness. Some [note: now most] states require fingerprinting before individuals are allowed to work with young people on a regular basis. At the very least, the administrator should ask for references and check them. In too many instances, people with pedophile tendencies and charming personalities have been assigned to positions of great trust. While no one can avert all possible tragedy, the wise administrator will have a procedure in place to gather the necessary background information on volunteers.

Diocesan and/or local administrators should consider an annual orientation for extracurricular moderators. Athletic coaches may be offered a separate orientation. In the unfortunate event of an injury, educational administrators could demonstrate that they had taken their responsibilities seriously and tried to ensure that moderators and coaches were competent.

Student Selection and Standards

Most administrators have received parent and student complaints on nonselection for an activity. Administrators should insist that moderators and coaches develop, publish, and implement clear standards for selection and participation. Obviously, selection is a somewhat subjective process. Feelings do get hurt. The administrator who insists on clear standards and monitors the performance of moderators and coaches can be satisfied that fairness requirements are met.

Administrators should guard against taking the side of a parent or student in a dispute over selection for or retention in an activity unless the moderator or coach is clearly in the wrong. One of the worst situations for a moderator and administrator to be in is second guessing the decisions of the moderator.

Each activity and moderator will have rules and regulations to which the student participant must adhere. Some may be general school rules. Others may be specific to the activity. In some cases, such as athletics and drama, state associations may provide other standards.

Rules and regulations should be as standardized as possible. It seems unfair for an athlete with a failing grade to be benched while another student with a similar grade is allowed to sing the lead in the school play. Some rules and regulations that might be considered include the following:

- Attendance during the school day to participate in an activity

- Academic requirements (minimum grade averages, for example) for participation

- Behavioral requirements (a student suspended from school should not be participating in an extracurricular activity)

Administrative Monitoring

Administrators need to be familiar with the rules and regulations of every activity in their schools. Certainly, they cannot be expected to recall every rule at any given moment, but they should have access to every rule and be able to obtain it if they cannot summon it from memory.

Administrators need to be physically present at athletic events and other extracurricular activities. No principal should be expected to attend every game or activity, but chief administrators should ensure some administrative supervision in the course of the year. Regular meetings with moderators and coaches will keep everyone informed and help minimize problems.

Numerous education and the law publications by NCEA can help administrators working to provide students with access to meaningful extracurricular activities.

Recent Developments: Liability for Sexual Abuse

A Texas federal district court heard the case of *Rosa H. v. San Elizario Independent School District,* W.D. Tex. (No. EP-94-CA-103DB, June 12, 1995), and ruled that a student who is sexually abused or harassed by an employee may be able to impute liability to the school district under Title IX, which prohibits sexual discrimination in any program or activity receiving federal funds. The court ruled that six factors should be present:

1. The school district is subject to Title IX.

2. The student was sexually abused or harassed.

3. A school district employee perpetrated the abuse or harassment.

4. The school district had notice, either actual or constructive, of the harassment or abuse. [Note: On appeal in 1997 at 106 F.3d 608, the Fifth Circuit Court held that liability could be imposed for actual knowledge as opposed to constructive knowledge. However, some more recent cases have held that constructive knowledge ("should have known") is enough.]

5. The school district failed to take prompt, effective remedial measures.

6. The conduct of the school district was negligent.

The *Rosa H.* case is particularly significant in light of a number of earlier cases holding that an employee who sexually abuses a student may be seen as acting ultra vires, outside the scope of employment. These cases resulted in a denial of plaintiff claims for school district liability. Although an isolated case at present, Rosa H. could [and indeed did] signal the beginning of a new line of judicial thought that makes it harder for schools and administrators to avoid responsibility for sexual abuse committed by school employees.

A second sexual abuse case, *Kendrick v. East DeLave Baptist Church* (E.D.Wis.), No. 92-C-727 May 31, 1995, followed the reasoning of earlier cases. An employee of a church school was charged with the sexual abuse of a student. Although the school may have breached its duty of conducting appropriate background checks or failing to make reports after another student's parents filed a complaint, the federal district court held that any such breaches were not the causes-in-fact of the injuries.

There was no evidence that the plaintiff had been abused after the first complaint or that the teacher would not have been hired even if a background check had revealed his dismissal from a previous church school for confessing to homosexual activity. Even if the school administrators had discovered the dismissal, the court found that it would have been reasonable to hire the individual anyway since there was no evidence that the person had engaged in sexual activity with children.

Kendrick reminds school officials of the four factors that must be present for a finding of legal negligence:

- Duty—the supervising entity had a duty to someone
- Violation of duty—the supervisor failed to supervise adequately
- Proximate cause—contributing factor; "but for" the action or inaction of the accused, the injury would not occurred
- Injury

Kendrick indicates that the causal factor was missing. Even if a clear duty was violated, the cause in fact of injury was the accused individual's actions.

These two cases, which appear to reach different results in similar circumstances, illustrate the ongoing dilemmas faced by courts. Young people have a right to safety. When someone breaches that right, the victim's rights should be respected and restitution made. Determining the party responsible for restitution continues to be problematic for the courts. Nonetheless, the reasonable administrator will know and understand the laws governing child welfare and abuse in the state where the school is located and will insist that all requirements of the law be met.

March 1996

Community Services Programs

Part of the mission of the Catholic school is to teach service. The philosophies of most Catholic schools clearly state that one goal is to develop people who consider service to others a primary responsibility. To that end, many Catholics schools have initiated service programs that range from preschool and kindergarten students visiting nursing homes or adopting a nursing home resident as a grandparent to sophisticated high school programs involving daily or weekly service at an off-campus site.

Many parents and students accept the service component of Catholic school curricula. Some, however, question the necessity and even the right of the school to insist on service of all students. A few remark that if you are forced to do the service, it isn't service at all, but a form of slavery.

Legal Basis

Public schools have also initiated service programs and have received many of the same complaints that Catholic school administrators have been fielding for years. A public school case decided January 2, 1996, pinpoints some of the problems presented by community service programs.

In *Immediato v. Rye Neck School District,* 1996 WL 5547, a second circuit New York case, a high school student and his parents brought a civil rights action against the district board of education. The Immediatos alleged that the district's mandatory community service program violated their constitutional rights, particularly the 13th Amendment's abolition of slavery and the 14th Amendment's due process clause. The district court granted summary judgment for the defendant school district, and the parents appealed to the U.S. Court of Appeals.

The district's mandatory program required all students to complete 40 hours of community service at some point during their high school careers and to participate in a classroom discussion about their service experiences. They must also complete a form documenting their service and describing what they learned from it. Students are allowed to set their own service schedules, and they must provide their own transportation. Student performance is graded on a pass/fail basis. No exceptions are made for students or parents who object to the service requirement. The program is governed by regulations on the types of organizations for which students may perform service and the nature of the work they undertake.

The students may not receive pay for their work. Twenty hours of the requirement may be satisfied by service to the school, but at least 20 hours must be completed off-campus.

The court found that the community service program and involuntary servitude were not the same thing and that community service was not prohibited by the 13th Amendment, as stated: "In application, courts have consistently found that the involuntary servitude standard is not so rigorous as to prohibit all forms of labor that one person is compelled to perform for the benefit for another. The 13th Amendment does not bar labor that an individual may, at least in some sense, choose not to perform."

Of interest to Catholic educators is the court's reference to the 1925 landmark case *Pierce v. the Society of Sisters,* 268 US 510, in which the right of parents to choose private education for their children was upheld in dictum. [Note: Dictum refers to something the court wants to make clear (in this case the right of parents) but cannot use as the basis for the case. The Sisters who brought the litigation could not sue for the rights of parents since they were not parents. They sued on the basis of their right to own property and operate a school.]

The *Immediato* case noted that those who choose one school system for their children are free to do so. The Immediatos could have chosen a school that did not require a service program, even if it would have been inconvenient or costly to make such a choice. Thus, the court of appeals found that the public school's community service program was lawful.

In a similar 1995 North Carolina case, *Herndon v. Chapel Hill-Carrboro City Board of Education,* 899 F. Supp. 1443, the U.S. District Court reached the same conclusion as *Immediato.*

Readers are aware that Catholic and other private schools are not required to protect the constitutional rights of students, particularly any guaranteed by the First, Fourth, Fifth, and 14th Amendments. The question of the 13th Amendment involuntary servitude has not been addressed in the private school setting. It is obvious that no institution, private or public, will be permitted to practice slavery. However, every action a student is required to take does not constitute involuntary servitude, even if the action is one the student would wish not to take.

The findings of the *Immediato* case provide important information for the Catholic school administrator. Since public schools, which are required to protect the constitutional rights of their students, may have mandatory service programs, Catholic schools certainly may have them. Administrators may wish to mention the Immediato case to questioning parents or students. Clearly, mandatory service programs are lawful. Having established their legal basis, let us now look at some of the other legal issues these programs present.

Parental Notification

The parent/student handbook is a good place to provide initial notification of a mandatory student service program. School administrators should require that all parents sign a statement, "We have read and agree to be governed by this handbook," before their children attend school.

In the year or semester in which the service program is held, the administrator or program supervisor should notify the parents of participating students in writing of the requirement, and the notification should reference the previously published statement in the handbook.

Parents should be required to sign a permission slip authorizing student participation. The permission slip should state where the student is providing the service and who is responsible for providing transportation. While some schools may transport students in school vehicles, most schools require that students or parents provide transportation.

A release from liability, prefaced with a statement that reasonable supervision will be provided, should be included. If a parent indicates a reluctance to sign, he or she should be reminded that the service program is part of the curriculum and parental signatures are required for many aspects of student life, such as course schedules for the coming year and participation in athletics and other cocurricular programs.

Supervision and Liability

It is highly advisable that school supervisors visit all service program sites. Such visits constitute appropriate diligence on the part of the school. Particularly if the service program involves release time from school, the supervisor should make spot checks of sites to ensure that students are in attendance and acting appropriately. If the sheer numbers and times of the service opportunities preclude some checks, the supervisor should be in regular phone contact with the site supervisor to ascertain that students are in attendance and that program objectives are being met.

The service program, like all off-campus programs, involves risks. One way to lessen school liability is to ask each site to provide a letter of invitation to the school. In this manner, any liability for injuries occurring on site should be largely borne by the site.

Community service programs comprise an important part of the Catholic educational experience. Care and vigilance in developing and administering such programs will enable all to reap the benefits of ministering to others in Jesus' name. 📜

November 1996

Student Retreats: Some Legal Concerns

Student retreats are important aspects of Catholic education. Whether these are day or overnight experiences, part of a school's religion curriculum or a religious education program, they can be powerful instruments for good in the lives of young people. At the same time, planning and implementing retreat programs pose special legal concerns for administrators, directors of religious education, teachers, and catechists.

This article addresses the following areas of particular legal concern: compulsory retreats, training of professional and volunteer leaders, permission slips, conduct rules, and confidentiality issues, including oral and written communication.

Compulsory or Not?

As much as administrators would like to believe that all students look forward to and profit from retreat experiences, not all students are enthusiastic or even willing participants. Administrators should consider the pros and cons of mandatory retreat experiences. It may be that the benefits outweigh the detriments, but potential problem areas are best addressed prospectively rather than retroactively.

Training of Leaders

Retreat leaders should be carefully trained. While the training need not be time consuming, it should nonetheless be thorough and cover aspects of group leadership, student contact, and confidentiality issues. Administrators should monitor the selection of leaders. Some people simply do not possess the maturity or good judgment to be effective leaders. It is better to decline someone's offer to be a retreat leader than to be forced to deal with the problems that can result from that individual's inappropriate decisions. Student leaders should also be carefully chosen and trained. It is important that they understand what constitutes appropriate sharing in group sessions and that they be given clear instructions to obtain adult help if serious or uncomfortable situations present themselves.

Permission Slips

Parents should be required to sign and submit permission slips for off-campus retreat experiences. On-campus retreat experiences that take place during regular school hours should simply be announced through letters or other written communications. It is good practice to give parents some idea of the schedule and content of retreat activities. If a parent objects to a particular aspect, the administrator has time before the retreat to discuss any perceived problems with the parent rather than deal with objections after the fact. Some administrators ask what should be done if a parent refuses to allow a child to participate in a required retreat experience. The ultimate penalty would be to require withdrawal from the school. However, administrators will want to make individual considerations for exceptional situations.

Conduct Rules

Normal school rules, particularly those on the use of controlled substances such as drugs or alcohol, should be in place. Parents should understand that they may be required to pick up a student involved in a serious violation of school rules. Teachers and sponsors must understand that enforcement of school rules and application of penalties is their responsibility. The special nature of retreats should not be used as an excuse to allow students to escape responsibility for their behavior. This author is aware of several retreat situations that involved alcohol consumption and retreat leaders made unauthorized decisions to let the students finish the retreat. Such an approach is unfair and could prove legally problematic if illness or violent behavior results.

Confidentiality

The very nature of the retreat experience encourages sharing of innermost thoughts and feelings. It is not uncommon for students to share feelings of suicide or other self-damage or to discuss experiences of physical and sexual abuse. A retreat leader may be reluctant to break a student's confidence and seek help from others. But the retreat leader has clear legal responsibilities.

An adult who receives information on a student's intent to harm himself or herself must reveal it to immediate supervisors and to the student's parent. Recent case law indicates that teachers can be held liable for student suicide or other injury if they had prior knowledge and failed to act. State law requires the reporting of physical and sexual abuse to the proper authorities. Retreats are valuable experiences that all young people should have. Attention to planning and training can help ensure an educationally and legally sound experience. 🖋

March 2000

Transportation to Off-Campus Activities

Many educators have questions about field trips. One of the most often-asked questions is "What kind of transportation must a school provide?" This article will discuss that question.

Many a person has observed, "If the school cannot afford a bus, it cannot afford the trip." Smaller schools or those with severely limited resources may believe that their students and parents will not be able to pay for a leased bus. No law requires that buses provide all field trip transportation, but in these days of increasing accidents and litigation, such a law may not be far away. Whatever mode of transportation is chosen, the principal, director of religious education, or youth minister must ensure that certain standards are maintained.

The means of transportation should be clearly noted in a cover letter or permission slip. The parents should specifically agree to that means of transportation. If the basketball team uses school buses for away games and parents have consented to the transportation, students should not be allowed to use any other transportation unless the parent has clearly given other directions for a specific instance or instances.

If parent drivers are used, the permission slip should contain a clause such as "We request that our child be allowed to ride in a car driven by a volunteer parent and we give permission." Since relatively few schools have insurance that covers volunteers, it is important for administrators to communicate clearly to parents that their insurance will be primary. Any school or diocesan insurance can be used only after the driver's insurance and assets are exhausted. Parents should be required to provide a copy of their proof of insurance and it should be kept on file.

Federal and state seat belt laws govern the use of seat belts. No driver should take more children than the number of seat belts in the car. Education officials should give drivers not only directions to the site, but also rules and procedures for student behavior in cars. Administrators must insist that drivers follow the schedule and not deviate from it, as sometimes happens when a parent decides to buy ice cream cones for those in his car while those in other cars go directly to the site. Case law is well established that such trips are not permissible.

At the high school level, it is not uncommon for students to transport themselves and their friends to activities. Often students make their own arrangements. Secondary administrators should ensure that no school officials assign particular students to a particular driver. In the unfortunate event of an accident or injury, a parent could allege that the supervisor was negligent if the supervisor assigned the student to a particular car. On the way to and from a site, as well as when on the site, high school drivers should not be permitted to take side trips to restaurants, movie houses, etc., unless such activities are part of the planned trip. In one high school case, a school was held liable when the priest supervisor allowed a high school boy to drive to a McDonald's after everyone had already eaten; the boy was involved in an accident. The court found the side trip unnecessary and ordered the school to pay more than $1 million in damages. Another possible approach is to require parents to provide transportation and to state that the school accepts no responsibility for that transportation.

Use of Teacher Cars

Administrators should clearly understand that no teacher or staff member can be required to transport students in his or her car. Sometimes, school or diocesan insurance will cover employees who transport students on official business; often, it will not. Thus, the administrator needs to check insurance coverage with the carrier or with the agent. In any case, use of teacher cars should be discouraged.

Following Diocesan and School Policies and Procedures

Failure to follow diocesan policies and procedures can result in tragedy. In one recent high school case, two athletic coaches failed to follow diocesan policy requiring school-owned or leased buses or vans to be used for transport. When one van failed to start, one coach took his own car and had another student drive students as well. The student was involved in a fatal accident. Certainly, no one wanted anyone to be hurt or killed. If the policy had been followed, however, there probably would have been no tragedy. The case was settled out of court, but a family was virtually destroyed and staff members have to live with the reality that their failure to follow policy may have caused a person's death.

Common sense is still a good guideline. Questions such as "How would I want this handled if my child were participating?" can help educators make good decisions. 𝒥𝑃

January 2001

Does a Student Have a Legal Right to Play Sports? To Participate in Extracurricular Activities?

CIIIO

The above questions arise fairly often in schools and other educational programs. In many cases, not everyone who tries out for an activity will be accepted. The students not selected for a team, and often their parents, are understandably disappointed. This disappointment can be expressed as a claim of a denial of legal rights. Principals, other administrators, athletic directors, and extracurricular moderators can often find themselves spending inordinate amounts of time with frustrated parents.

When this author was a Catholic high school principal some years ago, a father complained about his daughter not making the softball team. When the author told the father that the coach made the decision on who is cut and who plays, the father insisted that a separate re-tryout be held for his daughter with the father, the coach, and the principal having one vote each. When his demand was not met, he went away angry because he said that his daughter had been denied her constitutional right to play softball.

Does the Constitution Say Anything About Participation in Sports and Activities?

Readers of this column are probably aware that the U.S. Constitution is silent on the subject of education. Catholic educational institutions are not bound by the Constitution and do not have to meet the demands of substantive and procedural due process that public schools must meet. Catholic institutions are expected to be fair and thus meet the contractual obligations of good faith and fair dealing, but are not required to recognize constitutional rights.

Does a public school student have a legal right to play sports and participate in activities? The answer is clearly "no," as several courts have ruled. An individual must be given the same fair chance that others are given. If the fair chance is not granted, constitutional due process rights will come into play, because public schools are governmental agencies. However, giving a person an opportunity to try out does not mean the student will have a place on the team or in the activity.

Catholic institutions are expected to give their students that same fair chance. However, contract law, not constitutional law, binds Catholic entities. Administrators would be well advised to adopt a policy similar to the following:

All qualified students may try out for membership on sports teams and in extracurricular activities. The school is committed to providing everyone a fair chance to participate. Unfortunately, not everyone who tries out can be accepted. The decision of the coach, in conjunction with the athletic director, or the decision of the moderator, in consultation with the principal, is final. Ordinarily, the principal will not intervene in nonselection decisions unless the decision is arbitrary and capricious. Parents are encouraged to help their children understand that not everyone will be selected.

This policy could be inserted into the parent/student, athletic, or extracurricular handbook, as appropriate. Parents should be required to sign a statement such as "We, the parents of _____ have read this handbook and agree to be governed by its provisions." Having a signed statement to reference when tempers flare is an objective means of justifying the decision. No one wants to be callous in the face of parental and student disappointment. But a lesson is learned when students find out that they cannot always get what they desire, no matter how loudly parents protest.

What About No-Cut Policies?

Some elementary schools have no-cut policies, which mean that everyone who tries out for a sport or activity will be accepted. The theory is that, at such a young age, everyone should be allowed to participate even if the playing time of more able students is shortened. Administrators not infrequently state that it is easier to live with not winning than it is to deal with disappointed students and parents.

A no-cut policy is an administrator's or coach's prerogative. Allowing everyone to play shows fairness and ensures that everyone who wants to learn a sport will. However, as students enter high school, they generally will not find no-cut policies. Care must be taken to help students through what can be a difficult phase in growing up. The competition of secondary sports and extracurricular activities does not generally lend itself to no-cut policies.

Conclusion

An administrator should ensure that (a) policies are clearly articulated and promulgated to those affected, (b) parents and students, when appropriate, submit a signed statement agreeing to be bound by policy, (c) all tryouts are conducted fairly and all who wish to try out are allowed to try out, (d) coaches and moderators understand the importance of impartiality, and (e) parents and students are allowed to meet with an administrator to express dissatisfaction with the outcome of a selection process. [Note: In keeping with the principle of subsidiarity, administrators should not meet with parents or students until they have first met with the coach or moderator who made the decision.] The administrator will not ordinarily intervene, but can intervene if policy or fairness appears to be compromised.

November 2005

Alcohol at School and Parish Functions: Can It Be Served? Should It Be Served?

⟨≋⟩

As the school year begins, school and parish administrators generally put the finishing touches on the calendar. Virtually all schools and parishes have some sort of adult fund-raisers, generally ones that promote both fellowship and profit making. Alcohol has been a staple of many of these fund-raisers—perhaps for many years. More and more, the author is being asked questions about the legality of serving alcohol (a) to adults on parish or school property, (b) to adults present at off-campus school or parish activities, and (c) at parish or school functions at which minors may be present as guests or workers. The answers to the issues are complex and involve ethical, moral, and legal issues.

Certainly, every adult aged 21 and over has the legal right to drink, unless that right has been relinquished because one is incarcerated or on probation. So the question generally has little or nothing to do with the adults' right to drink. However, some states, cities, and towns may have regulations forbidding the use of alcohol on school or church grounds or within a certain number of feet of the institution. In those cases, of course, the legal regulation must be followed.

What should an administrator do when considering the continuation of a long-cherished event at which alcohol is served? Should an administrator even consider inaugurating a new event at which alcohol will be served? These are hard questions. Today, people know much more about the harmful effects of alcohol than was known even 20 years ago, long after many events were begun. More than one in every 10 adults is an alcoholic.

Twenty years ago, most people felt sorry for a drunk driver who caused an accident that killed or injured someone, but today one would be hard-pressed to find a significant number of people who would be sympathetic to the drunk driver. The organization Mothers Against Drunk Driving has made a significant impact on both the numbers of people who drive while intoxicated and on public response to people guilty of such behavior.

Parish and school picnics, generally involving raffles, pull-tabs, and other gambling, have long served alcohol and beer. The author recalls some 10 years ago being at such a picnic when the announcer stated over the loud speaker, "We are required to remind everyone serving beer and wine that the law forbids serving it to minors. We don't have time to check IDs, so look at purchasers carefully. You, not the parish, will be held responsible if you serve a minor." While astonished at such a statement, the author noticed that no one else seemed to be concerned or even surprised. Obviously, no people serving alcohol should state that they "don't have time to check IDs" and no institution can make such a statement and pass sole liability on to the server. In some areas, people mistakenly believe that because liquor has always been served and nothing has ever happened that nothing ever will.

If school or parish administrators decide to sponsor events at which drinking alcohol is allowed, some cautions are in order. Wherever alcohol and young people are present underage drinking is possible, so an adults-only policy is recommended. Further recommendations follow.

For On-Site Events

1. Check with your insurance carrier to see if you have host liquor liability coverage. If you do not, purchase it either on an event-by-event basis or as blanket coverage (which is becoming increasingly difficult to get).

2. Be very clear about who can authorize an event at which liquor can be served. In a parish, it might be the pastor. In a school, the president or principal may make the decision. The fewer people with authority to authorize such events, the better.

3. Use a certified bartender. One can be found by checking with the American Bartenders Association chapter in your town or city.

For Both On- and Off-Site Events

1. Require that all drinks be measured.

2. Limit the number of drinks each person may consume. If liquor is free, give people two or three tokens or coupons for a three- to four-hour event. If a cash bar is available, instruct the bartender to monitor consumption carefully.

3. Instruct the bartender to stop serving anyone who appears to be intoxicated.

4. Do not let an intoxicated person drive. Call and pay for a cab or have a nondrinker drive the person home. Consider having designated drivers to take people home.

5. Hire a police officer or other security. If an intoxicated person becomes abusive or poses harm to self or others, police or security can intervene. 𝔍𝔑

Liability

and NEGLIGENCE

March 1991

Tort Law in Catholic Schools: For What Are Educators Liable?

Tort cases are the most common form of lawsuit against educators. A tort is a civil or private wrong other than a breach of contract. The four main types of education tort cases are corporal punishment, search and seizure, defamation of character, and negligence. Negligence suits outnumber the other three types put together.

Corporal Punishment

Although some states permit corporal punishment, Catholic schools would be well advised to avoid it. While the administration of the punishment might not be illegal, injuring the child physically, mentally, or psychologically is. The risks of student harm and educator liability make corporal punishment a poor disciplinary choice. [See author's note in January 1991 column.]

Search and Seizure

The 1985 Supreme Court decision of New Jersey v. T.L.O., holding that public school officials must use reasonable cause in searching students or their possessions, does not apply to Catholic schools. Catholic schools should, nonetheless, have some kind of policy for searching students and seizing their possessions. Searching a student should require more cause than searching a locker.

Catholic schools can be subject to tort suits of assault and battery and invasion of privacy if a student is harmed because of an unreasonable search. Carefully developed policies should guide any search and seizure. A commonsense "balancing test" should be applied in each case: Is this search and its possible effects worth finding whatever school officials are seeking?

Defamation of Character

Defamation is an unprivileged communication that harms the reputation of another. Defamation can be either spoken (slander) or written (libel). Truth may not be an absolute defense for an educator, who is generally held to a higher standard than the ordinary person.

The potential for defamation to be alleged certainly exists in Catholic schools. It is important that school officials be factual in their comments, whether written or oral, about the conduct of students, parents, teachers, and other employees.

Catholic schools can protect themselves and their students and teachers by ensuring that record-keeping policies are in place that (a) limit contents of records to what is absolutely necessary, (b) provide for periodic culling of older records, and (c) limit access to records to people who have legitimate reasons to read them.

Negligence

If a principal or teacher is sued, odds are that the suit will allege negligence. Since negligence is an unintentional act that results in injury, a person charged with negligence generally does not face criminal charges. People who bring successful negligence suits are usually awarded monetary damages in an amount calculated to compensate for the actual injury suffered. It is possible, though rare, for a court to award punitive or exemplary damages if the court is shocked by the negligent behavior. Four elements must be present before legal negligence can be found: duty, violation of duty, proximate cause, and injury.

The person charged with negligence must have had a *duty* in the situation. Educators are not responsible for injuries occurring at a place where or a time when they had no responsibility. A principal or teacher walking through a mall on a weekend does not have a legal duty to students who are also walking through the mall. In the school setting, students have a right to safety and teachers and administrators have a duty to protect the safety of all those entrusted to their care. Teachers have a duty to provide reasonable supervision of students. Administrators have a duty to develop and implement rules and regulations guiding teachers in providing for student safety.

Negligence cannot exist if the second element, *violation of duty*, is not present. Courts understand that accidents and spontaneous actions can occur. If a teacher is properly supervising a playground and one child picks up a rock, throws it, and injures another child, the teacher cannot be held liable. However, if a teacher responsible for the supervision were to allow rock throwing to continue without attempting to stop it and a student were injured, the teacher would probably be found to have violated a duty.

Similarly, a teacher who leaves a classroom unattended to take a coffee break will generally be found to have violated a duty if a student is injured and it can be shown that the teacher's presence could have prevented the injury. If it can be shown that teachers often left students unattended while the principal, through inaction or inattention, did nothing about the situation, the principal has violated a duty as well. Under the legal doctrine of respondent superior (let the superior answer), principals are often held responsible for the actions of subordinates.

The violation of duty must be the *proximate cause* of the injury. The court or jury has to decide whether proper supervision could have prevented the injury and, in so deciding, the court has to look at the facts of each individual case. William Valente, in his text *Law and the Schools* (1980), observed, "To be proximate, a cause need not be the immediate, or even the primary cause of injury, but it must be a *material and substantial* factor in producing the harm, 'but for' which the harm would not have occurred" (p. 351).

Mary Angela Shaughnessy, SCN, J.D., Ph.D.

The tragic case of *Levandoski v. Jackson City School District*, 328 So.2d 339 (1976), illustrates. A teacher failed to report that a 13-year-old girl was missing from class. The child was later found murdered. The child's mother filed suit against the school district and alleged that if the child's absence had been reported, the murder would not have happened. The court found that no evidence existed proving a causal link between the violation of duty and the injury. Thus, the case failed in proximate cause.

One can easily see how a slight change in the facts could produce a different ruling. Had the child been found dead on or near school property, a court might well have found that proximate cause existed. It is not the act itself that results in legal negligence; it is the causal relationship between the act and the injury. If the relationship is too remote, legal negligence will not be found. Any reasonable educator will try to be as careful as possible, of course, and not gamble on the causal connection.

A well-known case that illustrates the concept of proximate cause is *Smith v. Archbishop of St. Louis,* 632 S.W.2d 516 (Mo. Ct. App. 1982). A second-grade teacher kept a lighted candle on her desk every morning during May. She gave no special instructions to the students on the dangers of lighted candles. One day a child, wearing a crepe paper costume for a school play, moved too close to the candle and the costume caught fire. The teacher had difficulty putting out the flames and the child sustained serious physical and resultant psychological injuries. The trial court ruled that the teacher was the proximate cause of the child's injuries. The court discussed the concept of foreseeability: It was not necessary for the defendant to have foreseen the particular injury, but only that a reasonable person should have foreseen that some injury was likely.

This discussion should indicate that proximate cause is a complex subject. It is difficult to predict what a court will determine to be the proximate cause in any particular allegation of negligence.

The fourth element necessary for a finding of negligence is *injury*. No matter how irresponsible the behavior of a teacher or administrator, there is no legal negligence if there is no injury. If a teacher leaves 20 first graders unattended and no one is injured, there is no negligence in a legal sense. To bring suit in a court of law, an individual has to have sustained an injury for which the court can award a remedy.

Courts follow the principle "the younger the child, chronologically or mentally, the greater is the standard of care." It might be acceptable to leave a group of high school seniors alone for 10 minutes when it would not be acceptable to leave a group of first graders alone.

In developing and implementing policies for supervision, the educator must ask, "Is this what one would expect a reasonable person in a similar situation to do?" The best defense for an administrator in a negligence suit is a reasonable attempt to provide for the safety of all through appropriate rules and regulations. The best defense for a teacher is a reasonable effort to implement rules and regulations.

Recent Developments

The right of a Catholic school to refuse to renew the contract of a teacher who acts in a manner that contradicts the teachings of the church was upheld in the 1990 Pennsylvania case *Little v. St. Mary Magdalene Parish,* 739 F.Supp. 1003. Ms. Little, a divorced, non-Catholic, tenured teacher, brought a civil rights action against the school when it did not renew her contract after she, without obtaining an annulment of her first marriage, entered into a second marriage with a Catholic man.

Ms. Little alleged that the parish's action was a violation of her rights under both Title VII of the Civil Rights Act of 1964 and state law, as well as a breach of contract. Catholic schools, like other religious organizations, are exempt from claims of religious discrimination under Title VII. Ms. Little argued that, by employing a non-Catholic, the school was waiving its right to the exemption. The court declined to find such a waiver.

Ms. Little had signed contracts containing a "Cardinal's Clause," which allowed the parish to terminate a teacher's employment for "public rejection of the official teachings, doctrine, or laws of the Roman Catholic Church." The parish maintained that her conduct, though permissible in her religion, violated the Cardinal's Clause.

In granting summary judgment for the parish, the court ruled that "[a] religious organization's right to make employment decisions based on religion exists throughout the employment relationship, not just during the hiring process" (p. 601).

This Pennsylvania decision suggests that the right of Catholic schools to hold teachers, regardless of religion, to strict standards of conduct compatible with the teachings of the Catholic Church will be upheld. [More recent case law, discussed in other columns, supports the earlier decisions.] 𝒥𝒫

September 1995

Negligence Revisited:
What Is The Legal Liability?

As the school year begins, educational administrators find themselves considering safety issues and negligence prevention. Negligence is the most common of all lawsuits filed against educators. In assessing whether a person's behavior is negligent, a court will use the "reasonable person" test: Would a reasonable person [educator] in the same situation have acted in this manner?

Courts also rely on the principle of "the younger the child chronologically or mentally, the greater the standard of care." Ninth-grade students, for example, would not ordinarily require the same level of supervision as kindergarten students.

Some people mistakenly believe that children and older students can never be left unattended. Courts recognize that emergencies can arise and that students might be left alone while the supervisor takes care of the emergency. Judges expect, however, that supervisors will have told students at other points, such as the beginning of the term and periodically thereafter, what they should do if the supervisor has to leave. At a minimum, rules might require that students remain in their seats when no adult is present.

Use of Volunteers

In some situations in which volunteers are used as substitutes in the absence of a teacher, the supervising volunteer may not even know the students' names. Administrators should insist that all individuals who supervise students, even those on the substitute list, participate in an orientation that addresses appropriate skills.

Elements of Negligence

Four elements must be present before legal negligence can be found—duty, violation of duty, proximate cause, and injury. If one of these elements is missing, legal negligence cannot be present.

The person charged with negligence must have had a *duty* in the situation. Educators are not responsible for injuries occurring at a place where or a time when they had no responsibility. In the educational setting, however, students have a right to safety and educators have a duty to protect and implement rules and regulations guiding teachers in providing for student safety.

Early Arrivals and Students Left After School

One situation that presents a negligence standpoint is that of the student who arrives early or is not picked up at dismissal time. All staff must understand that students must be supervised from the time they arrive at school until they leave. If parents are late picking up their children, an adult staff member must remain with the students until the parents arrive.

Administrators may want consider a penalty for repeated violations. A fine can be imposed, or in schools sponsoring extended-care programs, students present at unauthorized times can be sent to the extended-care site and parents can be billed for services. Such a policy should, of course, be noted in the parent/student handbook.

Whatever procedure an administrator chooses, at no time should a student be let unattended (particularly outside in front of a locked door) to await the arrival of parents. Courts have indicated that administrators and staff members can be held responsible for student behavior occurring on school property before or after programs and for the consequences of this behavior. This situation might well be taken to the education board for the development of a policy statement. Courts expect some policy on when students may arrive, what rules they are to follow, and what supervision will be provided.

Common sense must prevail in any situation. Textbook solutions are rarely available for individuals working with young people. For example, a teacher may return to school for a forgotten item and discover that a student is waiting for a ride and no other adult is present. The reasonable teacher would wait with the child until parents arrive or some other transportation arrangement can be made. In such situations, teachers may be tempted to take students home in their cars. However, should a teacher elect to take such an action and an accident occur, the teacher may be held liable for any injuries.

Negligence cannot exist if *violation of duty*, the second element, does not occur. Courts understand that accidents and spontaneous actions can occur. If a teacher is properly supervising students during a break and one student picks up an object, throws it, and injures another student, the teacher is not responsible. However, if a teacher responsible for supervision were to allow object throwing to continue without attempting to stop it and a student were injured, the teacher would probably be found to have violated a duty.

Similarly, a teacher who leaves a classroom unattended to make a personal or nonemergency telephone call will usually be found to have violated a duty if a student is injured and it can be shown that the adult's presence could have prevented the injury. If it can be shown that teachers often left students unattended while the administrator, through inaction or inattention, did nothing about the situation, the administrator has violated a duty as well. In determining whether the superior is liable, courts pose questions such as the following:

- Has the administrator developed a clear policy for staff conduct in dealing with situations such as the one resulting in injury?
- Has the supervisor implemented the policy?
- Are staff members supervised?

The violation of duty must be the *proximate cause* of the injury, the third element of negligence. The judge or jury has to decide whether proper supervision could have prevented the injury. Proximate cause is not necessarily synonymous with direct cause. For example, in the object-throwing example cited above, the student throwing the object would be the direct cause of the injury. However, the teacher's failure to intervene in the situation would be the proximate cause of the injury.

A well-known case that illustrates the concept of proximate cause is *Smith v. Archbishop of St. Louis,* 632 S.W.2d 516 (Mo. Ct. app. 1982). A second-grade teacher kept a lighted candle on her desk every morning during the month of May. One day a child, wearing a crepe paper costume for a play, moved too close to the candle and the costume caught fire. The teacher had difficulty putting out the flames and the child sustained serious physical and resultant psychological injuries.

The trial court ruled that the teacher's act of keeping the lighted candle on her desk was the proximate cause of the child's injury. The court discussed the concept of foreseeability. It was not necessary that the teacher have foreseen the particular injury, but only that a reasonable person should have foreseen that some injury was likely. The concept of foreseeability is important: Would a reasonable person foresee the likelihood of injury? Classrooms contain the potential for injuries like the one in Smith.

Administrators would be wise to hold regular staff meetings to discuss the curriculum, teacher expectations, and foreseeable problems. These matters can then be analyzed in light of health and safety requirements.

The fourth element necessary for a finding of negligence is *injury*. No matter how irresponsible the behavior of an educator, there is no legal negligence if there is no injury.

In developing and implementing policies for supervision, the administrator must ask, "Is this what one would expect a reasonable person in a similar situation to do?" The best defense for an administrator in a negligence suit is a reasonable attempt to provide for the safety of all through appropriate rules and regulations. The best defense for an educator is a reasonable effort to implement rules and regulations. Further, teachers are expected to keep all equipment in working order and to render areas used by young people as hazard free as possible.

Thus, educational administrators must take an offensive approach to the elimination of hazards. All activities should be carefully monitored. All staff, paid and volunteer, should receive thorough and ongoing orientation and instruction. The reasonable administrator supervises staff. The administrator who practices prevention by constantly striving to eliminate foreseeable risks will avoid both injuries and costly lawsuits.

Recent Developments: Sexual Abuse Claims

Today, more and more claims of sexual abuse are being made against teachers and other adults holding positions of trust over children. Two recent cases raise issues on statutes of limitation.

In the 1994 case of *Sanchez v. the Archdiocese of San Antonio,* 873 S.W. 2d 87, the plaintiff appealed a judgment that did not allow her to avail herself of the discovery rule in a child abuse case brought against a Catholic school. The 57-year-old woman claimed to have been abused as a child by a teacher at the school. She recently remembered the abuse, but everyone who might also have known of the abuse had died. The discovery rule normally delays the beginning of the statute of limitations until injury is, or could have been, discovered through reasonable efforts.

In this case, the court ruled that since there had been a significant time lapse and there was no one to corroborate the woman's claims, state precedent did not allow the use of the discovery rule to stay the statutes of limitations.

In the 1995 case of *Isley v. Capuchin Province,* 878 F.Supp. 1021 (E.D. Mich.), a former seminary student brought suit against a religious order and alleged that priests had sexually abused him. The incidents occurred in two separate states, Michigan and Wisconsin, and the court had to determine which state's laws would govern the statute of limitations. The court ruled that Wisconsin law could apply to tort allegations filed in Michigan but based on incidents in Wisconsin, while Michigan law would determine the statute of limitations.

Instances such as the one above are not uncommon. While the situation of a student under the control of an order in two separate states might seem rare, cases involving "choice of law" are not. A litigant may bring a lawsuit in the state where an action occurred, in the state where the defendant is domiciled (i.e., has residence), or in any state where the defendant/respondent does business. Since different states have different laws governing the statute of limitations, the state law selected may determine whether a person can even get a hearing in court.

These two cases illustrate the concept of statute of limitations. While it is harder to litigate an old claim of abuse than it is to litigate a more recent one, the outcome of a suit may depend on whether anyone is alive who can corroborate the claim and on the governing law of the state where the action is brought. [Note: While it may appear that cases brought since 2000 have not depended on when the abuse occurred, it must be noted that the vast majority of such cases and claims were settled out of court. Very few proceeded to trial. Thus, it is difficult to predict what today's judges and juries might do with cases similar to those discussed above.]

January 2000

Dangerous Activities and Young People:
How Responsible are Teachers and Administrators?

On November 18, 1999, 11 students at Texas A&M University died when they fell from the top of a log pyramid constructed for a homecoming bonfire. This tradition dates back 90 years and is viewed as one of the ultimate bonding experiences. But to the families and friends who bury young people, words about tradition and pride may ring hollow.

Helen O'Neill of the Associated Press wrote three days after the incident, "Tradition and danger have always formed a potent mix on college campuses." Another AP writer, Mike Crissey, reported, "Past A&M engineering professors said they tried over the years to warn students that the bonfire design contained perilous flaws."

What, then, is the lesson of this tragedy for those who work with elementary, middle, and secondary students? Rather than thinking such problems are the concern of only college administrators, teachers and educators in schools and programs must be particularly vigilant in guarding the safety of students. Young people generally do not seem to understand the ramifications of injury and death, and adults must help them. What seems like fun on one day may be a prelude to disaster on another.

Students will always value traditions. Making new ones, as well as keeping old ones, is very important. Often a principal will contact the author and say, "This field trip, senior class trip, altar server outing scares me to death. But it's tradition. The parents want it and the kids want it. The last principal who tried to do away with the tradition finally gave in because it was easier than putting up with the grief." Basically, however, the bottom line is the safety of students, not the convenience of the administrator.

It is the job of educators to do the following:

1. Identify and assess potential problem areas and practices.

2. Develop plans for dealing with these areas and practices.

3. Monitor ongoing progress toward lessening or eliminating the danger.

In a number of cases involving eighth graders and high schoolers, courts have generally not shown much sympathy to educators who, honoring the tradition, allowed students to engage in unsafe activity. Two cases involving falls from school roofs will illustrate. In one case the senior class wished to have their class picture taken on the roof of the building. The yearbook moderator agreed, told everyone to be particularly careful, and took the entire class to the roof. The combined weight of the group put extra stress on the roof, a mechanism surrounding a skylight gave way, and one girl plummeted to her death. In a similar case, students were gathered on the roof for class, and a girl walked too close to the edge, fell off, and died. Tradition or not, these deaths cannot be justified.

Adults must set limits for children and adolescents because so often they are unable or unwilling to do so themselves. The wise administrator will pay close attention to what staff members say about the safety of activities. Every educational program administrator should ensure that some group or committee regularly monitors safety in the school or program.

Negligence

Who's responsible for injuries that occur as a result of traditional activities? Under the doctrine of *respondeat superior,* let the superior answer, administrators can and often are held liable for the acts of their subordinates. If an injury occurs, the administrator will generally be charged with negligence. A plaintiff will probably argue that the accident was foreseeable. Courts will ask, "Should a reasonable teacher or administrator have foreseen that allowing this activity could result in serious injury?"

Some may say, "Well, life's dangerous." It is true that life offers no guarantees, but there are situations that sensible people would avoid. Using the traditional four-part test for legal negligence, the reader can see how easily legal liability can escalate.

First, the individual must have a duty in the situation. Administrators are expected to know what is occurring in their schools and how to respond. Second, the individual must violate the duty. An administrator who knew that a traditional but dangerous activity would take place could be held liable for letting it happen. Third, the violation of duty has to be the proximate cause of the injury. Returning to the roof case cited earlier, the moderator violated his duty and that violation resulted in injury. "But for" the senior picture on the roof, the student would still be alive. Fourth, someone must sustain an injury, mental or physical. Without an injury, there can be no legal negligence.

Recent incidents in higher education should be warning signals for administrators at all levels. Administrators should not always say "no" to student activity requests, but neither should they rush to say "yes." The well-being of students should be the primary focus of all educators. ⅅⅉ

September 2000

Negligence:
A Back-to-School/Program Review

⟨✺⟩

As the new school or program year begins, educators tackle many tasks. While litigation is perhaps one area most educators would prefer to forget, the beginning of the year is a good time to review potential hazards and dangerous practices. It is also a good time to brush up on the definition of negligence and its application.

Negligence has been defined in many ways; one of the best definitions is "an absence of care." The educator's lack of care can be causally linked to an injury. Four elements must be present before an educator can be found negligent. All four elements must be present; if any one is missing, legal negligence cannot be found.

The first element is *duty*. A person cannot be liable if he or she had no particular duty in a given situation. A youth minister who witnesses three of his youth group members fighting in a bowling alley has no legal obligation to intervene. It is not the youth minister's job to police the bowling alley. If, however, the same behavior occurred during basketball practice, the youth minister would have a clear duty to take appropriate measures.

The second element is *violation of duty.* The person charged with a duty must violate the duty. In a dated, but still applicable, Oregon case, a teacher was sued for negligence because a bee flew into a bus full of children on a field trip. The bee stung the bus driver, who lost control of the vehicle, and children were injured. In effect, the parents of injured students alleged that if the teacher had been properly doing her duty, she would have either kept the bee from flying in the bus or kept the bee from stinging the bus driver. The presiding judge stated that there were no Oregon statutes applicable to bees entering school buses; therefore, the teacher could not have violated her duty. Some events are beyond the control even of teachers.

The third element is *proximate cause.* The violation of duty must be the proximate cause of the injury. In an often-quoted 1982 Missouri case, *Smith v. the Archdiocese of St. Louis,* 632 S.W.2d 516 (Mo. Ct. App.), a second grader was burned by the flame on a candle that her teacher kept burning all day during the month of May to honor the Mother of God. If the teacher had not kept the candle burning in violation of her duty to protect the children's safety, no one would have been injured. Here the teacher's action was clearly the proximate cause of the injury. But for the burning candle, the child would have been unharmed.

The fourth element is *injury*. No matter how irresponsible an individual's actions, if no one is injured, there can be no finding of legal negligence. To bring a lawsuit, the plaintiff must have sustained an injury. The purpose of a judicial remedy is "to make whole" an injured person. The injury does not have to be physical. It can be mental, emotional, or psychological, but an injury must have resulted from the inaction or action of the supervisor. If a teacher were to tell a student to climb a steep roof to retrieve a softball and the student does so without injury, the teacher cannot be found legally negligent. Such a teacher would be professionally negligent, but without an injury, professional negligence will not result in a judgment of negligence in court.

Reviewing these elements and discussing situations that happened or almost happened in past years can be helpful. Staff members can contribute to the overall safety of the school or program by giving thought to the following questions and discussing their responses.

1. Are there any hazardous conditions in my classroom or other instructional areas? If yes, can I eliminate them on my own? If I cannot, do I know whom to contact and how to record the conditions and actions taken?

2. Have I noticed any hazardous conditions in the building or on the school or parish grounds? Whom should I inform? If the condition is not corrected, then I need to document that fact and notify my superior.

3. Have I noticed any patterns of dangerous behavior among the young people I supervise? What steps can I take to lessen, if not completely eliminate, these behaviors? Are my rules clear and consistently enforced? Do I understand it is more important for students to be safe than to have their own way? If I do, do I make decisions based on student safety first?

4. Have I ever observed suspicious individuals in or around the building? Have I reported these observations to my supervisor? Are signs directing visitors to the office clearly in evidence? Do people obey the signs?

January 2007

Liability for Unsponsored Off-site Activities

Parents, educators, and the media express concern about teenage and younger students' drinking, drug use, irresponsible driving, and sexual activity. Administrators often state that, while abhorring such behavior, they can do little about it when it occurs off campus. Even when school officials learn about "wild" parties scheduled to take place when parents are out of town (or worse, with the parents' consent or presence), phone calls or other contacts with parents may result in stony silence or statements such as "Thank you, but that's really none of your concern." Yet when injury or tragedy occurs, regardless of when or where, a first question often is "Did anyone at the school know?" If the answer is "yes," the next question is "Why didn't someone do something?" If the answer to the first question is "no," the next question may be "Well, shouldn't someone have known?"

These questions are not new. Unfortunately, there have always been young people who have friends over to drink or engage in other dangerous activities when parents are away—or even when parents are there. Twenty-five years ago, this writer was dealing with these very same questions in a state where the legal drinking age was 18 at the time. She remembers well calling a parent whose daughter was one of several who came to school intoxicated one morning after drinking in the area surrounding a lake. The mother said, "Sister, she's of legal age. If she's not drinking at school, you can't do anything about it." Of course, the writer did do something about it. Such a mind-set, however, is not a thing of the past. There are parents and even some teachers and administrators who think that what happens off campus is not the school's or parish's problem. But it is and can be—from both moral and legal standpoints.

The vast majority of Catholic schools and programs now have handbooks that parents are asked to sign. One component often addresses off-site conduct that can reflect badly on the church or school. Such regulations are needed. Being a good Catholic, Christian, or citizen is not something that should be expected only during a certain number of hours a day or during the school week. What young people do reflects on the school. A student who attends a drinking party on Saturday, drives a car, and injures or kills someone will be identified by the media not only as a high school student but also as one who attends a particular Catholic high school.

Obviously, the safety and well-being of young people are more important considerations for administrators than the effect bad behavior will have on the reputation of the school. No one would like to think that he or she could have prevented the death or injury of a student if a few words of notification or prohibition had been spoken. But administrators may ask, "How can it be my legal responsibility to do something about what occurs off campus, after hours, and not under my control?" The courts have not yet offered a definitive answer, but all indications are that they may be moving toward one.

A few recent cases that have not yet been decided involve allegations that the school knew or should have known that students planned to engage in dangerous activities, and officials failed to warn parents or took no action. Although this is a yet-uncharted area of law, one must remember that the usual standard for liability is "Did the administrator do what a reasonable administrator would be expected to do?" This is a question for a jury to answer when considering whether the four traditional elements of legal negligence are present: duty, violation of duty, proximate cause, and injury. While it may appear that most jury members will decline to find educators liable, what a jury will do is never a certainty, particularly today.

The wise administrator who cares for both the safety of students and the reputation of the institution will follow these reasonable procedures when dealing with rumors of dangerous activities:

1. Include in handbooks statements such as "We are partners with parents in their children's education. We notify parents of concerns about student life or behavior, even when off campus."

2. Instruct teachers, volunteers and staff to (a) take seriously conversation or information about potentially harmful activities or behaviors and (b) report that information to an administrator.

3. Administrators will contact parents when concerned about students' behavior.

Responsibility for student life and health does not begin or end on campus, nor is its primary goal the avoidance of legal liability. Both civil law and the Gospel demand that whatever can be done to protect God's children must be done. 🖎

MARCH 2002

RECENT LEGAL CASES OF INTEREST TO CATHOLIC EDUCATORS

The year 2001 witnessed a number of legal decisions with potential significance for Catholic schools. This column will offer a snapshot of selected cases.

Field Trip Negligence

In the case of *Doe v. Archbishop Stepinac High School,* 729 N.Y.S.2d 538, a Catholic school student sued seeking compensation for injuries he alleged were sustained when three students sexually assaulted him during an overseas field trip. The student claimed he had told teachers he was in danger. The court ruled that (a) the school could not be held liable for negligent or intentional infliction of emotional distress as school officials had taken reasonable precautions, (b) the school failed to produce convincing evidence that parents had signed a liability release, and (c) the liability release did not clearly and unequivocally express a release from liability. The court refused summary judgment and required a trial to determine, among other things, whether the school had sufficient knowledge of threats to harm the student. [Note: Ultimately, this case was settled out of court.]

This case reminds administrators of the importance of carefully drafted, legally reviewed permission slips and of the necessity of ensuring that each student who goes on a field trip submits a properly signed form. Administrators should see this case as a wake-up call and review field trip procedures and forms.

Release of Student to Noncustodial Parent

In the case of *Pauley v. Anchorage School District,* Alaska 31 P.3d 1284 (2001), the court refused to find a school principal liable after he released a student to his noncustodial mother in advance of the mother's Christmas visitation rights. The court ruled that the principal acted within his discretion because he notified the father, verified the mother's identification, discussed the matter with a police officer accompanying the mother, and reviewed the mother's court documents.

This case may appear surprising at first glance. It does illustrate, however, that courts can and do give school administrators the benefit of the doubt when it appears that they have acted with due diligence.

Threat to Kill Classmate Considered Protected Out-of-School Speech

The case of *Doe ex rel. Doe v. Pulaski County Special School District,* 263 F.3d 833 (8th Cir. 2001), involved an eighth-grade student who had written a composition containing references to killing a classmate. The student wrote the composition at home and stored it in his bedroom, where a visiting classmate discovered it during summer vacation. The visitor reported the writing to school officials, who expelled the writer. The court ruled that the student's writing was protected First Amendment speech in his home and was not a "true threat." Employing a totality of the circumstances test, the court stated that a reasonable person would not have foreseen that a visiting classmate might find the composition and construe it as a true threat.

This case, considered surprising by some, illustrates that courts do not expect schools to police everything that students do outside the school. This case involved a public school. Had such a situation occurred in a Catholic school that had a policy (often recommended by this author) prohibiting "conduct, whether inside or outside school, that is detrimental to the school," the expulsion would probably have been upheld.

Private School Tuition Was Reasonably Necessary Expense of Chapter 13 Debtors

In re Webb (Texas), 2001 WL 585674, involved parents who had filed for Chapter 13 debtor relief. The court ruled that the private school tuition of their son with Attention Deficit Hyperactivity Disorder (ADHD) and Generalized Anxiety Disorder was a necessary expense and school officials could collect tuition. The court stated that the existence of a public school alternative did not mean that the parents could not choose a private education.

This case provides some hope to administrators who often find themselves relegated to the ranks of unsecured and therefore unpaid debtors in bankruptcy proceedings involving parents of students.

False Statements Made by Parents Were Actionable Defamation Per Se

In *Huxen v. Villasenor* (La. App.) 2001 WL 1119574, a parent made allegations to a parent volunteer that a teacher was physically abusing a student. No evidence supported the allegations, which would have, if true, constituted criminal acts. The teacher could sue the parent making the statements for defamation.

For quite some time, most lawyers have advised teachers who wanted to know if they could sue parents for what they said about them that a certain amount of "grief" (i.e., defamation) went with the territory. Some states have passed laws making assaults or threats to teachers crimes. This case may illustrate the willingness of courts to take a tougher line against parents who make unsubstantiated claims against teachers.

Conclusion

These cases may signal some changing winds in education law. This column will carry future updates as some of these cases are heard in trial courts. ✐

Violence, ABUSE and HARASSMENT

September 1991

Child Abuse and the Catholic School

One of the most serious issues confronting educators today is child abuse. The media carry daily reports of adults causing children physical and emotional pain. The educator is in a particularly sensitive position. Children and adolescents often choose teachers as confidants in their struggles to deal with abuse and its effects. For this reason, principals must ensure that teachers and all school employees are as prepared as possible to deal with the realities of abuse and neglect. As the new school year begins, principals would be well advised to review pertinent state law and school policies and provide at least a few minutes of discussion on the topic at one of the first faculty meetings. If a separate meeting is not provided for other school employees such as secretaries, custodians, and cafeteria workers, the principal should consider having them present for the appropriate portion of the faculty meeting.

Statutory Considerations

All 50 states have laws requiring educators to report suspected abuse or neglect. While the actual wording varies from state to state, the statue ordinarily will be somewhat like that in Kentucky Revised Statute 199.335(2):

> Any physician, osteopathic physician, nurse, teacher, school personnel, social worker . . . child-caring personnel . . . who knows or has reasonable cause to believe that a child is an abused or neglected child, shall report or cause a report to be made in accordance with the provisions of this section. When any of the above persons is attending a child as part of his professional duties, he shall report or cause a report to be made.

Statutes generally mandate reporting procedures. The reporting individual usually makes a phone report followed by a written report within a specified time period, often 48 hours. Statutes usually provide protection for a person who makes a good-faith report of child abuse that later is discovered to be unfounded. Such a good-faith reporter will not be liable to the alleged abuser for defamation of character. However, a person can usually be held liable for making what is referred to as a "malicious report," one that has no basis in fact and that was made by a person who knows that no factual basis existed. Conversely, statutes usually mandate that a person who knew of child abuse or neglect and failed to report it be fined and/or charged with a misdemeanor or felony.

Defining Abuse

What is child abuse? This author once heard an attorney define it as "corporal punishment gone too far." Although it excludes sexual abuse, the definition has merit. However, it poses questions: How far is too far? Who makes the final determination? Can what one person considers abuse be considered valid parental corporal punishment by another? Are there any allowances for differing cultural practices? It is difficult, if not impossible, to give a precise definition that will cover all eventualities. Certainly, some situations are so extreme that there can be little argument that abuse has occurred. A student who appears at school with cigarette burns has been abused by someone. When a child alleges sexual abuse, only two conclusions probably exist: The child is telling the truth or the child is lying. The investigating agency will have to determine which conclusion is true.

The majority of cases will probably not be clear-cut and an educator may struggle to decide if a report should be made. Many law enforcement officials and some attorneys instruct educators to report everything a student tells them that could possibly constitute abuse or negligence. They further caution teachers that it is not their job to determine if abuse has occurred. As a reporter, the teacher's function is to present the information. Appropriate officials will determine whether the report should be investigated further or simply screened out as a well-intentioned report that does not appear to be abuse.

In-Service Education

School administrators should provide teachers, other employees, and volunteers with in-service training on the indicators of child abuse and neglect and the legal procedures for reporting such conditions. Many excellent written resources are available. Local police departments and social service agencies are usually happy to make both materials and speakers available to schools. If a school does not provide its teachers with education and materials on this topic, a phone call to appropriate sources should provide the teacher with needed materials.

Some of the most helpful material will identify warning signs or situations that abuse may be happening. For example, the National Council for Child Abuse Specialized Training has identified the following six indicators of child neglect: (a) lack of supervision, (b) lack of adequate clothing and good hygiene, (c) lack of medical or dental care, (d) lack of adequate education, (e) lack of adequate nutrition, and (f) lack of adequate shelter. The center cautions people to be sensitive to issues of poverty versus neglect. Poverty is not synonymous with neglect. Poor children may need social services; they may or may not be neglected.

The National Center states that children who are abused physically or emotionally will display certain types of behavior that are survival responses to what is occurring in the home. Four categories of these behaviors include (a) overly compliant, passive, and undemanding behaviors; (a) extremely aggressive, demanding, and rageful behaviors; (c) role-reversed "parental" behavior or extremely dependent behavior; and (d) lags in development.

Who Should File the Report?

Many experts advise that the school administrator, usually the principal, make all child abuse and neglect reports so that the same person reports all situations in a given school. However, individual state laws may vary on this point. Each staff member must understand that if for some reason the principal refuses to make the report, the staff member must file the report. If a staff member files a report, the principal must be notified that a report has been made. It is legally dangerous for the school when a police officer or other official appears to investigate a report of child abuse and the principal does not know that a report has been filed.

Schools officials should decide in advance how visits and requests from police and social workers will be handled. Many states require that school personnel allow officials to examine and question students. Principals should seek legal counsel in determining the applicable law for a given state. If the school permits the examination and questioning of a child, a school official should always be present.

Teachers and Abuse

A survey of recent educational cases decided in courts of record reveals that the number of lawsuits alleging teacher or other school employee abuse of children is increasing. While administrators can be found responsible for the acts of subordinates, courts appear unwilling to hold administrators liable unless there is clear evidence of administrative misconduct. In the 1990 case Medlin v. Bass, 398 S.E. 2d 460 (discussed in the May 1991 issue of NCEA Notes), school officials were found innocent of misconduct in their supervision of an educator guilty of abuse. The abuser's crime was outside the scope of employment and no compelling reasons existed for his superiors to investigate his background more thoroughly than they did.

In the 1990 case *D.T. et al. v. Ind. School District No. 16 of Pawnee County*, 894 F. 2d 1176, the court declined to hold school officials responsible for teacher abuse of students occurring during summer fund-raising. A particularly troubling aspect of this case was the fact that the teacher had a previous conviction for sodomy. The decision notwithstanding, it is possible that, in situations in which a school employee has a criminal record involving child abuse, other courts may find administrators guilty of negligence if they failed to take reasonable steps to check references.

[Note: In 2007 courts may well reach different decisions in similar cases. The sexual abuse crisis in the Catholic Church and heightened awareness of sexual abuse in general have resulted in a shift in both public perception of and court decisions on administrative responsibility for teacher sexual abuse of students. Today, judicial decisions depend on a determination of whether administrators had actual or constructive knowledge—whether they knew or should have known that abuse was occurring or was likely to occur.]

It is well established that schools can attract people with abusive tendencies seeking children on whom to prey. Thus, it is important that school officials do everything in their power to investigate the backgrounds of applicants before employment.

Some states now mandate that people who work with children be fingerprinted. Each applicant must also sign an authorization of a police check of his or her name for any criminal arrest or convictions. Conviction of a crime is not an automatic, permanent bar to employment. Many states bar people who have been convicted of a violent crime or sexual offense against children in the 10 years immediately preceding employment. Administrators may wish to include a statement such as the following on applications: "Conviction of a crime is not an automatic bar to employment. Please give all pertinent details. Decisions will be made as required by state law."

Any student or parent complaint alleging child abuse by a teacher must be thoroughly investigated. Failure to do so can put the school and its officials at grave legal risk. Principals, pastors, and school board should adopt policies governing reporting child abuse and neglect and investigating allegations of abuse by staff before the need for such policies surfaces. It is preferable to have a policy that is never needed than to have no policy and be forced to try to construct one when faced with a need.

Other Recent Developments

In the case of *Means v. Sidiropolis,* 401 S.E. 2d 447 (W.Va. 1990), the court upheld a student's challenge to the constitutionality of a statute requiring school attendance, unless excused for circumstances beyond a person's control, as a condition for the issuance or continuance of a driver's license to people between the ages of 16 and 18. The court ruled that the state's interest in young people's attending school is sufficient to uphold the statute. As more states adopt such rules governing students and drivers' licenses, high schools need to be aware of the laws of their states and be willing to cooperate with law enforcement officials in implementing those laws.

A divorced mother brought suit in *Cooper v. Farrell,* 566 N.Y.S. 2d 347 (A.D.2 Dept. 1991), to compel her ex-husband to pay 50% of the costs of educating their child in the private school she had selected. In holding for the father, the court found, "Absent special circumstances or voluntary agreement, a parent is not obligated to pay for the cost of a child's private schooling" (p. 347). Catholic school officials should take note of this case. It indicates that a court will not hold a parent responsible for half the tuition costs of a child if that parent has not agreed to the responsibility. 𝒩𝒩

November 1994

Sexual Harassment

Today's Catholic education administrator has probably heard much about sexual harassment. Newspapers carry stories of alleged sexual harassment and resultant law suits. No longer are adults the only culprits. School children claim they have been harassed by peers. The news stories can seem overwhelming and the potential for legal liability great. What can the Catholic administrator do?

Administrators should first understand what sexual harassment is. Every comment made about gender is not sexual harassment. For example, a male student who says, "Everyone knows boys are better at math than girls," or a teacher who declares, "I'd rather teach girls since they are not as rowdy as boys," is not guilty of sexual harassment. Title VII of the Civil Rights Act of 1964 mandated that the workplace be free of harassment based on sex. Title IX requires that educational programs receiving federal funding be free of sexual harassment. Both of these titled laws are antidiscrimination statutes.

Federal antidiscrimination law can bind Catholic institutions. Most schools now file statements of compliance with discrimination laws with appropriate local, state, and national authorities. Antidiscrimination legislation can have an impact on Catholic schools because the government has a compelling interest in the equal treatment of all citizens. Compliance with statutory law can be required if there is no less burdensome way to meet the requirements of the law.

The U.S. Equal Employment Opportunities Commission has issued guidelines that define sexual harassment, forbidden by Title VII, as "Unwelcomed sexual advances, requests for sexual favors, and other verbal or physical conduct of a sexual nature when:

- Submission to such conduct by an individual is made explicitly or implicitly a term of employment;

- Submission to, or rejection of, such conduct by an individual is used as the basis for an employment decision;

- And such conduct has the purpose or effect to interfere with an individual's work performance, or creates a hostile or intimidating environment."

The above definition concerns employment conditions, but "education" can be substituted for "employment" in the definitions and the basis for Title IX violations would be evident. Specifically, Title IX states: "No person in the United States shall, on the basis of sex, be excluded from participation in, be denied the benefits of, or be subjected to discrimination under any education program or activity receiving Federal financial assistance."

While the amount of financial assistance necessary for protection has not been established, most Catholic schools have taken some government funds or services at some time and would be well advised to comply with Title IX as far as possible. Courts, including the Supreme Court, are vigorously supporting individuals' rights to be free from sexual harassment.

In the case of *Franklin v. Gwinnett County Pub. Sch.,* 112 S. Ct. 1028 (1992), the U.S. Supreme Court ruled that monetary damages can be awarded students whose rights under Title IX have been violated. In this case a teacher had allegedly sexually harassed a student for several years. The harassment consisted of conversations, kissing, telephone calls, and forced sexual relations. The school system maintained that no relief could be given the student since Title IX remedies had been limited to back pay and employment relief. The court disagreed, held that students who suffer harassment are entitled to damages, and remanded the case to the lower court for a determination.

Thus, it would appear that if Title IX applies to the Catholic school (and no case to date has held that it does not), students are protected against sexual harassment in much the same manner that employees are protected.

Actions as Harassment

The following behaviors could constitute sexual harassment: sexual propositions, off-color jokes, inappropriate physical contact, innuendoes, sexual offers, looks, and gestures. In a number of recent public school cases, female students alleged that male students made sexual statements to them and that school officials, after being informed, declined to take action, stating, "Boys will be boys." The majority of these cases have been settled out of court and money has been paid to the alleged victims.

Although one can argue that the person who sexually harasses another should be liable and not the school and its administrators, case law suggests that administrators who ignore such behavior or do not take it seriously can be held liable to the offended parties. (See Jane Doe v. Special Sch. Dist. of St. Louis County, 901 F.2d 642 8th Cir. 1990.)

Suggested Policies

One of the most important actions an administrator can take on sexual harassment is to implement clear policies defining sexual harassment and detailing procedures for dealing with claims that sexual harassment has occurred. The following is one suggestion for a policy statement:

Sexual harassment is defined as (a) threatening to impose adverse employment, academic, or disciplinary or other sanctions on a person, unless favors are given; and/or (b) conduct, containing sexual matter or suggestions, that would be offensive to a reasonable person.

Sexual harassment includes, but is not limited to, the following behaviors:
1. Verbal conduct such as epithets, derogatory jokes or comments, slurs or unwanted sexual advances, imitations, or comments
2. Visual contact such as derogatory or sexually oriented posters, photography, cartoons, drawings, or gestures
3. Physical contact such as assault, unwanted touching, blocking of normal movements, or interfering with work, study, or play because of sex

4. Threats and demands to submit to sexual requests as a condition of continued employment or grades or other benefits or to avoid some other loss and offers of benefits in return for sexual favors

5. Retaliation for having reported or threatened to report sexual harassment

Procedures for reporting should include a statement such as "All allegations will be taken seriously and promptly investigated." Confidentiality should be stressed. Concern should be expressed for both the alleged victim and the alleged perpetrator. Any forms to be used should be included in the procedures.

Every employee should be required to sign a statement that he or she has been given a copy of the policies on sexual harassment and other sexual misconduct, has read the material, and agrees to be bound by it. Parent/student handbooks should contain at least a general statement that sexual harassment is not condoned in a Christian atmosphere, and both parents and students should sign a statement that they agree to be governed by the handbook.

Prevention

It is far easier to prevent claims of sexual harassment than it is to defend them. To that end, teachers and other employees should participate in in-service training that raises awareness of sexual harassment and other gender issues. Staff members must understand what sorts of behaviors can be construed as sexual harassment.

Teachers should discuss issues of fair treatment of others with their students and promptly correct any students who demean others. Defenses such as "I was only kidding" will not be accepted if the alleged victim states that the behavior was offensive and unwelcome and a court finds that a reasonable person could find the behavior offensive and unwelcome.

Finally, of course, sexual harassment and other forms of demeaning behavior have no place in a Catholic school or other educational program. Guarding the dignity of all members of the school community should be a priority for all administrators. 🕮

March 1997

Ministering to Sexual Abuse Victims

Sexual abuse is an ugly reality, and Catholic educators are often faced with the need to minister to victims of sexual abuse. Yet attorneys may rightly caution administrators to be aware of the legal ramifications of responding to victims. One would certainly expect a Catholic educator to comfort people who have experienced such trauma. At that same time, care must be taken to observe civil law and appropriate procedures.

Compliance with Reporting Laws

First and foremost, the Catholic educational administrator must ensure that all staff members and volunteers understand the requirements of state laws on reporting child abuse. While these laws vary from state to state, all require at minimum that an educator who suspects sexual or other child abuse has occurred or is occurring contact the appropriate agency.

Sometimes, well-meaning individuals may attempt to deal with sexual abuse victims without involving police or child protective services. Other people may decide to conduct fact-finding investigations on their own. The law clearly does not permit such actions, but requires that the person who suspects child abuse promptly make a report to the authorities. People who do not follow the law may unwittingly expose themselves, their schools, and their parishes to legal liability for failure to report or to report in a timely manner. In the process of investigating reported sexual abuse, social workers and law enforcement officials may come to the school or parish to interview the alleged victim. Administrators will expect that they or staff they designate may remain in the room with the individual while he or she is being questioned.

Several states now require that investigators be allowed to question alleged victims without anyone else present. This requirement can add to the suffering of a child or young person. However, the administrator has no legal choice but to comply with the mandate and have someone available for the young person after the interview is completed.

Providing Support to Victims

It is natural that victims and their parents or other family members will want to talk to the administrator or other staff member, who will want to be warm, supportive, and nurturing. Care must be taken, though, to avoid giving advice that would best be offered by a counseling professional.

Educators should be ready to offer names and phone numbers of counselors and doctors with expertise in dealing with sexual abuse situations. The temptation can be great for the administrator or staff member to become too deeply involved in the suffering of victims and their families and, thus, unable to provide the objective assistance needed. In extreme cases, a victim or family could sue for malpractice.

Avoiding Judgments

Staff members, of course, will avoid making any kind of judgments about how the alleged victim could have avoided being abused. At the same time, the educator must remember that an allegation is simply that—an allegation and not a proven fact—until there is an admission or adjudication of guilt. It must be remembered that the U.S. system of law holds that people are innocent until proven guilty.

Confidentiality

Educators must understand that only two legal privileges protect confidentiality of communications in this country—priest/penitent and attorney/client. Educators, including counselors, and doctors can be subpoenaed and compelled to testify about confidential conversations under penalty of perjury. When asked by a student or parent if a conversation is confidential, the wise educator will reply that confidences will be kept to the extent permitted by law.

Documentation

In this era of increasing litigation, educators would be well advised to keep good documentation of events and conversations on sexual abuse. All such documentation should be written in factual terms and should avoid statements of opinion. Copies of reports to agencies and police department should be kept and written memoranda should be made about phone calls and other conversations.

Past Abuse

Occasionally, a staff member or parent may reveal past abuse. Perhaps the abuse has already been reported or the statute of limitations for reporting abuse may have passed. If there is any doubt about whether the listener has an obligation to report, legal counsel should be sought.

Summary

The following recommendations may be helpful in working with victims of sexual abuse:

- Comply with all reporting requirements of civil law.
- Support the victim and family and be willing to listen, but avoid giving advice best offered by a professional in abuse counseling.
- Be able to refer people to appropriate professionals.
- Avoid making judgments.
- Keep good written documentation.
- Keep superiors, such as principals, pastors, and superintendents, informed as appropriate.

January 1998

What Should Administrators and Staff Do About Gangs?

In the last decade or so, the word "gang" has taken on a very different meaning than it had 20, 30, or 50 years ago. Many readers remember their parents or grandparents referring to the good times they had while they "ran around with a gang of friends." Today, "gang" has a sinister meaning connoting fear, violence, and domination. Suddenly, everyone is clamoring for schools to do something about the presence and activities of gangs, and many dioceses are writing and implementing policies on them.

The first step in developing policy is to define exactly what a gang is. A 1991 California case, *The People v. Ralph Gamez* (235 Cal. App. 3d 957, 286 Cal. Rptr. 8941), was significant in its definition of gangs. The court stated that the proper term to use when discussing problematic gangs is "criminal gang-like behavior." Unless state law has a different term or definition, diocesan staff and local administrators would be well advised to adopt such a designation.

An analysis of *Gamez* and similar cases leads to a clearer definition of criminal gang-like activity. The Archdiocese of Louisville offers this definition: "Criminal gang-like activity involving membership in a criminal gang is defined as an ongoing organization, association, or group of three or more persons, whether formal or informal, having as one of its primary activities the commission of one or more criminal acts."

Both educator and young person should understand that the intent to commit criminal acts is what distinguishes criminal gang-like activity from other types of group activities. Moreover, it is not membership that is the problem; it is the criminal activity.

Some may be tempted to think that enumerating all possible criminal offenses is useful in policy writing. In actuality, the issue of gangs is one better dealt with in general rather than specific terms. The term "criminal-like gang activity" includes all possible offenses. Attempts to enumerate all offenses can result in omission of some or an argument by an aggrieved student that what he or she did was not terroristic threatening or property damage, for example.

Gang Attire, Symbols, and Behaviors

The wearing of colors has long indicated membership in a gang. Any school is well within its rights to forbid such displays. However, it is not always easy to identify the display of gang colors exactly. In one state, for example, two university athletic teams have different school colors, so gang members wear university sweatshirts, jackets, etc., to denote their membership in a particular gang. Certainly, there is nothing wrong with wearing a college sweatshirt, but it is difficult, if not impossible, to determine who is supporting a team and who is displaying gang colors.

Many public schools now require students to wear uniforms. While the constitutionality of this mandate has yet to be tested, one result is lessening the wearing of gang colors. Catholic educators should enforce uniform regulations and dress codes and be attentive to violations of the codes.

Disciplinary Steps

If a teacher suspects or notices criminal gang-like activity at any time during educational and related activities, the principal, director of religious education, or other chief administrator should be notified immediately. The administrator should seek appropriate advice about investigating the suspicion or allegation and proceed to gather data. If the administrator determines or strongly suspects that the young person is involved in criminal gang-like activity, the student's parents or guardians should be notified and disciplinary action taken when appropriate. In the case of suspicion without any convincing evidence, a warning on the consequences for anyone who engages in criminal gang-like activity may be given. Written documentation of any meetings should be kept. If a criminal act has occurred, the administrator has a legal responsibility to notify local law enforcement officials and to assist the officials as far as possible in their investigation.

Keeping a Focus

An administrator should focus on what was actually done that was wrong, rather than on membership in a gang. If a school rule has been broken, the breaking of the rule should be discussed and appropriate sanctions given. If a crime has been committed, the focus should be on the crime and its consequences.

Sometimes a student needs help to avoid or terminate membership in a gang. Counselors should have some training or know where to contact trained individuals so that students can be helped to avoid gangs.

The days of simply announcing that some activity or association is wrong and expecting immediate student compliance are gone. It is every educator's responsibility to help create a community in which individuals have no desire to engage in criminal gang-like activity.

November 1998
School Violence: How to Prevent It; How to Deal With It

The all-too-familiar headline "Student Kills Other Students" causes most Catholic educational administrators to sigh in relief that such occurrences have not happened in Catholic schools. But only the most naïve would think that such violence could occur only in public schools.

Most Catholic educational administrators have at least considered the need for policies and procedures to deal with student violence. And a number of administrators have learned that it is far better (and easier) to write a policy that you never use than to try to write one to cover a present situation. Attempting to write polices after the fact leaves alleged offenders believing that they are being personally singled out for punishment. Thus, every school should have mechanisms in place to deal with the threat or actual occurrence of violence.

Policy Development

First, administrators, teachers, and board members must agree on a definition of violence. It is not necessary to use a legal definition, but the definition should be clear to the average reader. Violence could be defined as causing physical harm to another. Threatened violence could be defined as threatening to cause physical harm to another. While this definition does not deal with emotional or verbal abuse or other intangible injuries, it is nonetheless a clear definition of violence.

An often-asked question is "Should we have zero tolerance for violence and threats of violence?" One mother of a kindergarten student said that the principal had told the kindergarten class that anyone who said "I'm going to kill you" would be suspended and possibly expelled. The mother was aghast that any principal would threaten a 5-year-old with such drastic action.

But desperate times, as the saying goes, call for drastic measures. "How would you, as a mother, feel," the author asks, "if a classmate made such a threat to your child, and then came to class the next day with some sort of weapon and frightened or harmed your child? Wouldn't you want something done?" The mother admitted that, yes, she would expect the threatening child to be punished.

Types of Penalties for Elementary Students

So should there be a zero-tolerance policy for threatened or actual violence? The answer is "yes." But zero tolerance can have more than one meaning. A kindergarten child should not be expelled for making a threatening statement. It is possible to have a range of penalties. For example, the parents of very young children who make threats may be required to come to a conference in which the student and parents are clearly told that any further threats will result in suspension and required counseling before the student will be allowed to return to school. Older elementary school students might be suspended and referred to counseling on the first offense. A second offense (or in the case of a very young child, a third offense) might result in dismissal from school. Actual violence might result in stiffer penalties. A student could be expelled or suspended for a long time and readmitted only after counselor clearance.

Definitions and penalties should be clear. The school should require parents to sign statements saying they have read and agree to be governed by the school's handbook. Including a violence policy in the handbook will make it part of the contract to which the parents have agreed. Educators should explain the policy in detail by appropriate grade level.

Types of Penalties for High School Students

What about secondary school students? High school administrators seem divided in response to threatened student violence. Many schools simply expel on the first offense. Such an approach is clear, although to some it may seem harsh. Other administrators permit a student to be reinstated after serving a suspension and presenting a professional counselor's note that recommends readmittance and states that the student does not present a threat. Actual violence should result in dismissal from school. Secondary school administrators should ensure that students know exactly what behavior is forbidden, especially since the penalty is so severe.

Room for Discussion

No matter how cautious and fair educators are, there will be some cases with extreme mitigating factors. A school handbook that states "The principal (and/or pastor or president) is the final recourse in all disciplinary situations and may waive any and all regulations for just cause at his or her discretion" gives the administrator room for some discretion, if discretion is ever needed. Violence is an ugly topic, but educators must be prepared to deal with both its causes and effects.

September 1999

Preparing for the New School Year: Issues of Violence

❦

September is a time of excitement for students, teachers, and administrators. This September, however, because of the recent tragedies in Littleton, CO, and other cities, the excitement may be tempered by the realization that schools are no longer quite the same safe places we thought they were. While it is true that Catholic schools have so far been spared the agony of a Columbine High School tragedy, all Catholic educators should understand that a Catholic school is no safer than a public school and violence could just as easily happen. Catholic school personnel must be as prepared as public school personnel.

One of the best ways to be prepared is to practice reflective prevention. It is far better to enact policies and procedures that are never needed than to try to enact them once they are needed. Below are some guidelines for developing and implementing policies:

1. Call a meeting of the faculty and other appropriate individuals. Discuss what has happened or almost happened in the past in terms of institutional and personnel safety. Could any of these happenings have been avoided? Do particular concerns emerge?

2. Decide on elements to be included in safety and violence policies.

3. Develop a system for gathering input from all segments of the school or parish community. Ask for written suggestions on building safety, hazards, and preventing violence. Ask staff members and students if they feel safe.

4. Conduct a safety audit. Consider having someone who is not a school or parish employee serve as the chair of the safety audit committee. The committee should consider not only obvious dangers, but also risky practices such as chaining doors, blocking exits, etc.

5. Using all appropriate data, set goals and a reasonable timetable for their implementation.

6. Develop and enforce rules on threats of violence and actual violence. Carefully consider the words used and the meaning behind the words. If the school's policy is zero tolerance for violence, it should be defined. Zero tolerance does not have to mean students are expelled for every threat or action that may occur. Two first graders involved in a fistfight probably should not be expelled, but should be disciplined appropriately. An eighth grader who pulls a knife on another student probably should be expelled.

If any exceptions to existing rules can be made, the principal should be the individual empowered to make those exceptions. Principals and other policy-makers should thoroughly consider the ramifications of exceptions and should develop rules and policies written in careful, clear language. Language such as "Threats and/or acts of violence can or may result in expulsion" leaves room for exceptions. "The student will be expelled" leaves no room for exception. The school handbook should always include a statement reserving the right to deviate from policy. Such a statement might read, "The principal is the final recourse in disciplinary situations and reserves the right to waive any and all regulations for just cause in his or her discretion." One potential problem area is that most parents will want their child to be the exception. However, it is better to encounter that problem than it is to be boxed in to a certain action with no leeway for extenuating circumstances.

7. Know state weapons and controlled substance laws and enforce them.

8. Remember that staff and students can be required to have psychological evaluations if evidence indicates a potential risk to safety.

9. Learn the warning signs of violence.

10. Establish and enforce rules for teacher/student confidentiality. Instruct teachers to tell students, "I will keep your confidence as long as no one's life, health, or safety is involved. If life, health, or safety is involved, I must reveal what you tell me." Lawsuits have been filed in the Paducah, KY, and Littleton, CO, situations alleging negligence, particularly failure to warn, on the part of teachers who received dark and potentially risk-filled writings or confidences from students.

11. If the unthinkable happens, be prepared. Get appropriate help in developing a crisis communication plan and do not deviate from it without serious reason.

12. Identify a safe place, such as a nearby park or department store, where students can be taken if violence or other unanticipated happenings occur.

13. Try to anticipate situations and stay calm during them. The students depend on the teachers and the principal and the teachers depend on the principal.

14. If a situation seems impossible, ask for help—from God and others.

Although the topic of violence is a sobering one for the beginning of the school year, there is no better time to address the challenges of violence and violence prevention.

May 2001

The Unthinkable Has Happened: Student Shoots Student in Catholic School

⟨ oment ⟩

On March 5, 2001, a teen killed two and wounded 13 in a Santee, CA, public school. Just two days later a 14-year-old wounded a 13-year-old classmate at a Pennsylvania Catholic school. She was charged as a juvenile with both aggravated assault and attempted homicide. Many people have stated, "This is the first time there has been a shooting in a Catholic school." In fact, it is not. There have been at least two other incidents. One resulted in the accidental death of a student.

Catholic educators are concerned. However, as a national network of schools, Catholic schools are probably safer than public schools. In addition, most Catholic schools and parishes have excellent safety and crisis management policies in place and hold regular emergency drills. The few who do not should view the Pennsylvania shooting as a wake-up call and move quickly to institute safety policies and procedures.

The Pennsylvania school had done everything right. The school had a zero-tolerance policy on weapons. It had installed security cameras and secured entrances. Students are required to store backpacks in lockers at the beginning of the day and to keep books in clear plastic book bags. Short of armed guards and metal detectors, the school had done everything possible. It is this author's opinion that Catholic schools should avoid armed guards and metal detectors as far as possible because of the impact on the character and environment of the Catholic school. In any case, all must understand that the safety of children cannot be guaranteed. A person who wants to shoot someone will find a way to get the gun into the school.

Be Prepared

Violence has been discussed before in this column, but it seems appropriate to once again reiterate the basics of preparedness. It is always a good idea to plan for the worst-case scenario: "What is the worst thing I can imagine happening here?" Once that question is answered, examine policies and procedures to see if they can be applied in this worst-case scenario. It is also useful to ask students, teachers, and parents about potential hazards they see.

Safety audits are essential. The administrator or board should appoint a safety committee that includes at least one nonschool or -parish employee with some expertise. The committee should walk through the school and look for safety problems, such as windows routinely left open. Some schools persist in chaining unused doors, but problems can occur when those doors are needed for a speedy exit. [Note: Six years later, the author sincerely hopes that no one is chaining doors. Such a practice is against fire codes and may result in tragedy.]

Educators must be alert for troubled students. Identifying them can be difficult, particularly because so far it has not been unruly students who have committed crimes. It is not the students you would expect to pose violence problems who do. The stereotype that many have of a violent student is a young minority male student, but middle-class white males have perpetrated almost all of the shootings in American schools. The shootings have not happened in the inner city or depressed areas but in suburbs and small towns.

Zero-Tolerance Policies

Many schools are publishing zero-tolerance policies for threats and violence. This zero tolerance does not necessarily mean that every student who says anything threatening should be dismissed. If a first grader tells another student or a teacher, "I'm going to hit you," the consequence should not be expulsion. A parent conference is certainly in order. Administrators must be able to make allowances for differences in age and circumstance.

Mission Based on the Gospel

There is a strong sense of ownership in Catholic schools and parishes. The mission is based on the teachings of Jesus Christ, a powerful foundation. Catholic educators strive to produce students who care about each other. Catholic educators can talk about God, a freedom that the public schools do not have. There is no substitute for the life lessons a Catholic institution teaches.

The wise educator will help students be safe and aware without causing undue panic. The author's generation got used to bomb drills. This generation will become accustomed to safety and disaster drills. But Catholic educators must ensure that students never lose a sense of preparedness and proper caution.

January 2002
September 11 Prompts Questions and Concerns

In the midst of recent tragedies in this country, administrators must make decisions. This article will address three current issues: responding to threats of violence, handling mail, and deciding whether to continue school trips.

What Should I Do About Threats of Violence?

Administrators may say, "I know that we are supposed to take all threats of violence seriously and I have been doing that when students make threats. But what am I supposed to do with bomb threats, for example? We could get them every day or even several times in one day."

The rule is all threats of violence must be taken seriously. In the 1970s and '80s, law enforcement officials often left the decision to evacuate buildings during a bomb threat to the administrator. Some people reading this article will probably remember deciding that "enough was enough" after four or five bomb threats in one week and ignoring the fifth or sixth threat in the belief that pranksters were behind the calls. Administrators no longer have the luxury of making those kinds of decisions.

Previous columns have discussed safety audits and plans and crisis procedures. If administrators have not already done so, they must determine that safety and crisis plans are current and accessible to all who need them.

Buildings must be evacuated immediately upon receipt of a bomb or similar threat. No one can be permitted to remain in the building at this time or during any drills. No one should reenter a building after vacating it. In schools and religious education and youth ministry programs that use multiple buildings, all buildings must be evacuated so that an accurate attendance count can be taken. All people should proceed immediately to a predetermined safe place. Administrators and previously identified key staff members should be in contact by cell phone or radio or should have a previously designated place to check in with each other.

Secretaries and others with phone-answering duties should be instructed to try to keep the caller on the line so the call can be traced and pertinent information gathered while someone else calls 911 on another line. While many callers will simply hang up, an effort should be made to get them to talk. Asking questions such as "Where is the bomb? What does it look like? When will it go off? Where are you calling from? Who are you? Why do you want to bomb the school or parish?" may elicit useful information. Now is a good time to have caller ID put on phones and to ensure that more than one phone line is available at all times.

What Should I Do About the Mail?

While government officials assure the public that the risk from mail is minimal, administrators should take prudent measures to protect mail handlers. The following are some minimum suggestions:

1. The mail sorter should wear gloves and work in a closed area. Some recommend the use of face masks, but health officials warn that such use probably provides little additional protection.

2. Suspicious mail should be placed in a closeable plastic bag and given to law enforcement officials.

3. Everyone should be told to consider throwing away mail with no return address or that appears questionable.

4. People handling mail should wash their hands when finished.

What Should I Do About School Trips? To Foreign Countries? On Airplanes?

Administrators express consternation in trying to make these decisions. On the one hand, people do not want to stop living and let the terrorists win. On the other hand, the safety of young people is the most important concern.

Some attorneys suggest that administrators involve parents in the decision-making. Others suggest having parents sign releases agreeing not to sue if accident or injury results from the trip. This attorney believes that the better action is to cancel or postpone trips involving air travel. While it is probably true that air travel is safer now than it was before September 11, it is also true that death is a likely outcome of a terrorist attack involving an airplane on which one is traveling. It is one thing for adults to decide to fly on airplanes and take their children. It is quite another for a school or parish to provide an opportunity and take other people's children on airplanes.

About 15 years ago, terrorists were targeting American tourists in European airports. Many administrators made the often-unpopular decision to cancel trips to foreign countries. Did these decisions avert tragedy? We shall never know, but it seems better to err on the side of caution.

[Note: With the clarity of hindsight, readers may find some suggestions already implemented and others judged unworkable. Nonetheless, the two *NCEA Notes articles* on the events of September 11, 2001, serve to remind us that it was only six years ago that they occurred. Now is a good time to review safety procedures, plans, and audits.]

September 2002

Respecting Boundaries and Avoiding Litigation:
Reflections on Sexual Abuse of Young People

The explosion of litigation alleging clerical abuse of minors has left most of the Catholic community feeling outraged, numb, and, perhaps to some extent, powerless. Administrators cannot guarantee student safety, as much as they may desire to do so. Educators fear that they may be unjustly accused. The beginning of the school, religious education, or youth ministry year, when state child abuse reporting laws are generally reviewed, is a good time to reflect on the reality the Catholic Church faces and to explore feelings and fears while planning for the protection of young people.

Sexual Abuse Policies and Procedures

Certainly no reality in recent times has caused greater pain in the Catholic Church than sexual abuse. No one can give a person back his or her innocence. Administrators must act swiftly, decisively, and appropriately with due care for both the victim and the alleged perpetrator. Every diocese has sexual abuse policies. It is imperative that proper procedures be followed and that administrators not decide to conduct investigations independent of the police and social service agencies. Obviously, some data has to be gathered. But administrators must realize that they cannot handle such accusations alone.

Avoiding the Appearance of Impropriety

Administrators must encourage all who work in the Catholic Church to avoid even the appearance of impropriety. It is easy to be naïve and fail to realize how one's actions may be interpreted. A male teacher who worked with the author when she was a high school principal once said, "I would never stay alone in a room with a girl unless the door was open or you could see in through a window." That is very good advice for all adults with young people. A reputation is a terrible thing to lose and is almost impossible to rebuild as people often remember the accusation, but not the exoneration.

Some public school officials, trying to avoid liability, have forbidden any physical contact between students and teachers. That may well be overreaction. A better approach is to ask oneself, "If I saw someone else touching a student in this way, would I think it is all right?" When in doubt, of course, don't touch.

Establishing Boundaries

A related issue raising legal concerns today is establishing boundaries. Relationships must have boundaries. Sometimes, well-meaning people get too close to others. People tell all and answer any question. Far from being open, they are destroying the boundary that the person being ministered to needs. Catechists and teachers, for example, do not have to answer questions such as, "Did you sleep with your husband before you were married?" An educator or minister should not share very personal information, as he or she is not a young person's peer, but an adult with ministerial responsibilities in a relationship that is inherently unequal. Boundaries are healthy, and personal boundaries help keep adults within the legal boundaries that surround ministry.

Unfortunately, sexual misconduct can be alleged in apparently innocent situations. Young people can misinterpret touching, and an individual could find himself or herself facing child abuse charges. Extreme caution is in order whenever an adult touches a minor.

A minor who believes that an adult has not responded to efforts to achieve a closer relationship poses another kind of problem. Such a student may accuse a teacher of inappropriate conduct as a retaliatory measure. Thus, it is imperative that educators and other ministers protect themselves and those they serve by practicing appropriate behavior. A good question to ask might be "If this were my child, would I have any objection to someone relating to him or her in this manner?"

Fear of teachers facing child abuse allegations has caused some public school districts in this country to adopt rules that prohibit any adult touching of students. Such rules preclude putting one's arm around students, patting a student on the back, and giving a student a hug. No Catholic minister would want to take such a position, but commonsense precautions must be taken for the protection of all.

Professional Safeguards

All Catholic educators must bear in mind that they are professionals rendering a service. Volunteers, while perhaps not professionally trained, are entrusted with certain ministerial functions. Just as a counselor or psychiatrist is professionally bound to avoid emotional involvement with a client, an educator should strive to avoid becoming so emotionally involved with a young person that fairness, objectivity, and ministerial effectiveness are compromised.

Serving as a Catholic educator/minister in these times is a privilege and a gift. It is indeed sad when an individual is forced to relinquish that gift because of inappropriate choices. Reflection and prudent behavior will help to ensure that young people are kept safe, ministry is protected, and boundaries are maintained. 🙟

MAY 2003

HARASSMENT AND BULLYING: LEGAL DUTIES OF EDUCATORS

In the midst of today's litigation involving the church, Catholic educators find their legal antennae more attuned than ever to potential problem areas. Two such areas of concern are bullying and harassment. While people are generally aware of issues surrounding sexual harassment, issues related to non-sexual harassment, including bullying, are less clear.

One may ask, "What exactly is harassment? We talk about it a great deal, but I've yet to see a good, general definition." The ultimate legal authority for definitions is *Black's Law Dictionary*, which defines harassment as follows:

> Used in variety of legal contexts to describe words, gestures and actions which tend to annoy, alarm and abuse (verbally) another person. A person commits a petty misdemeanor if, with purpose to harass another, he: (1) makes a telephone call without purpose of legitimate communication; or (2) insults, taunts or challenges another in a manner likely to promote a disorderly response; or (3) makes repeated communications anonymously or at extremely inconvenient hours, or in offensively coarse language; or (4) subjects another to an offensive touching; or (5) engages in any other course of alarming conduct serving no legitimate purpose of the actor.

Harassment occurs, then, when one person makes repeated verbal or physical contacts with another person who does not want these contacts. Sexual harassment is a particular type of harassment that involves sexual comments, innuendo, invitations, or requests for sexual favors. Sexual harassment is generally fairly clear, while other types of harassment can be more blurred and harder to identify.

Bullying is a type of harassment that involves some sort of force, whether overt or subtle. Today, for example, exclusion is widely considered to be a form of bullying, even though there may be no apparent contact. By ignoring or excluding an individual from participation, the bully shows his or her power.

The real problem in harassment cases is a failure to respect the dignity of another. Since there are many ways to exhibit disrespect, administrators would be well advised to consider having a rule that simply forbids all demeaning behavior. There is a place, of course, for more detailed listings of possible offenses, but more general catchall clauses ensure that most inappropriate behaviors can be caught and individuals held accountable.

Under the doctrine of *respondeat superior*, let the superior answer, teachers and other supervisors can be held liable for one young person's harassment or bullying of another. If a teacher or other educator knows or has been informed that one student is harassing another and fails to act, the teacher can be held liable for the harassment. Although the majority of such cases involve sexual harassment, the potential for liability for other types of harassment exists as well. Thus, students exhibiting demeaning behaviors must be immediately corrected.

Educators really have five main duties under the broad, general category of demeaning behavior:

1. The duty to minimize risks. Teachers should periodically examine practices and routines to see if there are times and places when bullying and harassment are more likely to occur and should make plans to minimize the likelihood of occurrence.

2. The duty to educate students. Teachers need to show in word and deed that demeaning behavior is not appropriate.

3. The duty to investigate complaints and concerns. If a student expresses discomfort, educator should carefully investigate the situation while remembering that things may not always be what they seem.

4. The duty to remedy violations. Teachers should swiftly and firmly correct students who engage in demeaning behaviors.

5. The duty to monitor students and situations. Teachers should remember the old "eyes in the back of the head" image and pay careful attention to students at all times.

Prevention and Intervention Techniques

Educators often ask for practical suggestions for meeting legal responsibilities. Knowledge of law and legal phrases is of little use if one cannot put the ethical principles that drive the law into practice. The following are 10 suggestions:

1. Create a climate where all students are valued.

2. Observe students at times when you're not in charge.

3. Watch for the warning signs of isolation, depression, and suppressed anger.

4. Err on the side of caution when expressing concerns about student behaviors and attitudes.

5. Do not keep secrets.

6. Tell students that you will keep confidences only if health, life, safety, and criminal activity are not at issue.

7. When assigning students to groups, use random methods rather than self-selection.

8. Do not allow name-calling or demeaning comments.

9. Listen to what students don't say as well as to what they do say.

10. Remember that supervision is a mental as well as a physical act.

March 2005

Hazing: What Is It?
What Should Be Done About It?

⟨⟨⟨⟨⟩⟩⟩⟩

Harassment and bullying are two topics that have claimed a great deal of media and educator attention. Obviously, Catholic educators are opposed to demeaning behavior in any form.

Hazing, a particular form of harassment, has been around schools for a long time. Most readers have probably experienced hazing in some form in their school careers, although it may have masqueraded under the title of initiation and seemed fairly harmless. It may have ranged from such actions as requiring students to wear signs stating "I am a lowly freshman" or "I am the slave of the varsity basketball team" to forbidding students to use a certain set of stairs or making them take a longer way to get to their classrooms. Some hazing, though, has escalated out of control as students have suffered severe injuries and even death.

The reader may wish to consider definitions of harassment and bullying. *Black's Law Dictionary* defines harassment as follows: "Used in variety of legal contexts to describe words, gestures and actions which tend to annoy, alarm and abuse another person."

Harassment occurs, then, when one person makes repeated verbal or physical contacts with another person who does not want these contacts. Sexual harassment is a particular type of harassment that involves sexual comments, innuendo, invitations, or requests for sexual favors. Sexual harassment is generally fairly clear; other types of harassment can be more blurred and harder to identify.

Bullying is a type of harassment that involves some sort of force, whether overt or subtle. Today, for example, exclusion is widely considered a form of bullying, even though there may be no apparent contact. By ignoring or excluding an individual from participation, the bully shows his or her power.

Of course, more traditional forms of bullying can still be found in schools. The student who "forces" another student to steal items from a grocery store or face some dire consequence is bullying the individual. When that kind of behavior is required as "payment" for belonging to a team or club, hazing is occurring.

StopHazing, an excellent organization with a Web site at StopHazing.org, defines hazing as follows:

"Hazing" refers to any activity expected of someone joining a group (or to maintain full status in a group) that humiliates, degrades or risks emotional and/or physical harm, regardless of the person's willingness to participate. . . . Hazing is a complex social problem that is shaped by power dynamics operating in a group and/or organization and within a particular cultural context.

Today, many forms of hazing are reported, from relatively simple ones to such activities as burning, branding, paddling, depriving people of sleep and food, forcing individuals to drink alcohol, often in large amounts, and compelling people to engage in unreasonable amounts of physical exercise, to name a few. Some popular high school hazing activities involve such actions as slapping an initiate on the arm, leg, thigh, or stomach until the body part turns red, forcing a student to urinate in public, forcing a student to put his or her head in a toilet (a practice called "swirling"), and requiring a student to eat until he or she vomits.

Administrators, athletic directors, coaches, teachers, and moderators need to pay close attention to student activities, "talk," and the proverbial rumor mill. If students are talking about hazing activities, the administration needs to be informed and an investigation begun.

Teachers, other supervisors, and even team captains can be held liable for one young person's harassment, bullying, or hazing of another if they knew or should have known about it. Including hazing in the list of prohibited behaviors may raise awareness.

Educators have five main duties in preventing harassment in general and hazing in particular:

1. Duty to minimize risks. Teachers should periodically examine practices and routines to see if there are times and places when harassment and hazing are more likely to occur and should take appropriate actions to minimize the likelihood of occurrence.

2. Duty to educate students. Educators need to show in word and deed that all demeaning behavior, including hazing, is not appropriate and is never "funny."

3. Duty to investigate. If a student expresses discomfort or reports being hazed or witnessing someone else being hazed, the educator should carefully investigate.

4. Duty to remedy violations. Students who engage in hazing should be disciplined.

5. Duty to monitor students and situations. Teachers are responsible for knowing what is going on. In some litigation involving hazing, allegations have been made that educators knew that students were being hazed and did nothing.

Catholic schools are faith and educational communities where students should feel safe and protected. Civil law, as well as the Gospel, requires that the physical and emotional well-being of students be protected.

September 2005

The Bishops' Revised Charter for the Protection of Children and Young People: Legal Implications for Administrators, Educators, and Volunteers

〜〜〜

In June 2005, the United States Conference of Catholic Bishops approved a revised version of the *Charter for the Protection of Children and Young People,* originally published in 2002. The Ad Hoc Committee for Sexual Abuse of the United States Conference of Catholic Bishops developed and recommended the revision. While retaining much of the spirit and content of the original document, the revision expands the scope of diocesan, parish, and other Catholic institutions' responsibilities for those who work and volunteer in ministry with minors.

Some people mistakenly believe that the charter is concerned only with the actions of members of the clergy, but as Article 6 of the charter states: "There are to be clear and well-publicized . . . standards of ministerial behavior and appropriate boundaries for clergy and for any other paid personnel and volunteers of the church in positions of trust who have regular contact with children and young people." Thus, all people who minister to minors and all who administer institutions and programs within the structure of the Catholic Church are bound by the charter's provisions. [The entire text of the charter is at http//www.usccb.org.ocyp/charter.shtml.]

The original charter established the above-mentioned Ad Hoc Committee on Sexual Abuse, which the revised charter has renamed the Committee for the Protection of Children and Young People, and makes a standing committee of the United States Conference of Catholic Bishops. This committee will be assisted by the National Review Board, which continues to aid in assessing diocesan compliance with the charter, authorize studies on the sexual abuse of minors, and issue its own reports.

The charter mandates certain policies and procedures, while also requiring compliance with civil law. Article 10 holds, "The whole Church, especially the laity, at both the diocesan and national levels, needs to be engaged in maintaining safe environments in the Church for children and young people."

The beginning of the academic year is a good time to consider key points of the charter, review the institution's policies and procedures on abuse and boundary issues, and plan ongoing education and formation of all employees and volunteers as administrators seek to ensure respect for the dignity and safety of young people. If such a review has not been done before classes and activities begin, administrators should ensure that one is planned for the near future. In the event of any allegation or claim, being able to show that the institution has kept its employees and volunteers informed and educated will provide evidence of administrative good faith.

The following are guidelines for administrators who seek to provide safe and legally sound environments for all in their institutions and programs:

1. Trust your instincts. If a situation makes you uncomfortable, investigate and ask questions. Avoid witch hunts, but don't neglect your responsibility as an administrator charged with the protection of young people. It is better to err on the side of caution than to hope that a situation won't amount to anything.

2. Be visible. You will have a much better idea of what is going on in your school or program if you practice "management by walking around." People who are used to seeing the leader everyday will not be on guard and the administrator should have a good sense of how employees and volunteers treat young people.

3. Make and follow policies and procedures for supervising teachers and staff. Much is learned in formal as well as informal supervisory sessions.

4. Take seriously any allegation or rumor that reaches you. Even if the story seems outrageous, you have a responsibility to follow policy and to obey civil law requiring reporting of alleged or suspected abuse.

5. Remember that even if you have to remove an accused person from the school or program, he or she is considered innocent until proven guilty.

6. While reasonable regulations are necessary for orderly operation, be sure that parents know they are welcome in the classroom or other educational setting. An atmosphere of secrecy or unwelcome helps no one.

7. Cooperate with diocesan officials in safe environment training. Ensure that all volunteers and employees participate in it.

8. Have an open-door policy for staff, volunteers, young people, and parents. This does not mean that anyone can see you at any time without an appointment, but it does mean that you will see anyone who asks within a reasonable time frame.

9. Keep specific, behaviorally oriented, and verifiable documentation of situations and behaviors that are or could be considered problematic.

10. Remember to ask for God's help and guidance each day. Pray. Prayer is not optional.

Confidentiality,
PRIVACY, and DEFAMATION

January 1992

Privacy, Confidentiality, and Defamation: Balancing Rights While Avoiding Harm

Privacy and confidentiality are two serious legal issues facing Catholic educators today. Both students and teachers expect that information about them will be revealed only to those with a right to know. School officials who fail to take reasonable measures to safeguard such information could face civil lawsuits for defamation of character.

Defamation of Character

Defamation is an unprivileged communication that harms the reputation of another. Defamation, which may involve invasion of privacy, can be either spoken (slander) or written (libel). While truth is an absolute defense in most defamation cases, it may not render an educator immune from liability. Because of the serious responsibilities educators have, they are generally held to a higher standard of behavior than are noneducators.

Educators should be concerned about protecting the reputations of all in their schools. Principals should exercise great care in keeping student and teacher records, as well as in speaking about student and teacher behavior. It is only just that an educator refrain from gossip or unnecessary derogatory remarks about teachers and students. The best advice for both teachers and administrators is to be as factual as possible in official documents and to refrain from editorial comments. Written information should meet the following three criteria: (a) It should be specific, (b) it should be behaviorally oriented, and (d) it should be verifiable.

It is more professional, and legally more appropriate, to write "Bobby has been absent four times this month, tardy for class eight times, and sent to the principal's office for fighting five times" than to write "Bobby is absent too much, late most of the time, and always in trouble." It is better to write "Susan is reading on a first-grade level" than "Susan can't read."

Similarly, comments in teacher records should be strictly factual. In documenting a disciplinary situation concerning a teacher, a principal would be wiser to write, for example, "On Tuesday, September 15, Ms. Jones entered her classroom 15 minutes after the bell and offered no reason for lateness" than to write "Ms. Jones was late." The latter sentence is open to such questions as "How late was Ms. Jones—one minute or 20 minutes? Was there any reason for the lateness?" Anything that is to become part of a teacher's file should be discussed with that individual, who should also be given a copy.

If there is no reason to have an item in a person's file, it should be stored elsewhere. Official student files should contain only the following: the academic transcript, records of education or related testing, an emergency sheet, and a health form. Everything else can and should be stored elsewhere. Disciplinary records, in particular, should not be stored in official files. Students are still in a formative stage, and school officials should exercise extreme caution in storing information that could be harmful to a student. Disciplinary records should not be a part of the information sent to another school when a student transfers or graduates. If the new school requires disciplinary information, the transferring school should consider preparing a document containing the information and having the parents sign a statement that they have seen the document and agree to its being sent.

Teacher files should contain (a) transcripts, (b) employment applications, (c) letters of recommendation, (d) records of administrative observations and follow-up conferences, (e) evaluation forms, including self-evaluation forms, and (f) any disciplinary records, including written reprimands. Disciplinary records are part of the teacher's file but not of the student's file. Teachers and other employees should be permitted to inspect their personnel records on request.

In today's litigious society, most administrators are familiar with the problems of writing legally noncontroversial recommendations for employees and students without sacrificing the truth. Further, most administrators have read recommendations that seem to say very little. Administrators must understand that no one has an absolute right to a recommendation.

[Note: Today many educational institutions follow what seems to have become standard business practice: Verify the employees' dates of employment and say nothing else. In the case of problematic students, dates of attendance and grades can be verified. Administrators need to check the laws of their particular states. Some states require that specific offenses, such as selling or trafficking in drugs, violence, or bringing weapons to school, be documented on the transcript or in other written communication to the school to which a student transfers.]

Teachers and students can be given letters verifying employment or enrollment and factual statements can be made about employment duties or educational credits earned. The guideline is to be as just as possible. School officials should strive to be fair and respectful of the dignity of others in all communications, whether official or not, and to say only what can be shown to have some valid relationship to the professional situation. In so doing, school officials protect themselves against possible lawsuits alleging defamation or invasion of privacy.

Confidentiality of Records

An issue related to invasion of privacy is confidentiality of records. If a principal follows the procedures outlined above, the risk of having problematic materials in student and teacher files is minimized. Permitting teachers and other employees access to their personnel files ensures the individual's knowledge of the contents of those files. Hence, a person would find it difficult to maintain either defamation or invasion of privacy actions if that individual authorized the access of another to the files, such as in a release of file contents to a prospective employer.

The contents of student files should be released only to authorized persons. Even faculty and staff should be given access to student files only for appropriate, school-related reasons. Parental signatures should be required before records are sent to anyone.

Many educators in Catholic schools can recall when neither they nor students' parents were permitted access to their student records. In 1975 Congress passed the Buckley Amendment granting students and parents the right to inspect school records. It must be frankly stated that some legal experts believe that the Buckley Amendment does not apply to private schools. The amendment contains a clause providing that the legislation does not apply to private schools solely because of the presence of government funds (e.g., federal commodities in cafeterias, bloc grant money, etc.). However, this belief has never been tested in court.

There are cases in which private sector officials have been required to comply with federal legislation, such as antidiscrimination statutes. The requirement was based on public policy considerations or commonly accepted standards of behavior. The author believes that it is better to comply voluntarily with legislation such as the Buckley Amendment than to risk becoming a test case for the courts. Legalities aside, it seems only just that people affected by records have the right to see them.

Confidentiality of Student Communication

Educators often find themselves the recipient of student confidences. Students have a right to expect that their communications with school officials will remain private. At the same time, parents reasonably expect that they will be informed of situations that affect the welfare of their children. Sometimes, the student's right to privacy conflicts with the parent's right to know.

States have different laws on protecting student confidences given to educators. In some states guidance counselors are afforded some immunity. For example, they may be able to refuse to testify about conversations they had with students. Such laws vary greatly from state to state. In any event, the immunity afforded counselors is not extended to teachers. [Note: In 2007 courts recognize no counselor immunity. Counselors who refuse to testify about conversations with students will, in all likelihood, be held in contempt of court.]

Educators, including counselors, have virtually no immunity from liability if they withhold information about a student who has indicated that harm to self or others may occur. In such a situation, there is a clear duty to report. Case law indicates that an educator can be held responsible for injury occurring after the student has told the educator that such injury might occur

People who advise students are particularly vulnerable to the type of liability described in the preceding paragraph. Often teachers function as counselors. Some schools, particularly elementary schools, have no counselors. In others, one counselor may be responsible for hundreds of students and a distressed student may seek advice from a trusted teacher.

Certain subject areas may pose more opportunities for privileged communication. Individuals, such as English or religion teachers, who require students to keep journals may find themselves particularly vulnerable. Educators should inform students that their confidences will be respected unless the educator believes that health or safety is at issue.

November 1993

Defamation of Character and the Catholic Educator

⟨⟨⟨⟨⟨

"Can I be sued for what I say about a student?" is a question often asked by educators who want to do the right thing for students, but protect themselves as well. The simple answer is "Yes, you can be sued." Educators are wise to be concerned about what they say. Some basic information may prove helpful in establishing a philosophical and practical framework for making statements about students.

What Is Defamation?

Defamation is a type of tort, a civil action. People who bring defamation suits will have their claims heard in civil, not criminal, courts. People who allege defamation seek money damages, not the criminal convictions of the person(s) who defamed them. Defamation of character involves twin torts: slander, which is spoken, and libel, which is written. Defamation is an unprivileged communication (i.e., a statement made by one person about another person to a third party who is not privileged to receive it).

In the educational setting, a court might inquire about the necessity for the communication. If the communication is found unnecessary, even if true, the court could find the individual charged liable for defamation. *Black's Law Dictionary* (1979) says, "A communication is defamatory if it tends so to harm the reputation of another as to lower him in the estimation of the community or to deter third persons from associating or dealing with him" (p. 375).

Some people mistakenly believe that the truth is an absolute defense to defamation. People who work with children and adolescents are generally held to a higher standard than the average adult in a defamation suit. When a teacher repeats confidential information about a student, the defense of truth may not be sustained because a teacher is a person who holds a position of trust and thus can be held to a higher standard. Staff members must ensure, then, that they state opinions and facts about students only to those with a right to know.

Any documentation about young people must be both accurate and protective of the rights of individuals whose behavior is being described. Records must be objective and factual. Communications should be measured against the standard "What is written should be specific, behaviorally oriented, and verifiable." It is better to say "Mary Louise often gazes into space or draws pictures on a notepad during class" than to say "Mary Louise never pays attention" or "Mary Louise never keeps her mind on the class." The less personal the opinion stated about a student, the better. Any opinions stated should be those of a professional making professional judgments in a professional setting.

Slander

Slander, or oral defamation, can arise in seemingly innocent situations. For example, faculty rooms have long been considered safe places in which faculty members can express themselves freely. As long as the only people present in the faculty room are professional staff members, an educator may speak without fear of being accused of slander. It is generally held that other faculty and staff members are people with a right to know the thoughts and perceptions of staff members.

But if other people such as visitors, parents, volunteers, and maintenance and cafeteria workers are present, the faculty room is no longer a place for privileged communication. In such a situation, a teacher making negative comments about students risks being accused of slander.

Social gatherings can present other problems. A parent may approach a teacher at a neighborhood party and state, "My son has been spending a great deal of time with Bobby X. I am not so sure that Bobby is a good influence. What is your opinion?" If the teacher responds, "I don't think Bobby is a good influence either," the teacher could be guilty of defamation of character, or unprivileged derogatory communication. Educators should avoid even the appearance of defamatory speech and should avoid giving opinions about students to those who have no real right to know.

Staff members should be extremely prudent in making any comments, whether oral or written, about young people. Comments to parents should be about the parents' own children, not about other people's children. Communications should be made only to those people with a legitimate right to know.

All should remember that a person has a right to reputation. Educators should treat the reputations of those entrusted to their supervision with at least as much care as they would want their own reputations to be treated.

Libel

Libel, or written defamation, is generally easier to prove than slander. Teachers must be sure that the comments made in student records, or in other documents available to people other than the student's parents, are based on verifiable occurrences rather than on conjecture.

Questions often arise about situations in which teachers are asked to write recommendations for students. Obviously, if a teacher wishes to praise a student, the likelihood that a student could object is minimal. The problem occurs when a staff member cannot, in conscience, write a favorable recommendation for a student.

The educator then has two possible courses of action. The educator can refuse to write a recommendation; no student has an absolute right to a recommendation. Some educators may feel uncomfortable refusing and, in some cases, a recommendation form will direct that a specific subject teacher or the homeroom teacher answer questions. Teachers may question the fairness of telling students that they cannot fill out forms when the forms are required for admission or other considerations.

In such circumstances, the teacher may opt for a general letter of reference, which does little more than verify that the teacher did indeed teach the student. A teacher has every right to decline to fill out a form and to attach a letter to the form instead. This letter can verify the student's grade and discuss topics such as concepts studied, activities pursued, and textbooks used.

This kind of letter says nothing derogatory about John, although it certainly says nothing very positive about him. What is written is specific, behaviorally oriented, and verifiable. The individual receiving the letter should be able to tell that it does not constitute an overwhelming endorsement of the student. Thus, the teacher does not compromise professional ethics and the student has the minimal documentation needed.

Teacher comments on student report cards and permanent record cards pose another concern. If student report cards are simply reporting mechanisms to parents and the permanent record card is the actual retained record, teachers have considerable leeway in making comments on report cards. Parents have a right to know, and while a parent might dispute a teacher's comment, it would be difficult to demonstrate any actual harm to student reputation. People whose opinion of a student may be affected by comments contained therein may see permanent record cards as distinct from report cards.

The days when individuals could not see their records ended with the Buckley Amendment. The amendment's applicability to private schools has never been tested in court, but it seems unwise to risk becoming a test case when compliance with the amendment is ethically sound. Who would want to be refused the right to see what a superior writes about him or her?

In the end, as St. Thomas More once observed, "It is a question of love, not law." If Catholic educators truly love their students, they will not ask, "How can I write so that I won't get sued?" but will ask, "How can I write so that I protect both the reputation of those in my care and my reputation as a Catholic professional educator who abides by the highest ethical standards?"

Recent Developments: Academic Consequences for Disciplinary Infractions

Principals often question whether an academic penalty, as well as a disciplinary one, can be assessed for misbehavior. A recent case indicates that at least in the public sector the answer is "no." In the Indiana case of *Smith v. School City of Hobart,* 811 F.Supp. 391 (N.D.Ind. 1993), the U.S. District Court ruled that academic sanctions for disciplinary infractions are violations of constitutional substantive due process. Pamela Smith, a senior at Hobart Senior High School in Hobart, IN, left school with two other students to attend an off-campus class. Before reaching the class site, the girls went to one girl's home and drank beer. After Smith admitted to drinking the beer in violation of the provisions of the student handbook, which proscribe knowingly possessing or consuming alcoholic beverages or intoxicants, she was suspended for five days. The handbook clearly stated that a student's grade would be reduced 4% for each day missed during suspension. As a result, Smith's grade was reduced 20%.

The judge noted early in the opinion that he was not attempting to violate the doctrine of judicial restraint, which requires that judges refrain from substituting their opinions for those of the professional decision-makers. The issue presented by this case is whether the school's rule is constitutional.

The court held: "A student's grade or credit should reflect the student's academic performance or achievement, including participation in class. Reducing grades unrelated to academic conduct results in a skewed and inaccurate reflection of a student's academic performance."

As the writer has often noted, the Constitution does not apply to the actions of private school officials, since they are not public, government agents. However, private schools are held to a fairness standard, and actions found to be arbitrary and capricious can be struck down. School officials should consider whether an academic penalty for disciplinary reasons is appropriate. If officials wish to tie grades to school attendance, the appropriate rule should be for all unexcused absences, not just ones caused by suspension.

Such a rule might read "Class attendance is necessary for full academic achievement. Students who are absent from school without a legitimate excuse will have their grades reduced 1%" or "The teacher will establish a policy for attendance and academic grades and will announce that policy to students."

While one could certainly debate the worth of an attendance rule that can be difficult to enforce and can encourage deception, an administrator who wishes to require attendance as part of the academic grade should base the rules on unexcused absences rather than on disciplinary actions.

January 1996

Keeping Student Confidences:
What Can You Tell? What Must You Tell?

⟲⟳

Students sharing confidential information present one of the more perplexing situations facing Catholic educators today. Young people in the 1990s may well face more pressures and problems than the youth of any other decade. Broken homes, alcoholism, drug addiction, sexual and physical abuse, depression, and violence seem to be more prevalent, or at least more openly acknowledged, than they were when the majority of today's practicing Catholic educators were students.

The responsibility for advising students and receiving their confidences in day-to-day situations and crises can be overwhelming. Busy teachers may ask, "What am I supposed to do? I'm not a professional counselor, psychiatrist, or social worker. But I'm the one the student trusts, the one the student has consulted. Are there legal issues involved in receiving student confidences? Are there matters I must make known to others, even when the student has asked for and received a promise of confidentiality?"

These are appropriate questions for any educator to ask. None of us can afford to think that we can help all students all the time. We cannot. If a student were to come to a teacher and tell the teacher he or she is experiencing shortness of breath and chest pain, the teacher would quickly summon medical assistance and the student's parents. Yet psychological problems are no less serious than physical ones, and the layperson who attempts to deal with such problems unaided may be courting tragedy for both self and student. Such tragedies are more likely to be averted if we fully understand the concepts of confidentiality and legal immunity.

Confidentiality

Confidentiality is generally held to mean that an individual or individuals will keep private and not reveal information given to them. For example, someone receiving the sacrament of reconciliation rightfully expects that the subject matter of confession will be held sacred and not divulged to anyone by the confessor. Indeed, there are accounts of priests who died rather than break the seal of confession.

Friends confide in each other. One friend may say to another, "This is confidential. You cannot repeat it." The person speaking in confidence has a right to expect that the confidant to whom the information has been given will keep the matter between them. But there are recognized limits to what friends will keep confidential. For example, if a friend confides that she has been stockpiling sleeping medication to commit suicide that evening, morality demands that the confidant communicate that knowledge to a spouse or other family member of the suicidal friend, or take some other intervening action.

Sometimes a teacher who would not hesitate to get help for a friend refuses to believe that a student who is talking about suicide is serious, or assumes the student can be talked out of the planned action or is incapable of carrying out a threatened suicide. As child and adolescent psychologists report, young people do not usually comprehend the finality of death, nor do they think through the long-term ramifications of a suicide attempt. Some young people also have a fascination with death, as seen by the idolization of famous people who have died young or committed suicide.

If a student tells a teacher that he or she is going to harm self or others, the teacher must reveal that information even if a promise of confidentiality has been given. In a number of lawsuits brought against teachers and school districts, parents sought damages from teachers who did not contact parents or other authorities when they were told by students in confidence that they planned to harm themselves or someone else. In some cases, the educators were held negligent in failing to give warning. The 1995 case of *Brooks v. Logan and Joint School District* (see below) illustrates the liability that can ensue to both teacher and school when a threatened suicide becomes a reality.

Legal Immunity

It is a widely held myth that counselors, physicians, psychologists, and social workers have legal immunity from responsibility for injuries that may arise from their not acting on confidential information presented to them. Most states have abolished counselor immunity, and the few that still have it on the books have imposed severe limitations on the practice. A counselor to whom a young person discloses plans to kill his or her parents and who does nothing about it will not be able to legally decline to answer questions under oath, nor will the counselor be held blameless for any resulting injuries. Counselors and teachers must make it very clear to confiding individuals that they will keep their confidences unless their health, life, or safety or those of another are involved.

The only two privileges from disclosure of confidentiality information that appear to remain in state law are that of priest/penitent and attorney/client. Even the husband/wife privilege, which allowed a spouse to refuse to testify against a spouse, has been abandoned in most jurisdictions.

In light of the above facts, a teacher must presume that no legal protection exists for those who receive student confidences. What should the teacher do who wants to be a role model for young people, who wants to be approachable and helpful? The answer is simple: Lay down the ground rules for confidentiality before you receive any confidences. Tell students you will respect their confidences except in cases of life, health, and safety. If a student asks to speak to you in confidence, reiterate the ground rules before the student begins to share.

Journal Writing

Teachers of religion, language arts, and English have long recognized the value of student journal writing. This practice does, however, carry a real risk of student disclosure of information that the teacher is compelled to reveal. Teachers must set the same rules for confidentiality discussed above. Teachers must understand that they are expected to read what students write. If a teacher cannot read the assignment, then the assignment should not be made. In particular, teachers should avoid telling students to clip together pages they do not wish the teacher to read or to write "Please do not read" at the top of such pages. Journal writing has a place in today's curriculum, but teachers must be sure that students understand the parameters of the assignments and of the teacher's responsibilities of reporting threatened danger.

Retreats

The retreat experience is extremely important for today's Catholic young people. However, students are often at their most vulnerable in such situations. They may share stories of child abuse, sexual harassment, family dysfunction, and even possible criminal activity. While encouraging students to share, group leaders must once again set the ground rules before the sharing begins. The use of peer leaders does not lessen the responsibility of the supervising adults. Student leaders must be told the ground rules and the necessity to communicate them to group members as well as the procedures to follow in notifying adults if a matter is revealed in sessions that must be reported.

Conclusion

The case study and the discussion in this article indicate the vulnerability of teachers who receive student confidences. The wise Catholic educator will establish and enforce ground rules for dealing with student confidences and will seek help from school officials and parents when appropriate.

Recent Developments

In the case cited above, *Brooks v. Logan and Joint District,* No 2 903 2d 73 (1995), parents of a student who had committed suicide filed an action for wrongful death and a claim for negligent infliction of emotional distress against a teacher who gave the assignment of keeping a journal.

Jeff Brooks, a student at Meridian High School, was assigned to Ms. Logan's English class. Students were asked to make entries in a daily journal as part of their English composition work. For four months before his death, Jeff wrote in his journal. After his death, Ms. Logan read through the entries and gave the journal to a school counselor, who delivered it to Jeff's parents. Jeff had made journal entries indicating that he was seriously depressed and contemplating suicide. One entry read as follows:

> Well, Edgar Allan Poe, I can live with studying about that stuff he wrote especially the one short story about the evil eye . . . I used to write poems until I pronounced myself dead in one of them and how I could write poems or stories if I was dead . . .

> Recently . . . see I went into a medium of depression and wrote poems about two special people . . . I told them it was too bad I had to say goodby [sic] this way like that but, it would be the only way and I felt better . . . (p. 81).

Ms. Logan maintained that Jeff had requested the she not read his entries so that he would feel free to express himself. A note in the journal reported that Ms. Logan would not read the journal for content, but only check for dates and length. The parents maintained that, in a conversation after their receipt of the journal, Ms. Logan had said "reread the entries." Ms. Logan denied the statement and contends that she did not read the entries in question until after Jeff's death.

The lower court granted summary judgment in favor of the teacher and the school district. However, the appellate court reversed the finding and held that there were issues of fact that could only be determined at a still-pending trial. Thus, a trial court will determine whether Ms. Logan's actions or inactions constituted negligence that contributed to Jeff's death. Part of the analysis will have to include a determination of whether, if Jeff Brooks' suicide was foreseeable, a reasonable person in Ms. Logan's place would have recognized the possibility and notified someone. The appellate court refers to case law in which jailers have been held liable for the suicide of prisoners when the prisoners had exhibited warning signs. ⁂

September 2001
Issues of Confidentiality as the Year Begins

As a new school or religious education year begins, administrators and staff members begin a mental checklist process. Do we have the policies and procedures we need? Does everyone know what they are? Are there any new laws that affect us? Are we prepared to deal with violence and threats of violence? What rules do we need to stress to students? One of the greatest areas of concern is confidentiality. The beginning of the year is the best time to establish and explain ground rules for confidentiality.

Some teachers, catechists, and youth ministers sincerely believe they should keep student confidences confidential. Some fear that if students believe information entrusted to staff members can be shared, students will not offer information that should be shared. The recent experiences of violence cause adults to consider the importance of students trusting adults to do the right thing with information shared.

The responsibility of advising students and receiving their trust is awesome. Teachers and other staff members must be able to recognize the difference between matters that can be kept safely between teacher and student and communications that must be shared. While it is tempting to think that we can help all our students all the time, the truth is we cannot. Two useful questions to ask in considering whether to tell are these: "What would I want a teacher or other adult to do if this were my child (or grandchild, niece, or nephew) sharing this information? What would I expect the adult to do?" The answers should provide guidance for adults receiving confidences.

A Definition

Black's Law Dictionary defines confidentiality as "1. Secrecy; the state of having the dissemination of certain information restricted. 2. The relation between lawyer and client . . . with regard to the trust that is placed in the one by the other" (p. 294).

The dissemination of some information can be restricted—for example, boyfriend/girlfriend troubles, parent/child conflicts, fears and hopes, but the dissemination of other information is mandatory.

Issues

One area that poses special issues is journal writing. Recent litigation indicates that teachers can be held liable for knowing information and failing to act on it. They can also be held liable for not reporting information that they should have known. One of the first confidentiality/journal cases was *Brooks v. Logan and Joint District No. 2*, 903 P.2d 73 (1995). Parents of a student who had committed suicide filed an action for wrongful death against a teacher who gave an assignment of keeping a journal to students in her English class, but who did not always read what the students wrote. The student was fascinated with the works of Edgar Allan Poe. He wrote about that fascination and ended his journal with, "Recently . . . see I went into a medium of depression and wrote poems about two special people. . . I told them it was too bad I had to say goodby [sic] this way like that but, it would be the only way and I felt better. . ." (p. 81).

After the student died, his parents were given the journal and argued that had they been notified about their son's writings, they might have been able to intervene and prevent the suicide. The teacher stated that the student had requested that she not read his entries so that he could better express himself. The teacher reported that she checked for dates and length, but did not read the content. She maintained that she did not read the entry until after the student's death. The court ruled that a teacher could be held negligent in the death of a student under such circumstances. These cases, and others like it, illustrate the importance of teachers reading what they assign. Similar plaintiff's arguments have been made in the Paducah, KY, and Columbine, CO, school shooting cases. A good rule is "If you assign it, read it."

Other activities, such as retreat experiences, hold opportunities for disclosure of secrets. Students may share stories of violence, child abuse, family dysfunction, drug abuse, and criminal activity. The question that should be asked when deciding whether to share information is "Does this information impact the health, safety, or life of the student or others?" If the answer is "yes," the information must be shared with the appropriate authorities.

Recommendations

The following is a brief list of dos:

- Do discuss the concept of confidentiality with your students.
- Do explain that, as a supervising adult, you have responsibilities to protect them.
- Do explain that you will keep their confidences, if you are able.
- Do tell students, "I will keep your confidences as long as no one's health, safety, or life is at stake. Once health, safety, or life is at stake, there can be no guarantee of confidentiality and I must report what you tell me."

May 2002

Students Grading Other Students' Papers:
Owasso v. Falvo Decided

The U.S. Supreme Court recently decided the case of *Owasso v. Falvo,* 122 S. Ct. 934, which put on trial the notion of whether students could grade each other's papers and captured the attention of educators everywhere. The plaintiff, Ms. Falvo, contended that the practice of "peer grading," in which a student "scores another student's tests, papers or assignments as the teachers explain the correct answers to the entire class" violated the Family Educational Rights and Privacy Act of 1974.

Ms. Falvo argued that her children's privacy rights under the act were violated when other students marked the papers, which she alleged then became records covered by the act. FERPA does authorize federal funds to be withheld from school districts that permit the release of educational records without parental consent. Ms. Falvo maintained that the very act of peer grading violated the privacy requirement. The question she believed had not been adequately answered by the courts was "What exactly is an educational record?" FERPA defines educational records as those that "are maintained by an educational agency or institution or by a person acting for an agency or institution."

Ms. Falvo claimed that peer grading embarrassed her children and asked that the public school district ban peer grading and require teachers either to grade assignments themselves or at least permit students to grade only their own papers.

As the case was pending, the author received numerous queries from principals around the country who wondered what would happen if Ms. Falvo won her case. Some defended the practice of peer grading as part of the learning process. Some questioned what would happen to the practice of having students view especially good samples of peer work. Others wondered if the honor roll would be considered illegal since others would be told students' scholastic averages, which are part of educational records. One principal observed that the National Honor Society would have to be abolished since some of the highest performing students would be clearly identified.

The Supreme Court cited two errors in the lower court's reasoning. First, an assignment is not an educational record as soon as another student grades it because the grade is not "maintained" until it has been recorded in the teacher's grade book. The Supreme Court opinion states, "The student graders only handle assignments for a few moments as the teacher calls out the answers. It is fanciful to say they maintain the papers in the same way the registrar maintains a students' folder in a permanent file."

The Court of Appeals' second error was "in concluding that each student grader is 'a person acting for' an educational institution." The Supreme Court said that students are not agents of the schools as are teachers and other employees. In fact, the court observed:

> Correcting a classmate's work can be as much a part of the assignment as taking the test itself. It is a way to teach material again in a new context, and it helps show students how to assist and respect fellow pupils. By explaining the answers to the class as the students correct the papers, the teacher not only reinforces the lesson but also discovers whether the students have understood the material and are ready to move on. . . . Even if one were to agree students are acting for a teacher when they correct the assignment, that is different from saying they are acting for the educational institution in maintaining it.

The Falvo case appears to settle the question of the legality of students grading each other's papers. Yet there are ethical as well as legal issues to consider. Some readers may recall their dread when a classmate called out a not-so-terrific grade for the teacher to record. While there are educational benefits to a certain amount of peer review, educators must exercise caution and remember that students' feelings are fragile. The following suggestions may be helpful.

1. Use peer grading only for drill and other objective tests.

2. Don't have students call out grades. Either collect the papers and record the grades at a later time or have students approach the teacher's desk privately.

3. Before permitting peer review, seriously consider whether it is appropriate for students to grade each other's work.

4. If the reason for allowing peer review is that the teacher doesn't have time to grade the papers, the teacher should probably reconsider the assignment.

5. Consider students' feelings when using peer grading. If students seem unduly upset, abandon the practice.

[Note: A few dioceses take the position that FERPA does not apply to Catholic schools. This author believes that it is better to comply voluntarily than to fight this particular battle in court.]

MARCH 2003
COUNSELING ISSUES AND CATHOLIC EDUCATION

Today, more than ever before, educators are asked to counsel students. Certainly, part of being an educator is guiding students. Educators want to show young people that they are interested in them. Unfortunately, today's litigious society demands both caution and information. Student needs can be met, but all involved in the education of youth must understand the legal ramifications of assuming counseling roles. This article will address the responsibilities of those who are counselors, as well as those who assume counselor-like roles.

Confidentiality: The Bottom Line

No one, counselor or educator, has an absolute right to keep information received from young people confidential. Whether the information can be kept confidential depends on the nature of the confidence. A student's complaint about a parent or a teacher can ordinarily be kept confidential. Other matters cannot.

Many school counselors mistakenly believe they are protected by a privilege that allows them to keep confidential information they receive from their students/clients. Currently, only two privileges exist in civil law—priest/penitent, which is absolute, and attorney/client, which is not. The law recognizes the relationship between a clergyperson and a penitent. In the Catholic Church, of course, that relationship exists when the penitent is receiving the sacrament of reconciliation. Some states limit the clergy/penitent privilege to only those religions that have some sort of private confession. The difficulty in not limiting the privilege to private confession is that the court may find itself determining what type of confidential information fits under the privilege and what does not. If the statute does not limit the privilege to confession, the situation can become even more problematic. Catholic priests who serve as campus ministers or confessors in the school must understand that the privilege is usually reserved to times of confession.

The vast majority of counselors are not members of the clergy. It is imperative that all counselors understand that, no matter what any counseling organization to which they belong may have as guiding principles, civil law will hold them accountable to its dictates. In practice this means that counselors must reveal any information that, if withheld, might contribute to injury to another. For example, if a student tells a counselor that he or she is planning to commit suicide, most counselors clearly understand that they need to contact the student's parent. Other areas are more challenging. For example, the student who is pregnant is not injured, but delay in seeking medical treatment could result in harm to mother and child. The counselor must make a judgment call. If the student does not inform her parents that she is pregnant within a reasonable time period (e.g., two weeks), the counselor should see that the parent is informed, perhaps through a facilitated meeting.

Another problematic area is alcohol use. If a high school counselor reported to every parent of students who claimed to have had a few beers that the students had done so, the counselor would soon have few clients. If, however, the counselor suspects alcohol abuse or a dependency problem, the counselor must see that parents are notified and that the student receives assessment and, if necessary, treatment.

The age of the confiding student must also be a consideration in deciding to notify parents. The younger the child, the more imperative the timeliness of notification.

Administrators: What Do They Have a Right to Know?

It is not unusual for a counselor to maintain that an administrator has no right to information he or she received from a student, while the administrator claims that the counselor works for the school and must report information sought. The student is the one who ultimately loses when administration and counselors lock horns. As a former high school principal, the author said to her counseling staff, "I will not seek information from you unless it is absolutely necessary. If I do ask for information, then I trust you will give it to me. I also trust that you will tell me what I need to know even if I do not ask you about the situation." This approach requires mutual trust, but the student's best interests are served.

Teachers and other staff members also receive confidential information. They are bound to the same reporting requirements if the confidence concerns possible injury. Everyone should say to young people before they begin to share confidences, "I will keep your confidence as long as health, life, safety, and criminal activity are not involved. If they are involved, I must reveal what you say."

A Final Thought

Catholic educators believe that Christ is the chief teacher. Asking oneself what Jesus would do in a given situation and asking for His guidance will keep educators faithful to the demands of both civil law and the Gospel.

MARCH 2006

TO TELL OR NOT TO TELL:
COUNSELORS, ADMINISTRATORS, AND CONFIDENTIALITY

Although the topic of confidentiality has been addressed in past NCEA Notes columns, questions continue to arise. Counselors, pastoral and campus ministers, chaplains, social workers, and psychologists (referred to as counselors in this article) often find themselves torn among various potential and conflicting duties, including (a) a promise of confidentiality given, (b) knowledge of potentially dangerous situations, (c) legal responsibilities and liabilities, (d) parents who demand information, and (e) the principal or other administrator's right and need to know. Teachers, catechists, and other staff members have responsibilities, too, but this article is concerned primarily with those who, given the nature of their jobs, offer counsel to young people.

Confidentiality

Confidentiality is generally held to mean that one individual will not reveal private information given by another. For example, the person who receives the sacrament of reconciliation rightfully expects that the subject matter of confession will be held sacred by the confessor and will not be revealed to anyone. This situation is addressed by church law and no U.S. civil court has ever mandated that the seal of confession be broken. Even though chaplains may be priests, everything they are told is not confidential, only what is revealed in the sacrament. Another example would be the high school student who tells his counselor that he is the father of an unborn child and he and his girlfriend are considering an abortion. Yet another would be the student who reveals she is thinking of killing herself because her uncle is abusing her and begs the counselor not to tell or the uncle will kill her.

The general rule, with which the vast majority of readers are familiar, is that adults will keep the confidences entrusted to them as long as life, health, and safety are not involved. If they are involved, the adult may not keep the confidence. The best time to inform young people of this constraint is at the beginning of an academic year or extended counseling or in response to a young person's statement, "I want to tell you something but you have to promise not to tell anyone." If a student reveals that he or she is going to harm self or others, the adult must reveal that information, even if a promise of confidentiality has previously been given. In a number of lawsuits, parents sought damages from staff members who were told by students in confidence that they planned to harm themselves or others and did not inform parents and other authorities. In some cases, the employees were brought to trial on a claim of negligence by failure to warn. More recent cases have found such nonreporting individuals being bound over for trial for the crimes of negligent homicide and voluntary or involuntary manslaughter.

What Rules Govern? Professional Association? Local Administrator? The Law?

Those in the counseling professions have been trained to keep confidences and not reveal what they know about those confiding in them. It is not unusual for a counselor to say, for example, "But the _____ Guidance Counselors Association states in its rules for membership that counselors cannot repeat confidences." One would hope that there is less of this mind-set today than there was a decade ago, but it still exists. In the two weeks' preceding the writing of this article, the author was twice told something like the above statement. No association or organization can place itself and its members outside the law. There are no exceptions for counselors in reporting laws, rules of testimony, discovery, etc. If one does not obey the law, one is subject to the penalty for not obeying.

Why and When Should the Administrator Be Told?

Counselors may balk at revealing confidential matters to administrators. In cases involving health, life, and safety, the counselor must tell the administrator. The administrator has a right to expect and require that such information be immediately shared with him or her. State law may mandate, for example, that the person learning of child abuse report it, but it is only reasonable to tell the administrator, whom authorities will in all likelihood visit. Sometimes, an outside agency rather than the specific individual employed by the school or parish supplies a counselor. Nonetheless, the administrator, under the doctrine of respondeat superior, let the superior answer, is responsible for virtually everything that occurs in the institution or program, including acts and omissions of employees and volunteers.

So What's the Bottom Line for Counselors?

The bottom line is simple: Matters of health, life, and safety must be reported to those with a right and need to know, one of whom is the administrator. *JP*

Health

ISSUES

March 1993

Substance Abuse and the Catholic School

❧

Substance abuse is a growing problem in today's society. Young people have no corner on the problem; adults of every age are vulnerable as well. School officials struggle to respond appropriately to problems of substance abuse among students and staff. Most people understand that addiction is a disease that can claim anyone. At the same time, the Catholic school administrator cannot condone the use of illicit drugs or the abuse of lawful drugs or alcohol. The wise administrator will strive to enact policies that allow people suffering from addictions to seek the treatment the need while still experiencing the support of the school community. Little is accomplished when a student or teacher is summarily dismissed from the school because of addictive behavior.

Nevertheless, both faculty and staff must understand that their behavior, even if it is not completely voluntary, can have consequences. Students or teachers who choose to drink at school, for example, are violating school rules and are probably violating civil law as well. Students are below the legal drinking age and local laws may prohibit adults drinking on school property.

The school principal, counselor, teacher, and disciplinarian may ask, "How do we hold people accountable and at the same time help them get treatment if they need it?"

First, all must understand that every student who comes to school or a school function under the influence of alcohol or drugs is not an alcoholic or drug addict. Some students experiment with these substances. Little is gained if a student who is not addicted is forced into attending Alcoholics Anonymous or Narcotics Anonymous meetings.

The principal or guidance counselor is not the person best equipped to determine that a student is suffering from alcohol or drug addiction. The services of a reliable, certified substance abuse counselor or addictions treatment facility should be used. A clear policy on the use of alcohol and drugs should be developed and promulgated to everyone who may be affected by it.

Student Policies

Every school should be committed to providing drug and alcohol education for its students. Many excellent programs are available for this purpose. The school may choose to use a commercially available program or develop its own.

School policies should clearly state that the school, during school hours for everyone and all the time for students, should be drug and alcohol free. The penalties for using alcohol or drugs or being under their influence should leave no room for misunderstanding. Penalties should be progressive. The following is a suggested model.

For the first offense, parents should be notified and an assessment should be required. If the result of the assessment is that the student does not have a substance abuse problem but rather made some unfortunate choices, the student should not be placed in a treatment program. Counseling, either by school or outside counselors, may be required. If the result of the assessment is a diagnosis of substance abuse, substance abuse counseling and attendance at a treatment program should be required.

A disciplinary sanction, such as suspension, should be imposed for all first offenses. Administrators should make it clear that the punishment is not for having an illness, but for violating school rules. A good analogy is the alcoholic who is convicted of driving under the influence of alcohol. The punishment for drunk driving is imposed not because the person was intoxicated but because the person chose to drive, or at least permitted himself or herself to get in a position in which drinking and driving were possible.

Second offenses call for sterner measures. Counseling may be intensified and a longer suspension may be imposed. The policy should allow the school to expel for subsequent offenses. The author recommends a statement such as "Subsequent offenses may result in expulsion." The use of the word "may" rather than "can" allows the administrator the freedom to permit a student to stay if there is some extenuating circumstance; "can" seems to demand that expulsion occur.

Adult Substance Abuse

Adults who suffer from substance abuse often give signs indicating that something is wrong. Administrators who suspect alcoholism or drug addiction should document the behaviors observed. Like all documentation, written observations should be specific, behaviorally oriented, and verifiable.

Rather than writing "Mrs. Thomas was drunk again today," the administrator should describe the behaviors in nonjudgmental terms: "Mrs. Thomas was unsteady on her feet; her eyes were glazed and red; I smelled what seemed to be gin on her breath." Argumentative or other inappropriate behavior should also be documented.

The administrator should confront the individual with his or her observations and should focus on job performance. Assessment and treatment should be offered. If the individual refuses the options presented and the problem behavior continues, suspension or termination may be in order. Each diocese should have an employee assistance plan that can be adopted by schools.

Alcoholism and other addictions may not garner as much sympathy as other deadly diseases, yet they are no less deadly in their own right. The Catholic school administrator has an obligation to provide opportunities that can lead to healing and wholeness for people suffering from addictions.

Recent Developments: Teacher Dismissal

In a recent California case, a school librarian in a private religious school alleged that she was terminated because of her out-of-wedlock pregnancy. The federal district court held that if the plaintiff could prove her charge, she would establish a Title VII sex discrimination violation since only women can become pregnant. (See *Vigars v. Valley Christian Center of Dublin,* California (N.D. Cal.), No. C91-2185 THE, May 20, 1992, Henderson, Chief Judge.) This case is similar to an older, often-cited one, *Dolter v. Wahlert High School,* 483 F. Supp. 266 (N.D. Iowa 1980), in which an unmarried teacher who became pregnant sought to prove that unmarried men who engaged in premarital sex were treated differently than unmarried female teachers who became pregnant. The court held that a Catholic school could not apply different standards of sexual morality to male and female teachers.

Catholic schools, then, must be consistent in holding people to standards of sexual conduct. If a woman is dismissed for premarital sexual activity resulting in pregnancy, a man who engages in such activity that becomes publicly known should also be dismissed. Courts do not question the right of Catholic and other religiously affiliated institutions to set standards of conduct, but those standards must be applied equally to males and females.

MAY 1993

AIDS and the Law

❦

The word "AIDS" evokes many emotions: fear, compassion, pity, and anxiety, to name a few. Today's Catholic educators are no strangers to these emotions. It is not surprising that Catholic school personnel, like other educators, have questions and concerns.

The principal who wishes to assess staff knowledge and attitudes about AIDS may use the following true-and-false pretest as a tool for beginning discussion and education. Each statement is followed by a brief discussion. For in-service purposes, a test sheet without answers and explanations should be prepared.

AIDS, the Law, and the Catholic School Teacher: A True-or-False Pretest

1. Students and teachers in Catholic schools have fewer rights than students and teachers in public schools. **(True)**

The rights of students and teachers in Catholic schools are governed by contract law, not constitutional law, since Catholic schools are private institutions, not government agencies. Thus, Catholic school students do not have the same freedom of speech and dress, for example, that public school students have. In essence, the Constitution, including the Bill of Rights, does not apply in the private sector.

2. Catholic school students and teachers are not protected by antidiscrimination laws. **(False)**

While the Constitution does not apply to Catholic schools, statutes and regulations do apply. Thus, a Catholic school may not discriminate on the basis of race, sex (unless it is a single-sex school), or national origin. Catholic schools may discriminate on the basis of religion, however.
Section 504 of the Rehabilitation Act of 1973 can apply to Catholic schools. Section 504 requires that people not be discriminated against solely on the basis of handicapping condition if they are otherwise qualified to meet the requirements of the position (student or teacher) being sought. The Americans with Disabilities Act of 1992 provides further protection for people facing discrimination because of disability.

3. A teacher has a legal right to know if a student in his or her class is HIV positive. **(False)**

A number of court cases protect the rights of individuals to privacy. There would have to be some overwhelming, compelling reason for privacy rights to be violated.

One example sometimes offered is the situation in which a student is prone to biting. Legal experts suggest that clear evidence must indicate a history of this kind of behavior, not merely a fear that such behavior might occur.

4. If two students begin fighting, a teacher has a legal right to refuse to become involved if there is any reason to believe that he or she might be exposed to student blood. **(False)**

The standard that determines a teacher's duty in any situation involving students is the reasonable person standard. The fact finder in a court case must determine whether the teacher acted the way a reasonable person in the teacher's position would act. A teacher has a higher responsibility to students than a stranger would have to them. There is a good possibility that a judge or jury would not accept fear of coming in contact with blood as a reason for a teacher to decline trying to protect students.

[When this article was written, most school law experts believed that the legal doctrine of in loco parentis (in the place of parents) was, for all intents and purposes, dead. In more recent times, it appears to have been resurrected. A teacher or other person who acts in loco parentis must treat the student in the same manner a parent would be expected to treat the young person. It is hard to imagine a parent who would not attempt to intervene in a situation posing possible danger to his or her child because of the fear of blood.

A theory more recently applied in some educational settings (though mentioned in law journal articles as early as the 1950s) is the fiduciary theory. Fiduciaries are held to the highest possible standard of care and are expected to take at least as much care of that trusted to them as they would take if the thing were a personal possession. By extension, then, teachers must take at least as much care of students as they would take of their own children—an extremely high standard.]

5. A parent has a legal right to know if a student in his or her child's class is HIV positive. **(False)**

Although parents may wish to know whether a child is HIV positive, current laws protect the rights of both parent and child to privacy. [Note: The 1996 Health Insurance Portability and Accountability Act (HIPAA) and the more recent Privacy Act provide even stronger privacy protection of medical information and records.]

6. A teacher may discuss a child's HIV status with someone who has an interest, other than mere curiosity, in the situation. **(False)**

A teacher told of a child's HIV status by the parents or, with the parents' consent, by the principal has no right to discuss that status with anyone other than the parents or principal.

7. The principal always has a right to know if a student or staff member is HIV positive. **(False)**

The same right of privacy discussed in questions 3 and 5 applies to the principal as well. [Note: In 2007 privacy rights are even more closely protected; HIPAA laws are one example. The bottom line is that no one has to reveal his or her HIV or AIDS status to anyone. Medical personnel with that information may not reveal it.]

8. If a student's parent or family member with whom he or she lives is HIV positive, the principal should be informed. **(False)**

While arguments can certainly be made that the school should be informed in such situations so that appropriate support can be offered the student, there is no legal requirement that such information be given to the principal. [Note: As indicated above, privacy laws protect those with HIV or AIDS. No administrator can require that such information be shared with him or her.]

9. Universal precautions should always be used when dealing with any situation involving body fluids. **(True)**

Even if teachers knew that certain students were HIV positive, there is no guarantee that other students are HIV negative. People who are HIV positive may not know that they are. Currently, medical experts suggest that it can be two weeks to six months before one tests positive for the HIV virus. It can take up to 10 years for symptoms to appear.

Thus, the prudent approach is to assume that everyone may be infected and to take universal precautions when dealing with body fluids. Every teacher and staff member should have gloves and disinfectant within easy access, and all schools should offer in-service training in this area.

10. Since Catholic schools are private institutions, they may legally deny admission to individuals who are HIV positive as long as HIV status is not given as the reason or the denial. **(False)**

Although there has not been a major case dealing with such a situation in a Catholic school, it appears safe to say that courts would not uphold a denial of admission or employment in a Catholic school to otherwise-qualified individuals solely because of their HIV status. An individual denied admission or employment would have to offer evidence that would convince a court that the HIV status was the real reason for denial. [Note: The school would have to offer a justifiable, nondiscriminatory reason for denial of admission and that reason cannot be a mere pretext.]

Nonetheless, an individual with AIDS could be denied employment on some other basis, if that other basis is job related. A person who is too ill to perform the duties of employment can be denied employment because he or she does not possess the bona fide occupational qualifications for the job, one of which would be the physical and mental capabilities to meet the reasonable demands of the job.

Recommendations

The following recommendations might be the basis for ongoing consideration after discussion of the pretest:

1. Remember that everyone, including people with AIDS, is protected against discrimination.

2. Remember that everyone has privacy rights. Medical information is confidential and only those with a legal right to know can be informed. [Note: Today, the categories and numbers of persons deemed to have a right to know are much more limited than in the past.]

3. Assume that any staff member or student may be HIV positive or may have a communicable disease.

4. Do not discuss the physical, psychological, mental, or emotional condition of any student with anyone except professional staff (when necessary), parents, or those the parents designate.

5. Attitudes are important and can be expressed as much by actions as by words.

6. Teachers and other professionals are held to a higher standard than are "ordinary" people.

Conclusion

It should be clear that the law requires that institutions be nondiscriminatory. While the fear of AIDS is real, the responsibility of Catholic school educators to model Christian behavior and values remains unchanged. The question that should always be asked is "What would Jesus do if He were faced with this situation?"

[Note: In talking with medical professionals in 2007, the author learned that a new attitude appears to be growing among young people. One hears of far fewer people dying of AIDS today than 14 years ago when this article appeared, and an increasing number of young people express opinions that getting AIDS is not the "big deal" it used to be because they think it can be cured. There is no cure for AIDS, only improved means of controlling the symptoms of the disease. A growing number of adolescents are known as "bug chasers," who intentionally engage in sexual practices in the hopes of catching AIDS. At work here seems to the personal myth that is too often exhibited by young people who just don't believe that they will get ill or die. In 1993 there was a sharp rise in the number of AIDS cases reported among adolescents—more than a 300% increase over the 1992 rate. Since then, there has no return to the lower rates of reported AIDS cases in years before 1993. Additionally, the number of female adolescents reporting AIDS continues to rise.]

Recent Developments

The Second Circuit Court of Appeals in Louisiana has ruled that a private school student had a right to receive an official transcript, despite his father's failure to pay tuition. School officials had allowed the young man to attend classes and submit all required work.

The court stated that the school would not have had to allow the student, who was a third-party beneficiary of the school's contract with the father, to remain in school since the father's nonpayment of tuition would constitute a breach of contract. However, since the young man did remain in school and complete all work, the court held that he was entitled to an official transcript on a theory of detrimental reliance. (See *McKee v. Southfield School* (La. App. 2 Cir.), No. 24336-CA, January 20, 1993, Norris, Judge.)

Many Catholic schools face the problem of nonpayment of tuition. This case demonstrates the dilemma: If administrators allow students to remain in school and complete work when tuition is unpaid, the school could be compelled to grant transcripts. Once a transcript is granted, the possibility of payment decreases.

Administrators should consider requiring parents to sign tuition contracts that have been approved by school or diocesan counsel. A properly constructed and implemented written contract can help address the problems presented in the above case.

January 1999

Dispensing Medication:
Policies and Procedures

ᘓᗏᗝ

"I have to take my medicine," says the second grader to the school secretary, who opens a cabinet reserved for student medications and begins to search for the appropriate bottle. "I took this bottle of pills away from this student. It is a prescription, and someone else's name is on the bottle," reports a teacher. "Here are Mary's medications, plus a bottle of Tylenol and an over-the-counter cough syrup," declares a mother, who opens a plastic bag and dumps medication bottles on the school counter or secretary's desk. How should staff respond? One of the more challenging tasks facing education administrators today is dispensing medicine.

Few schools have full-time nurses on their staffs. Whether or not a school has a nurse, administrators must grapple with appropriate policies and procedures. Some approaches include the following:

- All medication must be brought to the office with a parent's note.

- Only prescription medication can be brought to school and it must be stored in a school office. No over-the-counter medication is allowed unless a written doctor's authorization is submitted.

- Prescription medication must be in the original bottle with the student's name on it and written parental permission must be submitted.

- The school will not dispense medication, so students are responsible for their own medication.

- The school does not dispense over-the-counter medication.

- The school uses variations of these positions.

Opinions vary on the best approach. Some medical professionals do not want to take time to write notes for over-the-counter prescriptions. Parents grumble about an extra trip to the doctor's office to get written authorization. Some high schools expect students to be responsible for self-administering all medication.

Attorneys can identify problems with almost any approach. Whenever a school official administers medication, he or she may be liable for any reaction that occurs. One dangerous policy allows parents to bring over-the-counter medications with the student's name written on it. The difficulty is that people are having increasing problems with aftereffects or reactions to nonprescription medicine.

In one case in which a student was given milk of magnesia, no one knew the student had an allergy to the product and he died. No action resulted, however, because it was the boy's mother, not a school official, who administered the medicine. One can imagine what the result could have been if a staff member had given the student the drug.

The practice of schools storing parent-supplied, over-the-counter medication appears to be growing. Even though written permission was on file, principals have been sued for administering parent-supplied medication that interacted with some other medicine the student was taking. Some parents allege that the school should have recognized the possibility of drug interaction and should have asked questions about other medication. Several cases of this type are making their way through the judicial system.

One question frequently asked in schools that do not have nurses is: Who should administer medication? The classroom teacher? The school secretary? The principal or another administrator? It should be readily apparent to the reader that the administration of medication warrants careful consideration in developing and implementing policies and procedures.

The following statements offer some suggestions to ponder when policies and procedures are being determined:

- The only students who have an absolute right to the administration of medication are those with serious chronic or life-threatening illnesses. For example, students who are allergic to bee stings must have the antidote serum readily available. A diabetic student must be able to have prescribed insulin injections. Diabetic students can, of course, be taught to administer and monitor their own medication, but students allergic to bees often need someone else to inject the antidote.

- People (at least two) must be identified and trained to administer injections or other drugs that a student cannot administer on his or her own.

- Students must be allowed to carry medication for life-threatening attacks. Asthma is one condition that may give little warning before an attack; if an inhaler is not immediately available, the student could be severely harmed.

- Adults who administer medication must place their whole attention on the task. The proper paperwork should be present (e.g., a prescription label in the student's name, a doctor's note of authorization, and a parent's written permission).

- If a teacher has a student with a life-threatening disease, the teacher must learn how to administer the medication. The reality is a matter of law, not choice.

- Young children should not be responsible for oral medication, other than inhalers. Oral medication should be brought to and kept in the office.

- High school students may be allowed to carry and monitor their own nonprescription medications, as long as the parent/student handbook contains a statement to that effect.

MAY 1999
HEALTH ISSUES AND THE LAW

As the school year draws to a close, administrators begin to focus on the next school year and its needs. Concern for the safety and well-being of all makes consideration of health issues most important.

Comparison of Public and Private School Health Laws

Although people in private schools do not have the same constitutional protections as those in public schools, statutory laws such as health regulations can bind both the public and the private sector. Administrators should carefully read all health-related communications from state or local agencies. Administrators who should have known what the law was will be held to the same standard that people who know the law are required to meet.

Planning

The first step in planning should be identifying any existing health or safety problems that the school can remedy. Inviting everyone in the school community to list problematic areas can help the administration identify the issues. Health and safety issues are related; failure to meet safety needs can result in health-related problems. A broken bleacher can lead to a person breaking a leg or arm. Courts expect principals to be proactive in identifying potential safety problems. At least once a year, the administration should complete a safety audit of all school buildings.

Teachers and Health Issues

Teachers and other staff members may be required to produce documentation stating that they will not pose a health threat for the school community. Tuberculosis poses a distinct threat. Many, but not all, states require new teachers to have a tuberculin skin test, chest X-ray, or both to rule out the presence of tuberculosis before the teacher starts work, but few states require further testing after a given number of years. It seems to this author that, whether required by law or not, teachers and other employees should be required to submit to tuberculosis testing at least once every five years. Medical experts report that tuberculosis is on the rise in the United States, so vigilance is appropriate. Someone may still contract tuberculosis, but the institution and its administrators will be able to demonstrate that the school has met the legal duty of due diligence.

HIV Status

All educators must understand that no one can legally be required to reveal personal HIV status or the fact that one has AIDS. If a student seeking to attend the school has AIDS, that student and his or her parents do not have to inform administrators. If administrators should discover after enrollment that a student is infected, they can do nothing to change the enrollment status of the student. These same principles apply to employing people with AIDS or who are HIV positive.

Universal Precautions

Staff members should use universal precautions whenever body fluids are present. No employee should be permitted to refuse to clean up body fluids or render aid to a bleeding student. Clear procedures stating exactly what to do will help ensure a calm, sound approach to situations involving body fluids.

The legal principle often applied in negligence cases, "the younger the child chronologically or mentally, the greater the standard of care," applies in body fluid situations. Teachers of smaller children are held to a higher standard, but those who teach older students are still held to the standard of taking whatever action a reasonable person would take.

Substance Abuse

Substance abuse is on the rise in America. Virtually no one is exempt from its effects. Administrators must understand that substance abuse is an illness, not a moral weakness. Just as people with other illnesses are protected by various disability laws, so too are substance abusers. Although a person's status may trigger disability protection, that status cannot be used to excuse behavior contrary to school rules. If a teacher keeps a bottle of vodka in her desk and is found drinking from it, the problem from a disciplinary standpoint is one of inappropriate conduct at school (bringing liquor to school for consumption) and not one of being a substance abuser. People who abuse substances and agree to enter treatment are protected; those who refuse assessment and treatment are not.

Student Athletes

Deaths of student athletes are becoming all too common. While many of the conditions precipitating the deaths could not have been foreseen, it is important for institutions to require that student athletes present doctors' authorization to play. In the case of illness, injury, or death, the school can then argue that administrators did everything they could do to avoid such injury. Now is the time to make a new year's resolution that this will be the year the school or institution gets its health policies in place and ensures implementation.

November 2004
Allergies and Allergic Reactions: Legal Responsibilities?

One type of legal question frequently raised concerns student allergies. More students than ever have allergies and parents request administrators to do the following:

1. Take appropriate measures to prevent exposure to allergens.

2. Keep and store medication.

3. Learn how to provide emergency medical treatment for allergic reactions.

4. Educate students and, indeed, the entire school community on the nature of allergic reactions.

Some staff members express fear or unwillingness to render aid to students experiencing allergic reactions. Teachers may ask if they must assume such responsibility. Administrators may be concerned about liability. This essay will attempt to answer some of the most commonly asked questions

Are Students With Allergies Protected by Disability Law?

Yes. A disability can generally be defined as any condition that interferes with one or more life activities. People with allergies to certain foods or bee stings can experience life-threatening allergic reactions. Students with allergies may be considered as having disabilities covered by Section 504 of the Rehabilitation Act of 1973 (amended 1974), which prohibits educational programs receiving federal funds from discriminating against otherwise qualified students if, with reasonable accommodation, they can meet the program or school requirements. Thus, students who need injections of adrenaline, for example, are protected. A student who cannot eat peanut butter or nuts is protected.

Must Our Schools and Programs Admit Such Students? Why?

As the aunt of a 7-year-old with the peanut allergy, this author was saddened to learn recently that some school and diocesan administrators are receiving requests from parents of students who are not allergic to certain foods, such as peanuts, to not allow allergic students to enroll in the school. The request seems to stem from the school's limitation on types of snacks that can be brought to school for parties and sometimes what is served in the cafeteria. Federal law protects such students, so they cannot be refused admission simply because they have an allergy that may inconvenience other students or their parents.

What About the Rights of Parents of Nonallergic Students? Must They Follow Restrictions Because a Few Students Have Allergies?

Parents of nonallergic students must comply with school directives to not send snacks with peanuts or other allergens to their children's classes. They may have to accept that peanut butter or items with peanuts or processed in plants that process peanuts may not be served in the cafeteria. These are simply reasonable accommodations. In one extreme case, parents of one student with the peanut allergy requested that no one be allowed to bring peanut products of any kind into the school. When contacted by an administrator in that school system, the author advised requiring the parent to produce a doctor's statement listing exactly what accommodations are necessary. A parent might believe that his or her child would be safest in a peanut-free environment, but if there is no medical necessity for that accommodation, the school is not obligated to make it. Thus, a school does not have to make every accommodation, but only reasonable ones that are medically necessary. In one case, a student may need a completely peanut-free environment; in another, he or she may only need to avoid the allergen.

These situations present opportunities for compassion. In discussing restrictions with parents, administrators should stress not only the legal requirements, but also the Gospel imperatives of "loving one's neighbor as oneself" and the importance of "doing unto others as you would have them do unto you."

What Are Teachers and Administrators Required To Do?

Teachers and administrators must do whatever is necessary to reasonably accommodate students with disabilities. A student must be allowed to carry an EpiPen® (device to inject epinephrine) if needed and the teacher must administer the injection if necessary. Failure to do so could result in serious injury to or the death of the student. Squeamishness must be set aside. Whatever a parent would reasonably do for a child, a teacher must do.

Summary

The following is a list of legal dos and don'ts when dealing with student allergies:

1. Students cannot be refused admission or continued enrollment simply because they have allergies to food, insects, or other substances.

2. Reasonable accommodations must be made.

3. If other students and parents are inconvenienced by the accommodations, they must accept the inconvenience.

4. Educators must be willing to learn about the allergies and the treatment needed.

5. Educators must be willing to administer medication when needed.

6. Educators should not isolate such students or take actions that might separate the student from other students or activities without parental permission.

7. Remind everyone that in every situation, all should act as Jesus would.

Technology
and MEDIA

May 1991

To Copy or Not to Copy?

Most educators realize the copyright law exists. If asked, many would probably respond that there are rules they should follow when making copies of articles, book chapters, computer programs, and television programs. Teachers have seen notices warning people making copies on copy machines that they are subject to the provisions of the copyright law.

For some individuals, the fact that apprehension and prosecution for breaking the copyright law rarely occur becomes a license to break the law. For others, the motive of helping students learn is an excuse for failing to comply with the law.

One commentator has observed: "Although this act [copying] may appear innocent on the surface, copyright infringement, whether malicious or not, is a criminal act. One's position as a teacher and having 'only the best interest of your students at heart' does not give anyone the right to copy indiscriminately" (*Merickel, The Educator's Rights to Fair Use of Copyrighted Works,* 51 Ed.Law Rep. 711, 1989).

Reasons to Copy

In the 1960s and '70s, budgetary considerations were the reasons churches, including Catholic churches, gave for copying songs from copyrighted works and compiling the copies in parish hymnals. Courts have consistently struck down such uses and have ordered the offending churches to pay damages.

Today, churches appear to be aware of the legal consequences of copying and many subscribe to the licensing arrangements of music companies: For a given sum, the institution can make as many copies of music as desired during the span of the contract.

On the other hand, it is not uncommon to find teachers copying such items as entire workbooks, other consumable materials, large portions of books, and print materials. The swift advance of technology has catapulted computer programs, videocassettes, and similar media into the sphere of teacher copying. This column will discuss copyright law as it applies to educational institutions, examine the tests of fair use, and offer guidelines for principals and teachers in Catholic schools.

Copyright Law

Upon reflection, most educators would agree that copyright protection is a just law. Both the Copyright Act of 1909 (the Old Law) and the Copyright Act of 1976 (the New Law) represent attempts to safeguard the rights of authors. People who create materials are entitled to the fruits of their labors. Those who use author's creations without paying royalties, buying copies, or seeking permission are guilty of stealing.

We may be tempted to think that copyright infringements and lawsuits are more or less the exclusive domain of large institutions. Certainly, we tend to hear about such abuses sooner than we learn of individual abuses.

Obviously, if a company is going to sue someone, it will seek a person or institution guilty of multiple infringements so that it can win larger damages. It simply doesn't make good economic sense to sue someone who will be ordered to pay only a small amount of damages.

Sometimes, though, lawsuits are brought solely to prove a point. A relatively recent legal case, *Marcus v. Rowley*, 695 F.2d 1171 (1983), involved a dispute between two teachers in the same school. One teacher had prepared and copyrighted a 20-page booklet on cake decorating. The second teacher copied about half the pages and included them in her own materials. The amount of money involved was negligible. The author had sold fewer than 100 copies at a price of $2. Nonetheless, the court found the second teacher guilty of copyright violation; her use of the other's materials was not "fair."

What Is Fair Use?

Section 107 of the 1976 Copyright Act deals with fair use and specifically states that the fair use of copies in teaching "is not an infringement of copyright."

The sticking point is what the term "fair use" means. The section lists four factors to be included in any determination of fair use:

- The purpose and character of the use, including whether such use is of a commercial nature or is for nonprofit educational purposes

- The nature of the copyrighted work

- The amount and substantiality of the portion used in relation to the copyrighted work as a whole

- The effect of the use on the potential market for or value of the copyrighted work

Educators should have little or no trouble complying with the "purpose and character of the work" factor. Teachers generally copy materials to aid the educational process. It should be noted, however, that recreational use of copied materials such as videocassettes or computer games is generally not allowed under the statute.

"The nature of the copyrighted work" factor can prove a bit more problematic than "character and purpose of the work." Who determines what is the nature of the work—the creator or copyright holder, the teacher, the judge, or the jury? Almost any material can be classified as educational in some context. Even a cartoon can be found to have some educational purpose if one is willing to look for it. It seems reasonable that, in determining nature, a court would look to the ordinary use of the work and to the author's intent in creating the work.

The "amount and substantiality" of the work copied is especially troublesome in the use of videocassettes and computer programs. Teachers understand that they are not supposed to copy a whole book, but may not understand that copying a television program or a movie onto videotape or copying a computer program for student use can violate the "amount and substantiality" factor.

In the case of *Encyclopedia Britannica v. Crooks,* 542 F.Supp. 1156 (W.D.N.Y. 1982), an educational company engaged in copying commercially available tapes and television programs for teachers was found to be in violation of the Copyright Act. The company argued that it was providing an educational service for students and teachers who would otherwise be deprived of important educational opportunities. The court rejected the argument.

Teachers may be tempted to think that their small-scale copying acts could not compare with the scope of the activities in this case. In the majority of instances involving single copying, there is no comparison. A relatively new practice, developing libraries of copies, is emerging in some schools. Whether the collections are of print materials or nonprint materials such as videotapes and computer programs, the practice of building collections can easily be subjected to the same scrutiny as the *Encyclopedia* case.

The last of the four factors, "effect on the market," is also difficult to apply in the educational setting. Arguments can be advanced that students would not rent or purchase commercially available items, even if copies weren't available. It appears, though, that use of an author's work without appropriate payment for the privilege is a form of economic harm. Good faith generally will not operate as an acceptable defense in educational copyright or infringement cases.

The court, in *Roy v. Columbia Broadcasting System,* 503 F.Supp. 1137 (S.D.N.Y. 1980), stated: "The federal copyright statute protects copyrighted works against mere copying, even when done in good faith and even when not done to obtain a competitive advantage over the owners of the copyright in the infringed works" (p. 1151).

Guidelines

A congressional committee developed "Guidelines for Classroom Copying in Not-for-Profit Educational Institutions," printed in House Report 94-1476, 94th Congress 2d Sess. (1976). Principals should ensure that teachers have access to copies of the guidelines, which are readily available from local libraries, the U.S. Copyright Office, and members of Congress. Although these guidelines do not have the force of law that the statute has, judges have used them in deciding cases. Some examples of the guidelines follow.

For poetry, copying of a complete poem of fewer than 250 words printed on no more than two pages or of an excerpt of 250 words from a longer poem is allowed. For prose, a complete work of fewer than 2,500 words or an excerpt from a longer work of not more than 1,000 words or 10% of the work is permissible. The guidelines mandate that copying meet this test of brevity.

The copying must be *spontaneous*. The teacher must have decided more or less on the spur of the moment to use an item. Spontaneity presumes that a teacher did not have time to secure permission for use from the copyright holder. A teacher who decided in September to use certain materials in December has ample time to seek permission. In such a situation, failure to seek permission means that the spontaneity requirement will not be met.

A last requirement is that the copying must not have a cumulative effect. Making copies of poems by one author would have a cumulative effect and would mean that collected works of the author would not be bought.

Similarly, the practice of "librarying" (building a collection of taped television programs, for example) is not permitted. Copying computer programs is never advisable, unless permission to make copies is included in the purchase or rental agreement.

Videotapes may be kept for 45 days only. During the first 10 days, a teacher may use the tape once in a class (although there is a provision for one repetition for legitimate instructional review). For the remaining 35 days, teachers may use the tape for evaluative purposes only.

Conclusion

Principals are responsible for supervising all aspects of the educational process. If a teacher is charged with copyright violation, it is likely that the principal will be charged as well. Clear policies and careful monitoring of those policies can lessen exposure to liability. As many legal authorities have observed, copyright violation is stealing. It appears, then, that "Thou shalt not steal" remains a good law.

Recent Developments

In the case of *Medlin v. Bass,* 397 S.E.2d 460 (1990), involving a principal who sexually abused a child, the school district and its officials were found innocent of any wrongdoing.

The child's mother had alleged that the principal's superiors should have known that he was a pedophile. The court, however, found that nothing in the record indicated the principal's criminal tendencies and that his behavior was not within the scope of his official duties.

Thus, district officials and the district itself could not be held liable in negligence or under an agency theory, respondent superior, let the superior answer.

This case indicates that principals and other supervisors will not be held liable for every act of a subordinate employee, but only for actions that occur within the scope of duty and that a reasonable person could have foreseen. 🖋

MAY 1997

TECHNOLOGY

⌒⟁⟁⟁⌒

Ten years ago most students had limited access to technology. Today, technological developments present challenges for the educator who seeks to act in ways that are morally, ethically, and legally correct. This article addresses the applicability of copyright law to technology and supervision of student use, including school censorship. It also presents a model for a technology acceptable-use policy handbook.

Applicability of Copyright Law

Much material available through electronic media, video programming, and computer software is subject to U.S. copyright law. Catholic schools are subject to such law in exactly the same manner as public schools. Copyright law is statutory and binds Catholic schools.

The Copyright Law of 1976, Section 102, clearly articulates the present and future parameters of applicability: "Copyright protection subsists . . . in original works of authorship fixed in any tangible medium of expression, now known or later developed, from which they can be perceived, reproduced, or otherwise communicated, either directly or with the aid of a machine or device." Thus, copyright law not only regulates print media, but other media as well.

Section 107 of the copyright law cites four factors used to determine fair use: (a) whether the use and character of the use is of a commercial nature or is for nonprofit educational purposes, (b) the nature of the copyrighted work, (c) the amount and substantiality of the portion used in relation to the copyrighted work as a whole, and (d) the effect of the use on the potential market for or value of the copyrighted work.

The 1976 "Congressional Guidelines for Classroom Copying in Not-for-Profit Educational Institutions" identifies three further factors: (a) brevity, or the amount of the work copied; (b) spontaneity, or when a decision was made to copy material and whether the timing of the decision allowed for contact with the copyright holder; and (c) cumulative effect, or how much of one author's or publisher's work is used. Administrators would be well advised to include these factors in any discussion of reproduction of copyrighted materials. (The May 1991 issue of *NCEA Notes* contained my article "To Copy or Not to Copy?" It provides detailed discussion of the four factors and the congressional guidelines.)

Supervision of Student Use

Students may consider censorship a negative word, but educational administrators have a clear duty to safeguard the minds of those entrusted to their care. While First Amendment issues of freedom of expression may affect public school censorship, they have no bearing on Catholic education, since the private school does not have to grant constitutional protection to students.

Congress attempted to help adults who supervise children when it passed the 1996 Communications Decency Act. Challenges to the act have reached the U.S. Supreme Court, which was expected to rule on its legality in June 1997.

Catholic educators need make no apologies for supervising student access to people and programs via the Internet. Students should not be allowed to enter Internet chat rooms freely. Some educational administrators have barred any access to chat rooms, and such action in the private sector appears to be lawful and appropriate. Continued development of software, V-Chips, and their progeny will provide educators with more supervisory aids.

Some educators ask for a definition of obscenity, which is not easy to find in the legal literature. Some courts have ruled that obscenity and pornography are recognizable when seen, so no hard-and-fast definition needs to be given. Courts have further ruled that standards of morality in a given community may govern.

An educational administrator may be tempted to view supervision of technology as an impossible task. Those searching for a rule of thumb should ask themselves: "Would I be comfortable with my child watching, using, or participating in this technological activity?" If the answer is "no," the activity should be prohibited.

A Model Handbook

The intricacies and wording of handbook components are beyond the scope of this essay. The following outline for contents of a technology acceptable-use handbook should provide guidance in its development.

    I.   Philosophy of the Catholic school

    II.   Brief history of technology in the Catholic school or in schools in general

    III.   Definition of acceptable use

    IV.   Types of technological abuse

        A.   Violations of privacy

        B.   Abuse of confidentiality

        C.   Theft

        D.   Vandalism or destruction of others' work

        E.   Stalking or harassment

        F.   Other issues

V.   Copyright law

VI.   Guidelines for acceptable use

VII.   List of parent/student responsibilities

VIII. Penalties for noncompliance

IX.   Signatures of parents and student 🖉

November 2003
The Promise and Peril of the Internet

The Internet and e-mail pose serious legal issues for today's Catholic educator. Students routinely use the Internet to communicate and they expect to use it to communicate with teachers as well. Parents are requesting, even demanding, that they be able to access information about their children's academic performance via the Internet. With the best of intentions, a teacher can find himself or herself accused of improper behavior in communications with students. Administrators can be accused of violations of privacy because of information posted on school Web sites.

In the past month alone, this writer has received a half dozen or so queries from administrators with Internet issues. This article will discuss two of those issues: posting information on school Web sites and legal etiquette in student/teacher e-mails.

School Web Sites

A growing number of schools give parents passwords and allow them to access their children's academic records. Some schools record progress grades every few weeks. In some schools teachers post all student grades on the Internet and a parent uses a password to view the grades the student has received. These are perfectly acceptable practices that will continue.

People value their privacy. Parents have a right to expect that personal information, such as addresses and phone numbers, that the school requires them to provide will not be shared with others, even other parents, without their express or implied consent.

Administrators need to insure the following:

1. The school Web site is secure.

2. Only individuals with passwords may access student records and only the records of their own children.

3. School information does not violate privacy. For example, if school administrators wish to publish a school directory with student and parent addresses and phone numbers, they should ensure that either parents give written permission to include such information or the school handbook states certain information will be published unless the parent notifies the school in writing by a certain date that such information should not be included for his or her family. Similarly, parents should have the right to request that their children's photos not be placed on the school's Web site.

E-mail Issues

E-mail and instant messaging are examples of the blessing and the curse technology brings to schools. Teachers must understand that there is no privacy on the Internet. The same boundary issues that must be respected in oral communications with students must be respected in written ones, particularly when e-mail is involved. Many people may view what is written, so the test of publicity must always be kept in mind: How would I feel if this correspondence suddenly ended up on the front page of the newspaper or on the evening news? The following guidelines can aid teachers and staff in the appropriate use of e-mail:

1. Use your school e-mail account. Never use your home or personal e-mail account. Using a personal account can give an appearance of secrecy.

2. Always remember you are a professional rendering a service to students. You are not the student's friend or buddy.

3. Communicate only about school matters or matters that are appropriate to be discussed in school. Most especially avoid any communication that might be construed as having sexual overtones. Do not reply to any such e-mail you receive from students. Make and keep a copy of any such inappropriate communication and notify the principal.

4. Write as though you are certain that others will read what you write. Remember that a student can share your message with students and others by a simple push of a button.

5. Remember there is no such thing as a private e-mail.

6. Do not use instant messaging. Do not put students on your "buddy list." If you find that a student has added you to his or her list, ask that your name be removed and keep a written record of your request. Remember—people can make copies of instant messages and they can come back to haunt you. If you are involved in an academic chat room, use it appropriately.

7. Ask yourself, "If my principal or anyone asked to see this communication, would I be embarrassed by what I have written?" If the answer is "yes," don't send the e-mail.

8. Remember that the student you are e-mailing is someone's child. How would your feel if your child received the e-mail you are about to send? If you think your e-mail might somehow be misunderstood, don't send it.

9. Remember that boundaries must be respected in written correspondence as well as in oral communication. Don't push the boundaries of teacher/student relationships.

10. Finally, e-mail can be misinterpreted. Before sending an e-mail, ask yourself if someone might read something into it that you didn't intend or if your message might be misinterpreted. Communicate in person whenever possible.

January 2006

Pagers and Cell Phones in Schools and Programs: Should They Be Permitted? What Are the Legal Issues?

Before September 11, 2001, the vast majority of schools and programs forbade student possession and use of pagers and cell phones. There were probably quite a few reasons for the prohibition: (a) preserving the peace of the classroom and school so that pagers and phones weren't ringing or buzzing at inappropriate times, (b) ensuring that students were not talking on phones and taking pager messages when they should have been paying attention, and (c) trying to make it difficult, if not impossible, for drug deals to be conducted during the school day.

Good administrators have always tried to head off problems by removing sources of temptation. So banning pagers and cell phones became an expected part of school discipline codes. Most rules stated something to the effect that if a student were found with a cell phone or pager, the item would be confiscated and kept (a) until the end of the quarter, semester, or year or (b) until the parent came to pick up the contraband. Of course, like anything else, forbidden fruit is always sweeter and many students sought to beat the system; vibrating phones and pagers provided one answer.

Some administrators, recognizing a need for parents and students to be able to communicate, allowed students to bring the phones or pagers to the office. Soon storing, keeping them straight, and returning the right phone to the right student became problematic. The answer then seemed to be requiring students to keep phones and pagers in their lockers. Anyone who has been an administrator very long can attest that, in such a scenario, students would attempt to spend a great deal of time at their lockers.

Then, 9/11 happened and prevailing views about many subjects changed. Shortly after the tragedy, the author was traveling in Minnesota and several Catholic school administrators related that a number of their students' parents were flight attendants or pilots on Northwest Airlines, headquartered in Minneapolis. Students, who according to school policy should not have had cell phones in school, pulled them out and attempted to call their parents. Fortunately, no student had a parent on one of the hijacked planes, but administrators saw clearly what could have happened. So what polices should a school or program have on pager and cell phone use?

Legal Issues

There are legal issues involved in permitting students to carry cell phones in schools. Perhaps the most serious is that mentioned above, the potential to communicate about drug deals and drop-offs or other illegal activity. A second is the school's responsibility to provide the best possible education in the best possible learning environment, which can be compromised by ringing phones.

So should schools and programs allow students to bring pagers and cell phones to school? School officials are legally free to allow or forbid cell phones in schools, but this author believes the wisest course is to permit students to bring cell phones to school with a number of conditions. There appears to be no compelling reason to allow students to bring pagers, so administrators should make what they believe to be the best decision about their use.

Suggested Policy Points

Administrators may wish to adopt a policy stating that students are allowed to bring cell phones to school, but that they are to stay in the off position during the school day. A school official who observes a student talking on a phone or who hears a phone ringing at an inappropriate time should confiscate the offender's phone. Return of the phone should follow already-established rules such as those suggested above.

Handbooks/policies should outline what is allowed in the use of cell phones. Harassment of any kind should be prohibited. Camera phones pose difficulties as they can be used to copy from students' papers or to make copies of exams. The growing practice of "skirting," taking a picture under a girl's skirt, certainly is disrespectful and violates privacy. Originally, some schools outlawed camera phones, but it is becoming increasingly difficult to find phones without cameras. So a broad statement about abuse of cell phone privileges might be in order. The following is a suggested protocol for cell phone possession and use:

Cell phones may be brought to school or class or activity under the following conditions:

1. Phones must be kept in the off position from _____ (time) to _____ (time).

2. No cell phones may be used to take pictures.

3. No harassment or threatening of individuals via the cell phone is permitted.

4. Cell phones may not be used for playing games, accessing Internet or e-mail, gambling, or making purchases of any kind.

5. Those who violate any of the rules on cell phones may forfeit their privileges of bringing them to school. 𝕁𝕋ℝ

MAY 2006

BLOGGING: HOW FAR CAN A CATHOLIC SCHOOL GO IN REGULATING STUDENT CONDUCT?

Each academic year offers at least one new legal issue demanding attention. This year's appears to be blogging. Not so long ago, many readers would not have recognized the term, which means the keeping of an online log or journal. The Web site myspace.com and its progeny began innocently enough. Adults were able to share thoughts with other bloggers and site visitors. Some people, unable to find publishers for articles, began to post them through blogs and eventually sell subscriptions to their sites or works. While blogs were generally more sophisticated than chat rooms in terms of conversation type and content, site providers provided little or no monitoring of content or bloggers. Sites often include a statement that all bloggers must be at least 16 or 18 years old, but there is no way to ensure that individuals under the minimum age will not have access.

In the past several months, the writer has received more phone calls and e-mail inquiries about blogging than any other topic. Students generally blog from home, not school, but two problem areas cause administrative concern: (a) blogger safety and (b) the appropriateness of what the blogger posts.

Safety

Bloggers often post identifying personal information that can have tragic consequences. Anyone with Internet access, including sexual predators and murderers, can log onto a blog. Many young people do not seem to understand mortality, at least their own. They believe that bad things happen only to other people. However, nothing prevents a predator from noting a child or adolescent's picture, address, phone number, school, extracurricular activities, etc., and making plans to intercept the young person. Recently, at a diocesan superintendent's request, the writer gave a brief talk on blogging and Internet safety to an audience of high school students who were attentive, polite, and challenging. However, most of them could not "get" it—that posting pictures and personal information on blogs or other sites could prove fatal. "Come on, Sister," protested one particularly attractive teenage girl, "Nothing like that would happen here. This isn't a big city; it's a small town." Students at Columbine High School probably held similar beliefs before tragedy occurred. No one's safety can be guaranteed.

Educator responsibilities do not begin and end with the school day. Student safety must be paramount. Whatever can be done to protect students and educate parents should be done, regardless of whether the law requires it.

Student Discipline

Any seasoned administrator has probably had at least one parent or student argue, "It happened outside school/the school day. You can't punish me for what I did on my own time." The fact, however, is that a Catholic school or program administrator can impose consequences for conduct occurring outside school. What students do off campus can have a detrimental impact on a school's or program's reputation. As long as the parent/student handbook, which can and should be a contract, states that the administration reserves the right to discipline students for off-campus conduct, courts will not interfere. The school should require that before the student's first day of attendance, parents sign a statement that they agree to be bound by the handbook's rules and regulations. Courts will uphold rules and regulations that are not illegal.

Educators are already familiar with the issues arising from student threats conveyed through e-mail. Blogging provides another venue for making threats. Threats are threats wherever they are made.

A more common problem occurs when students make negative, often untruthful statements about staff and other students. The Web site Ratemyteachers.com, in addition to blogs, offers opportunities to post potentially defamatory statements. Holding that teachers were, in effect, quasi-public figures and had to expect a certain amount of "grief" from parents and students, courts in the past were reluctant to find in favor of teachers who brought defamation suits against parents or students. Such is no longer the case. Several state courts have ruled that teachers and administrators have the same right to their reputations as other people. If defamed, therefore, educators have a right to sue.

Additionally, school administrators can punish students who defame others in the school community. Deliberate defamation of others is not consistent with Christian values and students should be held accountable for intentional harm they cause others.

Use of School Name and Logo

The school or parish owns the school or program's name and administrators have the right to restrict its use. An administrator can determine that a Saturday trip to an amusement park organized by parents is not a school event and can decline to allow the use of the school name. In the same way, rules can prohibit unauthorized use of names and logos on blogs.

What Would Jesus Do?

In prayer, administrators will find direction as they seek to keep people and their reputations safe, just as Jesus would. 〽️

Policy, GOVERNANCE, and BOARDS

March 1992

Catholic Schools and Finance: How Does the Law Apply?

⌒〰〰〰⌒

Principals spend much of their time budgeting, collecting tuition, attempting to raise money, and worrying about money. It can be very easy to overlook the fact that civil law must be considered when financial policies are developed and implemented.

Contract Law

One aspect of civil law that affects the operation of Catholic schools and their financial policies is contract law. The Catholic school is a private institution that is not required to grant constitutional protection. People in Catholic schools surrender their constitutional protection, as it were, when they enter. These people are not, however, left unprotected. The provisions of the contract they have with the school determine their rights.

Since the school and those who set its policy determine the contents of contracts, principals should ensure that contracts clearly state financial expectations (e.g., amount of tuition charged, payment arrangements, penalties for delayed payments). Carefully written documents that leave little, if any, room for disagreement on their meaning are administrators' best protection against allegations of unfairness and civil lawsuits.

A contract is an agreement between two parties. Five elements must be present in a legal contract: (a) mutual assent (b) by legally competent parties (c) for consideration (d) to subject matter that is legal and (e) in the form of an agreement that is legal.

Mutual consent implies that two parties entering into a contract agree to its provisions. A Catholic school agrees to provide an education to a student and, in return, parents accept that offer.

Legally competent parties imply that the parties entering into the contract are legally qualified to make the agreement. Parents are legally competent to agree to pay tuition and to meet other obligations. Minor students are not legally competent, so parents or guardians must sign contracts on their behalf.

Consideration is what each party agrees to do for the other. The Catholic school agrees to provide educational services to a student in return for payment of tuition and adherence to school rules.

Legal subject matter assumes that the provisions of the contract are lawful. Caution is in order here. Some Catholic schools may consider requiring parents to work at bingo games or Las Vegas nights a condition of enrollment. Most states do not permit organizations to use nonvoluntary workers in operations that state law considers to be gambling. Catholic schools can require service of parents and that service can be given in bingo games or church festivals, but options should be given for people who do not wish to participate in games of chance.

Legal form may vary from state to state. Some states require contracts to be in writing or to be witnessed. It is advisable that contracts be in writing because such a practice lessens the possibility of argument later.

Contracts are not limited to the documents that people sign. Courts can and do construe school handbooks as contractual documents. A school's parent/student handbook constitutes a contract between the parent and the school. To protect everyone, parents should be required to sign a statement such as "We have read this handbook and agree to be governed by it." Certainly, there is an assumption that a person who enrolls a child in a school agrees to be bound by the rules and regulations of the school. That assumption, however, becomes fact when a written statement to that effect is on file in the school.

Tuition Contracts

Many schools now require parents to sign tuition contracts or include all financial policies in the parent/student handbook. Tuition contracts provide evidence that a debt is owed the school. In the 1987 case of *Thomas Jefferson School v. Kapros,* 728 S.W.2d 315, the court held that a school could expel a student according to its rules and that parents could be required to pay the full year's tuition since they had signed a contract binding them to the payment of liquidated damages if the child did not complete the school year. Such a judgment may seem harsh at first glance.

Administrators, however, budget for expenses based on a certain number of students. Those expenses remain even if students withdraw. As difficult as it may be, those responsible for Catholic schools must remember that the school, while primarily a ministry, is also a business that must pay bills.

Principals and other policymakers should remember that exceptions to a policy can always be made. For example, if a parent signs a tuition contract and is later transferred to another city, the principal should be able to waive the payment of the remainder of the tuition. If, however, a student decides he or she would rather go to a different school, the principal may require the parents to pay the remaining tuition.

Tithing as Tuition

The practice of requiring parents to tithe or make a certain contribution in the collection basket weekly so that their children can attend the parish school poses special problems if those parents then take income tax deductions for the contributions. Section 170 of the Internal Revenue Code governs such a practice and does not allow charitable deductions for tuition. Revenue Ruling 83-104 states in part: "Payments made by a taxpayer on behalf of children attending parochial or other church-sponsored SCHOOLS are not allowable deductions as CONTRIBUTIONS either to the SCHOOL or to the religious organization operating the SCHOOL if the payments are earmarked for such children."

A noted authority on tax law, Professor Norvie Lay of the University of Louisville's School of Law, cautions against any quid pro quo arrangement:

> When attendance at a school which is tuition-driven is equated with making contributions to the organization, Treasury will disallow the deduction. A donative intent is necessary for a deduction to be allowed. If children of parents who don't contribute are not permitted to attend school, Treasury will probably view the contribution as a tuition substitute and it will be disallowed.

Professor Lay suggests that an appropriate question is "How can we accomplish what we want without violating the law?" He offers one answer:

> If everyone is eligible to attend the school and contributions are made directly to the church whose budget officers determine what amount goes to the school, a quid pro quo situation can be avoided, and a charitable deduction will probably be allowed.

Thus, one approach to tithing is a suggested minimum contribution for all parishioners. Any contributing parishioner would be entitled to participate in all parish programs, including the school. The issue is complex. Pastors, principals, and boards, however, should be aware of ramifications involving the IRS when tuition is tied to contributions made to the parish. They should never suggest that parents can procure an education for their children, support the church, and earn a tax deduction for a charitable contribution with one expenditure of funds. Administrators wishing to use tithing as tuition should consult with diocesan attorneys to ensure that the parish operates within existing laws.

Fees and Fund-Raising

Pastors, principals, and boards should give serious consideration to developing a policy governing fees, particularly in the area of refunds. The wisest course is to state that all fees are nonrefundable. The administrator could retain the right to make exceptions when appropriate.

Fund-raising is a fact of life in Catholic schools. Principals should ensure that parents and students understand what is expected of them in this regard. The parent/student handbook is a good place for this information.

Careful planning, consultation with diocesan or school attorneys, and periodic review of policies and procedures should help the school and those responsible for it to keep it functioning in a financially and legally sound manner.

Recent Developments

A Louisiana public school was found guilty of negligence in the case of a 6-year-old boy who left the school grounds and was injured, *Sutton v. Duplessis,* 584 So2d 362 (La., 1991). The school had an early dismissal, and school officials testified that a notice of the early dismissal had been sent to parents via their children. The child's mother claimed she had never received the notice.

When the mother did not call for her two children, they were sent to the principal's office and were instructed not to leave the school. A secretary was present, but she was working and did not notice that one child did leave the grounds. In returning to the school, he ran into a moving automobile and sustained injuries.

The appeals court ruled that the board's failure to supervise the child in a reasonable manner was the sole legal cause of the injuries. The court overruled a portion of the lower court's ruling that found the mother partially responsible and stated that the school's negligence was both the cause and the legal cause of the injuries: "The fact that [the child] was able to leave the school grounds alone, unnoticed by any school authority, is the sole legal cause of his injury."

Educators can be held liable for injuries that could have been foreseen. The court found that this child's injuries were foreseeable and the school should have provided appropriate supervision: "The possibility that parents occasionally will not show up on time to get their children . . . is certainly foreseeable by school authorities. Therefore, the school must have a policy to ensure that younger students are properly supervised and do not leave the school unattended."

This case illustrates the necessity for supervision plans for students who are present on school grounds before and after school. School officials cannot evade responsibility by adopting policies stating that the school is not responsible for students who arrive before or remain after a certain time.

The age of the student is certainly a factor. Elementary school administrators should give serious consideration to establishing an extended-care program and to adopting a policy that students present when no supervision is available will be placed in the program and parents will be billed for the service. People responsible for older students, even those in high school, should ensure that there is a plan for supervising early arrivals and those who remain after school has been dismissed. Both the welfare of the students and the legal well-being of the school will profit by observance of these guidelines. 📰

January 1994
Policy Development: Some Considerations

The development, adoption, and implementation of policies are tasks claiming much of Catholic school administrators, board members, and pastors today. Gone are the days when policy was whatever Sister or Father said it was. Today, those affected by policies want the right to at least be heard on policy development. Thus, all involved in the operation of Catholic schools should understand what is meant by the term policy, including what is covered and what is not. Every administrative act is not a policy; wise individuals understand the parameters of policy-making.

As most people are aware, the number of lawsuits brought against the Catholic Church is growing. The reluctance that used to keep individuals from attempting to settle differences with the church in court has largely disappeared. Proper policy formation can help ensure that Catholic schools have the best possible legal position should they face lawsuits in the future.

A Working Definition

A policy is a guide for discretionary action. Policy determines what is to be done, not how it is to be done. For example, a school may have a policy mandating a dress code or a uniform. The details of the dress code (what types of clothes can and cannot be worn) and the color and style of a uniform are matters of administration, or how the policy is implemented. Boards set policies; principals implement them.

The principal has a right to expect that the administration of the school is his or her responsibility and that board members will not interfere in the day-to-day running of the school. It is often easy for a board member to succumb to the temptation to get involved in disciplinary matters, academic disputes, or faculty/principal problems. A board member has to remember that his or her responsibilities are twofold: (a) Develop policies and (b) support the people and activities that implement those policies.

Administration is the principal's job, policy recommendation is the board's job, and ratification is the pastor's job. Policies are broad, general guidelines. Unfortunately, many people do not understand these distinctions and the result is a blurring of roles. When the pastor or board begins to interfere in the day-to-day operation of the school, the principal's authority is undermined. If parents and teachers know that they can get a pastor or a board to intervene in disputes over the principal's administration of the school before the grievance is presented to the principal, an unhealthy dynamic occurs and no one truly benefits.

Subsidiarity

Subsidiarity, solving all problems at the lowest possible level, should be one principle guiding policy development in the Catholic school. Thus, a parent or student who wants to register a complaint about a teacher must first speak with the teacher before making that complaint to the teacher's superior. A person who wants to complain about the action of a principal must meet with the principal before voicing the grievance to a pastor or school board.

If everyone in Catholic schools practiced these principles, schools would be much happier places. More problems would get solved at the lowest level, with the person about whom a complaint is lodged. If the complainant does not want to face the source of the problem, the complaint may well be unjustified. Only problems that have been presented to the appropriate individual would progress to the next level if a solution could not be found at the lower level. Obviously, in a few cases this procedure would not be implemented. For example, one might not require an 8-year-old to face a teacher accused of molesting the student. In a situation in which a person claims that he or she cannot face the individual because of fear of retribution, the superior can offer to attend the conference. Subsidiarity, then, can be a powerful value in policy formulation, adoption, and implementation.

Subsidiarity is Gospel-based. Jesus tells us, "If you are bringing your gift to the altar and you remember that your brother or sister has something against you, leave your gift at the altar and go and have it out with your brother or your sister." The Gospel does not direct us to discuss the problem with someone other than or superior to the brother or sister.

Principals' Legal Duties

Principals have two legal duties: (a) to make, develop, and communicate rules and policies and (b) to supervise teachers. Someone else, such as a board of directors, a pastor, or a religious community, may approve the policies, but it seems appropriate for the principal to write and present at least the first drafts of policies.

School board members are not usually professional educators, nor are pastors. The role of the school board may be to advise on or approve policy, but the principal should be considered the educational expert. Thus, it is the principal's task to formulate educational policies. Once formulated, the policies can be presented to boards, pastors, or other appropriate bodies for adoption.

Adoption of policies should not be a pro forma activity. Board members should discuss the policy and be able to ask the principal questions about it. If the board decides it cannot adopt the policy as presented by the principal, the board should call an executive session in which board members can state their views and listen to those of the principal. The principal might be asked to develop different policy implementation plans.

Goals and objectives are ways of implementing policies. The principal may be able to make modifications acceptable to the board. Ideally, the board and the principal can come to some understanding or compromise. If no compromise can be reached that both parties can support, the board may have to call in an outside facilitator or arbitrator.

The principal should be an ex officio member of all board committees. While the principal may not be able to attend every committee meeting, he or she should be present whenever possible and certainly when policy additions, deletions, or modifications are discussed.

Local Policies and Dioceses

Those who make policy in a local situation must understand that they have duties to the diocese and to the larger church. If a parish or diocese owns the school, policies must be consistent with those established by the diocese. If the policy-makers cannot support a given diocesan policy, change must be sought through appropriate channels. A Catholic institution is not free to adopt a policy at variance with established diocesan policy. An institution's responsibility is clear: to uphold the policies of the diocese and to develop local policies that are in harmony with those of the diocese.

The same principles apply to an institution sponsored by a religious congregation. The philosophy and goals of the sponsoring group must be apparent in any policy. Since a Catholic institution exists under the primary authority of the bishop and is subject to him in matters of faith and morals, local policies in such matters should be consistent with those of the diocese.

Handbooks and Policy

The beginning point for policy development should be the school's philosophy. Every school should have a clearly written philosophy available to teachers, parents, and, as far as possible, students. The life of the school should flow from the philosophy.

The school board (or other appropriate party) should annually review and accept all faculty, parent, and student handbooks as a matter of policy. If policies are clearly written, there is less possibility of misunderstanding.

Recent Developments

Two recent cases should be of interest to the Catholic school administrator. In the 1993 case of *Geary v. Visitation of Blessed Virgin Mary Parish School* (C.A. Pa.), No. 93-1062, the Third Circuit ruled that the Age Discrimination in Employment Act (ADEA) could be applied to the lay faculty of a religious school and that such application does not violate the First Amendment's requirement of separation of church and state. However, if a religious principle is involved, the ADEA will apply only if the plaintiff does not violate accepted religious practices and beliefs.

Catholic school administrators must ensure that employment practices are free from age bias. If a person over 40 is denied employment in favor of a younger person who draws a lower salary, age discrimination can be involved. Federal antidiscrimination law can apply to Catholic schools; this case serves as an illustration of this reality.

In a 1993 New York appellate case, *Mix v. South Seneca Cent. of School Dist.* (N.Y.A.D. 4 Dept.), the court ruled that a public elementary school was not liable for injuries when one child struck another with a screwdriver on the playground when school was not in session. In ruling for the school district, the court held that the school did not create the condition or have notice of it, and that the throwing of the screwdriver constituted a superseding cause. In light of these factors, the school was absolved of liability.

However, the court did not say that schools were not liable for accidents occurring when school is not in session. Here, the screwdriver and the child's misuse of the tool resulted in injury. One can easily see how a dangerous condition, such as a damaged swing, could be within the school's control. A child injured by damaged equipment could have a cause of action even if the injury occurred during hours when the school was not in session. 🖎

September 1994
Catholic School Boards and the Law

School year beginnings offer many activities and challenges for the principal, the pastor, and others who work in the ministry of Catholic education. One important activity is the opening board meeting. Since new board members may be attending their first meeting, many questions and concerns may surface. Good orientation helps board members understand their roles and those of the principal and pastor. Board members with a clear understanding of board operating procedures have a greater chance of functioning efficiently and effectively than those without such an understanding.

The relationships between and among pastors, administrators, and board members should be mutually beneficial. Thus, it is important that the legal role of the board be carefully outlined and the scope of its authority delineated. Board members have a right to the information and documents they need to perform their job effectively.

Canon Law

Canon law governs the functioning of boards, just as civil law does. There is no such creature as a board with absolute jurisdiction, even if the educational institution is separately incorporated. Any school or program that calls itself Catholic is subject to the authority of the bishop in what was traditionally called "matters of faith and morals." Canon 803, Section 3, states, "No school, even if it in fact is Catholic, may bear the title 'Catholic school' except by the consent of the competent ecclesiastical authority."

Types of Boards

Two types of boards function in Catholic schools: consultative boards and boards with limited jurisdiction. A consultative board is generally established by the pastor or by diocesan policy. This board is responsible for developing and/or approving policies. The pastor has the final authority to accept the recommendations of the consultative board. This structure seems to be in place in the majority of parish schools in this country.

A board with limited jurisdiction has been defined as one "constituted by the pastor to govern the parish education program, subject to certain decisions which are reserved to the pastor and the bishop" (CACE/NABE, *A Primer on Educational Governance,* p. 27). This board has more freedom in decision- making than the consultative board. Pastors and bishops can delegate power, but they cannot delegate responsibility.

The civil law doctrine of *respondeat superior* requires that a superior answer for the acts of subordinates. Generally if a Catholic school board is sued for its actions, the pastor and bishop will be sued as well. Private schools owned by religious congregations or other structures such as boards of trustees may have either consultative boards or boards with limited jurisdiction.

Authority

The school board has the power to recommend and/or adopt certain courses of action. Board members must understand that power is vested in the board as a body, not in individual members. The role of the board is development of policy, even if policy has to be approved at a higher level.

Policy is usually defined as a guide for discretionary action. Thus, policy will dictate what the board wishes to be done. Policy is not concerned with administration or implementation; the board should not become involved in how its directives will be implemented or with the people who will implement them. For example, a board might state as a policy that students are to wear uniforms. The board would not be concerned with what company supplies the uniforms or what color is selected. Such questions are administrative ones and should be dealt with by the principal, who is the chief executive officer of the school.

The principal, as the educational leader, should certainly suggest policies and perhaps write the first drafts of policies. The board then recommends or sets policy, the implementation of which is the principal's responsibility. Administrative decisions are the day-to-day management choices of the principal. It is important for everyone involved to understand these distinctions.

Generally boards will recommend or set policies in the major areas of program, finance, personnel, and plant. A board might approve the budget, approve programs and handbooks, set tuition, determine hiring and dismissal policies, and possibly oversee school facility planning. Other areas of board action might include grievance procedures, extra- and cocurricular activities, building safety and usage, and disciplinary code approval.

When tensions arise, board members must keep their responsibilities to the diocese and to the church in view. If a board member cannot support a policy (support does not necessarily mean agreement, but it does mean a willingness to live with and support the decision), then the member must seek change through appropriate channels. If change cannot be achieved and a board member still cannot support the policy in question, then the person's only real choice is to resign from the board. The board of a parish or diocesan school is not free to adopt a policy at variance with those of the diocese.

This author believes that schools owned by religious communities or other legal entities should strive to abide by reasonable diocesan directives and be able to articulate a rationale for difference when those directives are not followed. For example, any school that calls itself Catholic should adhere to all regulations relating to the Catholic character of the school. In other areas, such as salary scales and benefits, there may be differences. Attempting to follow diocesan guidelines whenever possible strengthens the school as part of the Catholic Church in a given diocese.

Board members, then, have two basic responsibilities: to recommend or approve policies and to support the people who implement those policies. Becoming involved in internal school conflicts only weakens the authority of both the board and the administrator. The principal, however, should keep board members informed about problematic or potentially problematic situations so that board members will be able to respond intelligently if questioned.

Board Handbooks

Board members will find a thorough handbook an invaluable aid in learning about the school and board membership. Orientation can be structured around the contents of the handbook. The handbook should begin with the school or program philosophy, a statement that answers the question "What do we as Catholic educators say that we are doing in this school, program, or activity?"

The handbook should also include the constitution and bylaws of the board. Parish and diocesan schools and programs may have set bylaws and constitutions from the bishop or his delegate. These documents, written by people with authority, should provide detailed information about the authority, accountability, role of the board, and practical aspects of membership, procedures, and meetings.

All policies, including diocesan policies and policies adopted by the board, should be included in the handbook. Policies should be dated and revisions clearly noted. Formal minutes of all meetings should be kept. Board members should be responsible for filing these minutes in their handbooks and keeping them in good order so that they can be passed on to their successors.

Appropriate financial information, such as budgets and audits, should be readily available in the handbook. Official school handbooks should be included in appendices or as separate documents in a board binder.

Confidentiality

Board members have a solemn responsibility to keep the confidences they receive in their capacities as board members. This responsibility should be noted in the handbook and stressed in orientation so that no board member loses sight of this trust.

Member Liability

Consultative board members may seem to be immune to civil liability for actions the board takes, since someone such as a pastor is free to take or decline the advice the board offers. Members serving on boards of limited jurisdiction, however, may be liable for actions taken within that jurisdiction if they knew or should have known that the actions violated people's rights. Same states have laws exempting people serving on boards of directors of nonprofit institutions from liability for good-faith actions. The law leaves open the question of liability for actions alleged to have been taken in bad faith.

Even though lawsuits against boards of directors of Catholic schools and parishes are rare, it seems only just that board members be protected from the threat of such action with board or director liability insurance.

[Note: The emerging trend in this country, particularly at the elementary school level, is to have advisory or consultative boards rather than ones with limited jurisdiction. Since the person or entity receiving the advice is not required to act on it, members of consultative boards will not be held liable for recommended actions unless the recommendation is outrageous and an injury occurs (e.g., advising the pastor to sell 600 tickets to a function held in a facility with an occupancy limit of 200, since the building inspector is an alumnus and probably wouldn't report the violation; if injury occurs or is exacerbated by the crowded conditions, the board could conceivably be held liable).]

MAY 2004
KEEPING LEGALLY SOUND MINUTES

Education board members and principals often ask questions about the keeping of minutes: "How do we best keep minutes? What should be in the minutes? Who should have access?"

Many theories abound. Some people advise recording everything that transpires in a meeting. Others advise writing as little as possible. Others suggest a compromise between the two positions. One reality is ever-present, however. What is written becomes a legal record and can be used both for and against the institution. Developing a planned, orderly, consistent approach to taking and keeping minutes is imperative.

Does State Law Govern Catholic Education Board Meetings?

Catholic education boards govern private, not-for-profit, 501 (c) 3 organizations, which are not generally subject to the same regulations as public organizations. Therefore, in the majority of cases, so-called sunshine laws requiring that meetings and records of meetings be open to public scrutiny will not apply.

What Are Minutes?

Minutes are the written, legal record of actions taken at an official meeting of an official body. Robert's Rules of Order, the bible for meeting process, states that the following should be included in minutes:

1. Name of the organization (school board, parish council, parents' organization, etc.)

2. Date of the meeting

3. Place of the meeting (particularly if the meeting is held at other than the customary meeting place)

4. Presence of the regular presiding officer (president, principal, chair) and recording secretary or their substitutes

5. Names of members present and absent

6. Approval of the minutes of the last scheduled meeting of the board (if the minutes are corrected, the corrections should be made in writing on the written minutes presented to the body for approval; new, corrected minutes should not be generated)

7. Officer and committee reports (the fact that a report was given is generally sufficient; the report can also be included as an attachment to the minutes)

8. All motions including (a) the name of the person who made the motion, (b) the fact that the motion was the seconded (the name of the person seconding the motion is not absolutely required), and (c) the complete text of the motion

9. The vote on the motion including (a) the number of votes for and against, and (b) if a roll call vote is taken, the names of those voting for and against

10. Any appeals or points of order taken (not an ordinary occurrence)

11. Beginning and ending times of the meeting

How Detailed Should the Minutes Be?

Conventional wisdom suggests that less, rather than more, is the acceptable norm. In preparing for this article, the author consulted a number of attorney colleagues practicing in the not-for-profit arena. To a person, the advice given was this: "Say as little as possible. Accurately record actions taken. Do not document discussion or who said what. Anything you write can be used against you in a court of law, especially when taken out of context."

How Should Executive Session Meetings Be Documented?

An executive session occurs when the board determines it will meet with only the members and guests invited for a specific reason, such as attorneys, in a confidential session. A wise course of action is to record only actions taken (motions passed). Much confidential information is often shared in executive sessions, such as personnel and financial information. The information and the discussion surrounding it should not be recorded in the minutes. Additionally, if legal counsel is present at an executive session, the attorney/client privilege may be lost if legal advice and discussion are recorded in the minutes.

Who Should Have Access to Minutes?

To a great extent, the answer to this question should be determined at the local level. Many parishes routinely publish the minutes of the parish council, for example, in the parish bulletin. Some schools post the minutes of their board meetings on the school's Web site.

Members of the board receive copies of the minutes. Policy should determine who else has access. A board might keep separate records of executive-session meetings and not allow access to those records to anyone other than board members.

Dos and Don'ts for Keeping Minutes

1. Do record only what must be recorded.

2. Don't document discussion. Do record the names of those making motions or, if a roll call vote is taken, who voted for and against a particular motion.

3. Do follow the rule "Whatever is written should be specific, behaviorally oriented, and verifiable." Example: "Mr. Jones made the following motion: 'The salary for beginning teachers with no experience will be $24,000 for the 2004–05 school year.' After being seconded, the motion passed unanimously."

4. Do enact a policy governing access to minutes.

5. Keep an accurate, complete set of official minutes in a safe, secure place.

MAY 2005
CONFLICT OF INTEREST

As the school year winds to an end, busy administrators and board chairs often meet to discuss plans for the next academic year and the policies and procedures that will guide that new year. One area that deserves and is getting increasing attention is conflict of interest. Historically, if the topic has been considered at all, it may have been only within the context of education boards. However, there is grist for the conflict of interest mill in many situations in Catholic schools and programs. This column offers a brief discussion of the topic and some recommendations.

A Definition

Black's Law Dictionary, the bible of all things legal, offers this definition of conflict of interest:

> Term used in connection with public officials and fiduciaries and their relationship to matters of private interest or gain to them. Generally, when used to suggest disqualification of a public official from performing his sworn duty, term "conflict of interest" refers to a clash between public interest and the private pecuniary interest of the individual concerned. . . . A situation in which regard for one duty tends to lead to disregard of another.

While once used only in public situations, the term is now routinely used in both public and private situations. A conflict of interest occurs when an official might be unable to be objective and make fair decisions because of his or her interest in both parties. For example, the situation may arise when a school needs the services of an architect, engineer, or contractor. It is not unusual for such an individual to be sitting on the board and to be prepared to offer services to the institution at a sizeable discount. Board members' first inclination may be to vote for the board member's company to provide the service. After all, everyone knows the individual and a discount is being offered. However, an observer as well as a competing firm might raise questions: "Were bids sought? If not, why not? If yes, did they follow procedure and was each provider asked to bid on the same services? And did the individual board member supplying the service or who was awarded the contract have any say in the decision?"

No board member whose company or self is being awarded a contract can honestly say that there is no conflict of interest in such a situation. At the very least, the board member should (a) declare the conflict, (b) absent himself or herself from discussion, and (c) abstain from any vote. The same actions should be taken if a board member's relative is being considered for a business contract or for employment at or termination from the institution.

Other Conflicts

Other types of conflicts of interest can arise among non-board members. A teacher whose son is in trouble can hardly be objective about the situation and clearly has a conflict of interest.

Friendship can pose conflicts as well. Since a Catholic school or program is first a community of faith, it is only natural that friendships will develop. Administrators in particular must ensure that they always take actions with the best interests of the school, parish, or program in view, without regard to how their friendship with another will be affected. If an administrator believes he or she cannot be objective, the honest approach is to make that belief known and to allow someone else to serve as decision-maker.

A conflict of interest is not necessarily a bad thing as long as the person with the conflict is open about it and does not attempt to influence decision-making on issues affecting his or her personal, business, or other interests.

Signing Conflict of Interest Statements

It is routine for members of boards of directors and trustees to be asked to sign statements declaring any known conflicts of interests and agreeing to make known any conflicts that may arise. Boards may wish to consider asking principals and employees to sign such statements as well. A conflict of interest statement can be complex or very simple. A person can be asked to sign a document in which he or she lists any known conflict and agrees to make known any conflict that may arise in the future.

A friend of the author once observed that every action taken in a school or other forum should pass three tests: (a) smell, (b) newspaper, and (c) Mom. Does the situation "smell" bad to the casual observer? If yes, there is more than likely a problem to be considered. Would the actor be ashamed to see the action reported on the front page of the newspaper or to tell his or her mother about it? If yes to either or both, there is a problem. Or perhaps the best test is the one most ask everyday: "Would Jesus do this?"

If we can answer that question, we will know what to do and we will avoid conflict of interest.

Beginning and
END-OF-YEAR Tips

September 1996
Back to School: A Legal Issues Checklist

᠀ᘉᗆᗞ

As back-to-school bells ring, the Catholic educational administrator probably prepares to-do lists of important tasks, relegating legal issues to a back burner. Yet the beginning of the year presents an opportunity to review existing policies and procedures one last time and to ensure that everything needed for a lawful school year is in place. This article offers a checklist of crucial legal needs.

Handbooks

Since the parent/student handbook can constitute part of the contract between the school and the parent, it is important that all parents be given a handbook and be required to sign a statement that they have read and agree to be governed it.

Teachers should have read the entire faculty handbook and the parent/student handbook as well. Many administrators require teachers and other staff members to sign a statement that they have received and read the handbooks. The principal should allow time at one of the first faculty meetings to discuss and clarify any issues. Changes in operational policy from the preceding year should be highlighted.

Child Abuse Reporting

Since all 50 states have child abuse reporting laws, the principal or other educational administrator will want to spend time at an early faculty/staff meeting reviewing the statutory requirements. The three types of reportable abuse—sexual, physical, and emotional—should be defined and discussed.

Particular attention should be paid to the concepts of suspicion and reason to believe. The procedure for making a report should be explained, and each teacher should have a copy of the current state law. The administrator should stress that the person responsible for reporting to the appropriate agency is the teacher or staff member who suspects that abuse may occur and that one is not relieved of that duty simply because a colleague or supervisor is told of the suspicion.

Facilities

Before teachers arrive, the administrator should conduct a walk-though of the buildings and campus with an eye to identifying any existing or potential hazards. At the first faculty meeting, teachers should be encouraged to examine their instructional areas and report any problems to the chief administrator or other designated individual.

Forms

Before teachers arrive, the administrator should ensure that all teachers have an adequate supply of forms and know how to use them. Any new forms and procedures should be explained.

A properly completed emergency sheet should be on file for each student enrolled. If this year seems a good time to update or revise the existing form, administrators should consider the following:

- Obtaining at least two, preferably three or four, names of people who can be contacted in the event of an emergency

- Obtaining parent or guardian authorization to seek medical attention and requiring that the signature(s) on the authorization be notarized

Supervision

The beginning of the year is an ideal time to highlight teacher and staff responsibility for supervising students. Staff must understand that they are never really off duty on campus if students are present and need their oversight. Courts will not relieve a teacher of liability for student injury simply because the teacher was not on duty when an injury occurred. Supervision is everyone's responsibility and everyone needs to understand that reality.

As has often been stated, supervision is a mental as well as a physical act. It is not enough that a supervising individual be physically present; he or she must be mentally present as well. Situations that present special problems should be addressed. For example, playground supervision is a veritable land mine of potential liability. Teachers must understand that they must focus their attention on the children, not on conversation with other adults who may share supervisory duties or on other distractions.

Volunteers

As parents and other volunteers prepare to assume their duties in the school, the administrator should schedule an orientation for all volunteers and require attendance at it. If no volunteer handbook is available, at least a few pages of instructions on school policies and procedures are in order. The administrator should assure volunteers that there is no such thing as a stupid question. It a volunteer is uncertain how to proceed in a given situation, a teacher or administrator should be consulted.

No checklist is perfect, but reflection on the topic areas discussed above may help to prevent legal problems during the year. 𝒯ℛ

May 1998
End-of-the-Year Legal Checklist

∾

The school year is over and the administrator realizes that a new academic year approaches. While compiling and filing end-of-year reports, teacher evaluations, report cards, and other student records, administrators must consider those ever-present legal concerns that seem to have a way of cropping up at inopportune times. This column presents a legal checklist, accompanied by suggestions.

Handbooks

Are the parent/student and faculty handbooks in good order? Are staff members satisfied with them? Have suggested revisions been entered under the appropriate categories? (See earlier columns or the NCEA publication School Handbooks for specific, issue-by-issue advice.)

Have all handbooks been checked against diocesan or other governing policies to be sure that no conflict exists? Have any new state or local laws and regulations been enacted that may affect existing policy and, if so, have handbooks been appropriately modified? If not, have plans been made to do so? Has the advisory board or board of directors reviewed and ratified the handbooks or recommended ratification to the pastor or other appropriate parties? Is the ratification noted in handbooks?

Have new or revised handbooks been distributed to parents and staff? If not, is there a plan for distribution? Are signed forms agreeing to be bound by handbook policy required from parents? Is there a plan for collecting such forms? Are penalties for not returning forms clearly articulated, and is there a plan for imposing those penalties?

Field Trip Policies and Forms

While field trip forms and policies should be found in the appropriate handbooks, they should receive special administrative attention before the beginning of the new year. Is there a standard form that must be used? Does that form include (a) parental request that the student be allowed to participate in the off-site activity, (b) parental permission for such participation, and (c) parental release/identification/waiver of school responsibility or liability in the event of accident or injury?

Does the school have parental signature cards for each student in the school? Does the school have a procedure for checking forms against signature cards for verification purposes before departure? Does a reliable person have responsibility for this task? Permission forms should be retained for at least one year after the trip. Are they? Where are they kept?

Is there a policy that no student will be allowed to participate in off-campus activities without a signed, official school permission slip? It should be noted that telephone calls will not be accepted in lieu of permission slips. Faxed permission slips may be permitted, if desired.

Medication and Medical Releases

Does the school have a policy, noted in the handbook, on the use of nonprescription and prescription drugs? Is it enforced? Are there clear consequences for failure to follow the policy?

Does the school have a medical release form in which the parent gives permission (or withholds it) for school officials to seek hospital or other emergency treatment for the student when necessary? Does the form request the names of physicians and preferred health care facilities? Does the form request insurance information? Does the school have a procedure for collecting and using this information? Are copies of forms (or the original forms) available to supervisors of off-site activities?

Extracurricular Activities

Do all activities have moderators? Rules for participation? Are issues of student presence on school grounds or in buildings before and after activities addressed?

Crisis and Safety Plans

Does the school have a crisis plan? Is there a code word or phrase, such as "Mr. Joe Smith (or other name), please come to the office," that advises teachers and other adult supervisors to take certain actions to ensure the security of students and physical spaces under their supervision?

Does the handbook tell parents what steps will be taken in the event of an emergency? Is there an alternate site where students and staff will be taken if the school or other buildings must be vacated? What radio and television stations will carry emergency information?

Have maintenance and cleaning personnel been asked to notify the administration of the existence of safety hazards? Is there a plan to correct these?

Contracts

Are all staff and administrative contracts signed for the coming year? Where will copies of these documents be kept? Has a list of individuals employed at the school or facility been sent to diocesan or other officials? What are the plans for filling vacant positions?

Are all contracts for goods and services current? If new contracts are needed, what are the procedures and time lines for procuring them?

A Last Consideration

Has the administrator planned a vacation? While this issue may not appear to be a legal one, a rested administrator will help to ensure a "lawful" new year.

September 1998

Written Records and Forms: A Beginning-of-the-Year Review

⟨〰〰〰⟩

As the school year begins, Catholic educators check student records for completeness, accuracy, and currency. Administrators ask, "How do we know our written records are appropriate? How do we know they contain everything we need?" One approach is to list every record that the school should or wishes to have and check that list against existing records, school and diocesan policies, and the needs of the school. This column will present such a checklist of minimum, legally recommended records.

Permanent File

Legal experts suggest that permanent files contain five items: (a) academic transcripts or report cards, (b) any academic testing, including testing under federal and state disability-type statutes, (c) registration forms, (d) an emergency form (unless kept in an office), and (e) a health form (unless kept in a nurse's office).

Registration Forms

Students' permanent files should also contain their registration forms. Parents should submit written agreements to abide by school rules. One suggested form simply states, "I/We, the parent(s) of _____, have read the handbook and agree to be governed by it."

What should an administrator do if a parent refuses to sign the form? This author believes that denying admission until the form is submitted is appropriate. Letting people bypass the system is not recommended. If a parent will not sign the form, he or she does not have a right to services, in the same way that an airline passenger does not have to submit to a metal detector search, but will not be permitted to board the plane without the search. There are some cases, such as this, in which one cannot have one's cake and eat it too.

Emergency/Medical Release and Health Forms

Every school should have on file, either in the cumulative folder or in a separate file, an emergency/medical release form. This form should require parents to list at least two emergency contacts other than themselves. Doctors' names and hospital preferences should also be given. Parents should submit or sign statements authorizing the school to seek medical attention for an injury or illness. Such statements should be notarized. It should be noted, however, that not every hospital will honor a notarized statement, but such a statement is the best legal protection for students and school officials. Parents should also be required to submit answers to health questions about their children. A form that includes these questions should be completed by either the parents or the physician.

Athletic Records

The beginning of the year is an excellent time to collect and examine all records pertaining to student athletes. Such records should include parental permission to play, medical examination reports, the physician clearance-to-play form, and a medical release. These records may be kept in an athletic or other administrative office. They should not be included in the cumulative folder.

Discipline Records

Student discipline records should never be placed in students' cumulative folders, but should be retained in separate files. Such a procedure can prevent defamation lawsuits if the school faces a legal proceeding that compels the submission of records. Each school should have a policy of not sending disciplinary records when transcripts are requested. Disciplinary records should be viewed as internal documents to which only parents and appropriate school officials have access, unless the records are subpoenaed.

Field Trip Permission Slips

The majority of Catholic school administrators have legally sound field trip forms. The following is a sample form:

> I/We, the parent(s) of _____, request that my/our child be allowed to participate in _____ on _____ (date). I/We give permission for my/our child to participate. In consideration for making arrangements for the trip, I/we hereby release, indemnify, and hold harmless the school, its employees, and other agencies from any and all liability for any and all harm. I/We give permission for my/our child to be transported by _____ (insert type of transportation and who will provide it). The educational purpose of this trip is _____. (Parental signatures should follow).

Driver Forms

School officials must know and follow diocesan and school procedures for parent drivers. Parents must be required to furnish copies of their drivers' licenses and proof of insurance. Preferably, parent drivers should be at least 25 years old, although some insurance companies permit drivers as young as 21.

In high school, students are sometimes allowed to drive themselves and others to events and should be required to furnish the above-mentioned documents. To avoid liability, school officials should not assign students to particular cars, but should have students sign up for cars. 𝒩𝓁

September 2003
Legal Checklist as the New School Year Begins

⟨≋⟩

In the midst of so much media coverage of litigation against the Catholic Church, educators may find themselves bewildered and perhaps frightened as the new school year begins. Can a person ministering in the Catholic Church take any steps to help prevent and avoid liability for student injury? The answer is a resounding "yes."

The beginning of the school year, like the beginning of the calendar year, is an excellent time to review the past and make resolutions for the future.

An examination of professional behavior—an exercise similar to an examination of conscience—might be helpful: Did I do anything last year that I know I should not have done? Anything that might have exposed the parish, school, or me to liability? Did I take chances that I should not have? Did I leave children unattended for less-than-sufficient reasons? Did I observe the boundaries of professional behavior? Did I keep confidences when appropriate and reveal them when necessary? Did I give the students my best? Did I remember my obligation to the Catholic Church and its teachings and did I present those teachings without apology?

Many educators have asked the author for a beginning-of-the-year checklist. After examining one's professional behavior over the past year, teachers should ensure that they can answer "yes" to the following.

Checklist

1. Have I read my contract and faculty handbook? Do I understand my responsibilities? If there are areas I do not understand, have I asked for clarification and explanation? Do I understand clearly what I am expected to do in the classroom and outside the classroom? Do I understand that I am a Catholic educator 24 hours a day, seven days a week and that I am responsible for my behavior at all times?

2. Have I checked my classroom and instruction areas for hazards? If there are conditions that could prove dangerous for my students and others, have I notified the principal or other administrator? (Writing a note to the janitor does not absolve one of further responsibility.)

3. Have I received necessary medical information for any of my students with special medical conditions? Do I know who has diabetes, epilepsy, or food or bee sting allergies? Do I know how to respond if a student has a medical emergency?

4. Do I understand the custody arrangements for children not living with both biological parents? Do I know (or can I readily locate) information about which parent has custody on which day of the week? Do I have or can I access a list of other relatives or adults authorized to pick up children?

5. Have I developed classroom rules and asked another teacher to review them to make sure they are clear? Have I posted them? Have I explained them to the students the first day of class?

6. Do I have a plan book? Do I understand that I am legally expected to keep a record of what I did and what I intended to do in terms of classroom instruction (even if the school administrator does not require me to keep such documentation)? Do I have a set of alternate lesson plans available for a substitute if I must be absent unexpectedly?

7. Am I familiar with the school's crisis plan? Do I know the code word indicating a crisis situation? Do I understand what I am expected to do? Do I have a plan for instructing the students in appropriate responses to the crisis plan?

8. Do I understand the child abuse reporting laws of the state? Do I understand what constitutes physical, sexual, and emotional abuse? Do I understand that the responsibility to report if I suspect child abuse is mine and that I cannot pass this responsibility on to someone else?

9. Do I understand that confidentiality is not absolute? Do I understand that I can keep student confidences only if no one's health, life, or safety is at stake? Do I know to whom I would report concerns about health, life, or safety? Do I have a plan for explaining the limits of confidentiality to my students?

10. Do I understand professional boundaries? Do I understand that anything I do must pass the test of publicity? Am I confident that I act appropriately?

11. Finally, am I a person of prayer? Will I commit to praying for my students and my educational community daily? Do I thank God for the priceless privilege of sharing in the education of these young people?

There are no surefire ways to avoid legal liability, but being able to answer "yes" to the above questions should help a teacher act in legal and ethical ways. ⬚

September 2006

It's That Time Again:
Legal Issues for Staff and Administrators

〇〽〇

It may seem as if the end of the school or program year was yesterday, yet the new year and its attendant issues are here. In the midst of readying rooms, schedules, supplies, and lesson plans, prudent educators should take at least a few minutes to ready themselves legally. The following list of issues may be helpful in the readiness reflection.

Background Checks

Every diocese has policies mandating that criminal background checks be completed before an employee or volunteer begins ministry involving young people. These policies and state law must be strictly followed, regardless of the inconvenience. It is not unusual for someone to be hired at the last minute. Needing a teacher or a catechist cannot overcome the requirement of background screening.

Handbooks

Administrators are legally responsible for ensuring that all employees and volunteers have copies of pertinent handbooks and have signed statements acknowledging receipt of the handbooks and agreeing to be bound by the contents. Even if someone is a veteran, he or she still needs to review the documents affecting that ministry, especially those affecting the safety, learning, and religious faith of young people. Policies and procedures can change from year to year.

While handbooks will certainly outline policy, administrators must articulate their expectations on instruction, homework, discipline, testing, and grading from the very beginning. Administrators should never assume that people just "know" anything or that because something has always been done a given way, everyone will do it that way without instruction or prompting.

Parents should be required to submit a signed statement affirming, "We have read and agree to be governed by the handbook." The vast majority of Catholic schools and programs probably have such a requirement, but the proof is in the proverbial pudding: Have all statements been collected and the consequences imposed for those who have not submitted them by the stated deadline?

Parent Information and Contact

Parent information sheets, as well as handbooks, should clearly delineate academic expectations, particularly in the areas referenced above. Parameters for parent behavior and contact should be clear from the beginning. Parents should know they have a right to visit and speak with the principal, but they should also be informed of time constraints.

Emergency information must be current. Each year parents should be required to submit updated sheets. Encourage parents to list the names of anyone whom they might ask to pick up their children or act for them if personnel are unable to reach them.

Safety Issues

Have all necessary audits and inspections been conducted? Have all necessary repairs been made? Does everyone know how to report unsafe conditions and to whom?

Do all staff members (paid and volunteer) have copies of crisis plans? Are crisis drills, as well as fire drills, scheduled for the year? Does the school or parish have a catastrophe plan? Hurricane Katrina has taught a forceful lesson: It's not just the intruder with a weapon or a person making a threat that constitutes danger; it is also unanticipated, unforeseen disasters. Administrators must be sure that adequate policies and procedures are in place and necessary supplies secured. What if no one could be released from the school building for a week because of an avian flu quarantine? It may be helpful to have staff and volunteers brainstorm on such topics, particularly if such policies are in an infancy stage. Role-playing and engaging in what-if scenarios can be helpful.

Does everyone know the four elements of legal negligence (duty, violation, proximate cause, and injury)? What areas appear most prone to negligence? Do adult supervisors understand the difference between mental and physical supervision and the importance of each?

Issues of Catholicity

The beginning of the year presents one of the best opportunities for reviewing and emphasizing what it means to be a teacher, staff member, or volunteer in the ministry of Catholic education. The Catholic school exists and is recognized as a Catholic school because the bishop has determined that it is indeed Catholic. If a school or program presents itself as Catholic, the first legal obligation of those who administer and teach in it is to be Catholic not only in name, but also in fact. Everyone who teaches in a Catholic school does not have to be Catholic, but all must agree to support the teachings of the Catholic Church and to do nothing that would cause the Catholicity of the program to be called into question. Ministering in Catholic education is not a five-day- or one-night-a-week job. One's actions and words both inside and outside the parish and school have ramifications for all. Today as always, serving as a Catholic educator is a sacred trust. 𝒩𝒩

May 2007

Catastrophe Planning:
How to Plan for What We Don't Like to Think About

〇〰〰〇

As the second anniversary of Hurricane Katrina and the resulting devastation approaches, memories of the horror may diminish for those not personally affected by it. Catholic schools and parishes across the country rallied in support of people left homeless and those who sought refuge in their cities and towns. New Orleans is recovering, as are other cities affected by Katrina. Before too much more time passes, administrators should consider what they would do in a catastrophe. Principals and pastors who experienced Katrina have shared their frustration and, in many cases, lack of preparedness.

Schools and parishes generally have crisis plans, many of which were implemented in the wake of the school shootings of the last decade. Dioceses invited speakers to help administrators develop crisis plans appropriate for their schools, parishes, and programs. Principals and other educational administrators developed such plans. For awhile, virtually every teacher in a Catholic school could locate his or her copy of the crisis plan. As time passed, copies of plans were misplaced and crisis drills neglected. The end of the year is a good time to review crisis plans and develop catastrophe plans if none are in place.

A catastrophe differs from a crisis, although crises may certainly be present in a catastrophe. A crisis usually passes quickly. The results of a catastrophe do not. Preparation can mean the difference between recovering from the damage and perishing as an institution or program. Even in a catastrophic situation, administrators have very real legal responsibilities to their communities.

To prepare for a review or development of a plan, administrators and their advisors should try to imagine the worst that could happen that would make normal operations impossible for a substantial time period. September 11, 2001, was a crisis for both New York City and the country, as well as a catastrophe for individuals. Yet few, if any, schools or churches were forced to remain closed for long.

Examples of catastrophes that could occur are (a) a pandemic of bird flu; (b) an earthquake; (c) a tornado; (d) a foreign invasion; (e) a bombing attack on the country, state, or city; or (6) a fire that destroys all or most of the school or program's buildings.

The following is a brief checklist to facilitate discussion:

1. What catastrophes can we envision that could affect the existence or operation of our school or program? How can we respond to each? How will we respond if we are closed for months? If our building is destroyed? If city or town services are unavailable?

2. Are there special circumstances that could influence our response? These include such issues as assisting students who live many miles from school who are caught at school even when some warning and evacuation time is given. Do certain members of our community have special needs? Disabilities? Our plan will have to include provision for these individuals.

3. What insurance coverage do we have? Understanding that it may take months after a catastrophe to gain access to insurance funds, the administrator should, nonetheless, know what the coverage is and where to locate copies of policies. Copies should be kept in more than one format and in more than one place.

4. If people are stranded in our facility, do we have adequate provisions? Public health officials offer guidelines for quantities and types of nonperishable food, water, first aid supplies, etc. As it may be impossible for some to leave the building, a good question to ask is "How long could we feed people if everyone in our school or program were to live here for an extended time period?"

5. How can we communicate with the outside? If there is no phone or Internet service, do we have other options?

6. What will we do if the electricity fails?

7. What provisions do we have or can we make for sanitation needs? If the plumbing fails, how will we deal with drinking water and toilet and bathing needs?

8. In the case of an operations shutdown, how will we continue to pay our employees? Can we?

9. Where are student records stored? Do we have electronic copies in case all paper copies are lost?

10. Finally, and perhaps most important for us as Catholic educators, how will we provide the spiritual leadership needed? How will we pray with our communities?

Many people comment to the author that they did not become Catholic educators to worry about legal issues. Assuredly, few, if any, foresaw the need to become catastrophe response planners. But this job is simply one more in the ever-emerging demands of Catholic educational leadership.

Handbooks

May 1995
Parent/Student Handbook Revision

As the school year draws to a close, principals may find that handbook revision is one of their remaining tasks. The construction of legally sound parent/student handbooks is a major concern as one plans for the next academic year. Now is the time to consider the changes that presented themselves as possibilities during the present school year.

This article will address some of the legal principles that should govern the construction and revision of parent/student handbooks and offer suggestions for content areas.

Legal Principles

The importance courts rightfully place on the development, promulgation, and implementation of rules is significant. Since handbooks and other written agreements can be construed as part of the contract between the school and its students and their parents, it is important that, as far as possible and practical, rules be in writing.

Courts look for evidence of good faith: Did the institution have a rule? Was that rule promulgated? Did students and parents know of the rule? The court does not concern itself with the wisdom of the rule or even with the rightness or wrongness of the professional opinion of educators. The court is concerned only with the existence of a properly promulgated rule and with evidence that the institution acted in good faith according to the procedures it stated would be followed. School officials, of course, should understand that they will never be able to write down everything a student could possibly do that might result in disciplinary action. Therefore, it is advisable to have some kind of catchall clause such as "other inappropriate conduct." No court will expect a school to have listed all possible offenses, but courts will expect that something is written and that parents and students have a reasonable idea of the school's expectations.

Philosophy

The beginning point for rules development should be the school's philosophy. Principals must ensure that a clearly written philosophy informs all school activities. The philosophy must be viewed as a living document, not something written, stored, and brought out when the occasion requires it.

Parents and students should understand and be able to articulate the philosophy. The life of the school should be seen as flowing from the philosophy. Courts may analyze rules to see if they are consistent with the philosophy.

Admission Policies

Diocesan superintendents generally require that school handbooks contain a statement of nondiscrimination. Catholic schools do not discriminate on the basis of race, sex (unless traditionally a single-sex school), national origin, age (in accordance with law), or disability (if, with reasonable accommodation, the disabled person can function in the school environment).

Catholic schools may discriminate on the basis of religion and give preference to Catholic students. Such preference should be clearly noted in this section of the handbook.

Financial policies should be clearly stated, including those on payment and refund of registration fees, tuition, and book rental or purchase. Much ill will and legal complication can be avoided if parents are told from the very beginning what the school's expectations are.

Academic Policies

This section should clearly outline the school's requirements on the type and amount of homework. Time expectations for each grade should be explained.

The grading policies of the school should be outlined. Whatever system is used (numerical, letter, or other type of grade) should be defined. Statements on what constitutes superior, satisfactory, and unsatisfactory work should be given.

Promotion and retention policies should be outlined. Many dioceses have clear guidelines on reasons a student may be retained in a grade.

Access to records should be discussed in this section. The school should state the procedures to follow if a parent or student wishes to view a record. For example, the school can ask for 24 or 48 hours' notice and can require that the request be made in writing.

Absence policies should be included in this section, particularly if the school imposes any academic penalties for absence. [Note: Recent court decisions suggest that such academic penalties must be clearly tied to participation grades and cannot be merely arbitrary.] If not discussed in this section, absence policies that require the parent to notify the school if the student is absent should be included elsewhere.

Discipline

Administrators should strive for simplicity and clarity in rule construction. Long lists of rules should probably be avoided. Phrases such as "other inappropriate behavior" or "conduct unbecoming a Christian student" cover many types of misbehavior.

The principal or other administrator should retain the right to make exceptions in cases in which mitigating circumstances call for a different response than policy suggests. Phrases such as "must" or "will result in a certain penalty" can result in little or no leeway. Phrases such as "can" or "may" give an administrator room to allow for individual circumstances.

Extracurricular Activities

All extracurricular activities sponsored by the school should be listed, along with requirements for participation. Academic, disciplinary, and attendance standards should be considered.

Field trips are privileges afforded to students, not absolute rights. The school handbook should state that students can be denied participation if they fail to meet academic or behavior requirements.

It is an excellent practice to include a copy of the school's permission form in the handbook. If a student forgets to bring the form home, a parent can copy the proper form and fill in the appropriate details.

Use of School Grounds

In these days of increasing litigation seeking damages for injuries occurring on school property at times and places where no supervision is present, school officials must state the school's rules and the consequences for deviation from those rules. Simply stating the rule is not enough; clear consequences must be enforced. Failure to enforce penalties can be interpreted as tacit approval of student presence at unauthorized times.

Other Considerations

The principal should reserve the right to amend the handbook for just cause. The handbook should indicate that parents will be promptly notified if changes are made.

The above listing of handbook components should be considered an absolute minimum. Readers may be interested in the NCEA publication *School Handbooks*, authored by the writer. It discusses parent/student and faculty handbook contents in detail.

For everyone's protection, parents and students should be asked to sign a statement such as "We have read and agree to be governed by this handbook." Students should not be permitted to attend classes until such a signed statement is submitted. Since courts can construe handbooks as part of the contract between the school and the parents, it is both legally and ethically advisable to ensure that all parties to the contract have read it and agree to be ruled by it.

Conclusion

All Catholic schools should develop clear procedures governing parent and student rights and responsibilities. Catholic educators must be concerned about being models of moral behavior. Policies and procedures must be examined in light of Gospel principles and the fundamental dignity that is the right of all people. The appropriate inquiry is not merely "Can we legally do this?" but "Even if we can legally do something, is it the right thing to do? Is it what Jesus would do?"

Recent Developments: Bargaining Agent Certification and Failure to Rehire Principal

Two cases involving Catholic education should be of interest to the administrator.

In the 1995 case *Central Catholic Educational Association v. Archdiocese of Portland*, 133 Or.App.280, the Central Catholic Educational Association sought to overturn the Employment Relations Board's dismissal of the association's petition for certification as the exclusive bargaining unit of lay teachers and other education-related personnel at a school operated by the Archdiocese of Portland. The board had determined that it lacked jurisdiction over the school.

The court recognized that the 1979 U.S. Supreme Court case *National Labor Relations Board v. Catholic Bishop of Chicago,* 440 U.S. 490, 99 S.Ct. 1313, 59 L.Ed.2d 533, held that the National Labor Relations Act does not generally confer jurisdiction on the NLRB for the labor-management relations of church-operated schools. Relying on the principles of that decision, the court affirmed the Portland board's decision that it lacked jurisdiction. However, citing some earlier noneducation cases, the court ruled that the archdiocese could be subject to the jurisdiction of the NLRB even though teachers and other personnel do not fall under its jurisdiction.

This case suggests that the findings of *NLRB v. Catholic Bishop of Chicago* will continue to be challenged by religious organization employees who seek NLRB protection.

In the 1994 case of *Sabatino v. St. Aloysisus Parish,* 654 A.2d 1033, a New Jersey Catholic school principal filed suit when she was not rehired as principal after several parishes formed a cosponsored school. Ms. Sabatino alleged breach of contract, since she had been previously hired for six years under a series of one-year contracts.

The process for filling positions in the new school required that all positions be opened, although incumbents could apply. After interviewing the incumbent principals, the search committee interviewed other candidates and recommended the appointment of a nonincumbent who is a religious sister. The pastors, who were responsible for the final decision, accepted the committee's recommendation.

The court upheld the pastors' right to appoint a principal who was not an incumbent. Since Ms. Sabatino had been employed on a year-to-year basis, she was not dismissed from her position; rather, her contract was not renewed, and she had no legal right to continued employment. *ℳ*

November 1997

School Handbooks

After the first weeks of school, an administrator may give a sigh of relief that the opening went well and the business of Catholic education is moving forward. Now, before the memories fade, is the time to evaluate beginning-of-the-year events and documents. No documents are more important than the faculty and parent/student handbooks.

Principals, teachers, and parents may ask why a certain item isn't covered by a handbook policy or procedure or may state that what is written in a handbook does not seem sufficient for situations that arise. These are important observations to capture and record when made, not six months later when it is time to revise the handbooks for the coming school year. Handbook development should be everyone's responsibility, not just the principal's.

A principal should consider using a simple index card method for revisions. Anyone who has a suggestion for inclusion or deletion in handbooks should note it on an index card. Only one suggestion per card is allowed. In the spring when handbooks are usually revised or updated, the administrator can sort cards by topic. Then the administrator or handbook committee can consider each idea. Such an approach makes revision much easier and does not result in frantic efforts to recall what people said at previous faculty or other meetings.

Minimum Components of Faculty Handbooks

Six minimum topic areas should be included in any faculty handbook:

- Philosophy of the school
- A list and explanation of teaching duties, including a working definition of what constitutes good teaching
- A list and explanation of nonteaching duties
- Policy and procedures for administrative supervision and evaluation of teachers
- A list and explanation of personnel policies
- Sample forms

These six areas are by no means exhaustive, but they provide a broad, legally sound framework. Almost everything that an administrator would want to include in a handbook can fit into one of these categories. For example, a policy on the law relating to child abuse reporting is a nonteaching duty. A policy that reflects an awareness of students with special needs can be placed under the category of teaching duties.

Parent/Student Handbooks

Parent/student handbooks are, in the opinion of this author, preferable to having simply a student handbook or two separate handbooks. The parents are the parties who contract with the school. Parents pay tuition or support the school in other ways in lieu of tuition, and in enrolling their children in school they are agreeing that both they and their children will abide by the rules and regulations of the school.

The parent/student handbook should include policies and procedures in the following areas:

- Philosophy

- Admission policies/notice of nondiscrimination

- Academic policies

- Communication between the parent(s) and teachers and administrators

- Discipline code, including rules, regulations, penalties, and exceptions

- Extracurricular activities, including policies on participation and exclusion from activities

- Parents' signed agreement to be bound by the handbook, on a detachable card or a separate sheet, stating: "We, the parent(s) of_____, agree to be governed by this school handbook for the school year. We recognize the right and responsibility of the school to make rules and enforce them."

An administrator may also wish to have the students sign, but it must be clearly understood that students, unless over age 18 and functioning as adults, cannot be held legally responsible for meeting the terms of a contract.

Right to Amend

Since situations can arise that were not foreseen when the handbook was written, the principal should always reserve the right to amend the handbook. Parents and students should be promptly notified of any amendments.

Binding Power

A sizable number of court cases hold that handbooks can be legally binding in the same way as other contracting documents. Some administrators have inserted disclaimers into handbooks stating that they are not legally binding contracts. Ethical issues should be considered before an administrator publishes a handbook that binds faculty, parents, or students, but that the administrator does not consider binding for the school or its administration. Since courts generally resolve any ambiguity in favor of the person who did not construct the document, it is easy to see how problems can arise. The wise administrator will always attempt to balance ethical and legal issues in decision-making.

MARCH 2007
HANDBOOKS: PRINCIPLES FOR REVISION

Now is the time when administrators begin to think about handbooks. Do they need revision? Are there parts that should be deleted or added? Should some policies be changed? Or, as this writer remembers thinking, "Will they work for another year?" Revising handbooks takes time. There are always other crises clamoring for attention and other fires to extinguish. NCEA Notes columns as well as various NCEA publications contain information about and content outlines for handbooks. This brief article offers a few points to consider as March Madness approaches and administrators consider handbook changes for the coming year.

Know the Law

Although most administrators are not lawyers, they can be held legally liable for activities or omissions that contribute to the injury of others. Informed administrators ensure that policies and procedures comply with existing law and should know when to seek competent legal advice.

Most administrators have taken a course in school law. Unfortunately, the vast majority of such courses are geared to public schools. As most readers know, the laws affecting public education and those affecting Catholic schools can be very different. Sometimes the best knowledge is knowing what you don't know. What you don't know can hurt you. The wise administrator reads current articles on legal issues, participates in workshops, and seeks advice. Having a competent attorney review contractual documents, including handbooks, for legal soundness is an excellent practice. If a qualified attorney is not available, administrators can read and critique each other's handbooks. Another set of eyes can be quite useful in determining the clarity of handbook contents.

Be Able to Apply the Law

All the knowledge in the world won't help administrators if they can't apply the law. Applying the law is not unlike driving a car. It's a skill one has to practice. After reading an article on field trips, an administrator should ask, "How does this apply to my situation? Are my school's policies and procedures in line with the principles expressed in the article? Are we doing some things that could be legally problematic? How can we address the issue in the handbooks?" Asking such questions when one reads an article is a far better approach than trying to remember what one read months later.

Know Your Situation

This author often asks people who call for advice, "What do you want to do?" Some people respond, "But I called you to find out what to do." The administrator is the real expert on his or her school or program. The best approaches are often found in answers to questions such as "In light of the situation we have, what could we do? Do our handbooks cover this problem? Do we need more specificity?"

Another question needing an answer is generally not "What can I legally do?" but "Given what I can legally do, what should I do?" Just because a certain course of action is legally permissible doesn't mean it is the right thing to do. For example, it may be perfectly legal to expel a student who comes to school under the influence of alcohol, but it may not be the right thing to do. Gospel mandates as well as civil law must be considered.

Protect the School Contractually

Contract law is the basic source of the law in Catholic schools and programs. Handbooks can be considered contracts. Administrators should take actions that comply with existing policies and procedures. If students facing suspension are entitled to a hearing, the principal should not suspend without having a hearing, no matter how heinous the offense or how much at wit's end the principal is. Policies must be clear and leave little room for differences in interpretation. Administrators must act in ways that are consistent with contractual documents as well as with commonly accepted standards of good faith and fair dealing—how reasonable people treat each other.

Always Have an Escape Clause

No matter how careful the handbook writer, unforeseen situations will arise. Handbooks should contain a right-to-amend clause such as the following: "The principal is the final recourse and reserves the right to amend this handbook. Parents will be given prompt notice."

Keeping Up With Handbook Revision

Handbook development and revision can be accomplished incrementally. An index card or computer entry approach is useful. When the administrator thinks of a handbook revision, the idea is entered onto an index card or into a computer file. Staff can be invited to submit suggestions. The administrator will then have a resource bank from which to draw when it is time to prepare next year's handbook.

About the Author
Sister Mary Angela Shaughnessy, SCN

Sister Mary Angela Shaughnessy is a Sister of Charity of Nazareth who has taught at all levels of Catholic education from elementary through graduate school. She served eight years as principal of a Catholic high school. Sister Mary Angela holds bachelor's and master's degrees in English, a master's degree in educational administration, a J.D. degree in law, and a Ph.D. in educational administration and supervision. Her research centers on the law as it affects Catholic education and church ministry. She is the author of more than 30 texts.

A consultant to numerous dioceses, Sister Mary Angela is a regular speaker at National Catholic Educational Association conventions. She has served as adjunct professor in various college and university programs. She spent 21 years at Spalding University in Louisville, KY, where she held various administrative posts, including vice president, legal counsel, and founding director of the doctoral program in education, and served as professor of education. She is a member of the bar in Kentucky.

Sister Mary Angela is now executive director of the Education Law Institute, sponsored by St. Catharine's College in Springfield, KY. She has received numerous awards and in 1997 was named one of the 25 most influential persons in Catholic education.